Women, Feminism and Italian Cinema

Women, Feminism and Italian Cinema
Archives from a Film Culture

Dalila Missero

EDINBURGH
University Press

Edinburgh University Press is one of the leading university presses in the UK. We publish academic books and journals in our selected subject areas across the humanities and social sciences, combining cutting-edge scholarship with high editorial and production values to produce academic works of lasting importance. For more information visit our website: edinburghuniversitypress.com

© Dalila Missero, 2022

Edinburgh University Press Ltd
The Tun – Holyrood Road
12 (2f) Jackson's Entry
Edinburgh EH8 8PJ

Typeset in Garamond MT Std by
Manila Typesetting Company

A CIP record for this book is available from the British Library

ISBN 978 1 4744 6324 9 (hardback)
ISBN 978 1 4744 6326 3 (webready PDF)
ISBN 978 1 4744 6327 0 (epub)

The right of Dalila Missero to be identified as author of this work has been asserted in accordance with the Copyright, Designs and Patents Act 1988 and the Copyright and Related Rights Regulations 2003 (SI No. 2498).

Contents

Acknowledgements — vii

Introduction — 1

Part I   Cultures of Film Consumption: Affective Spectators and Activist Audiences
1. Searching for Gender in the Audience: Cultural Discourses and Opinion Surveys — 17
2. The Spectator in the Magazine: Cinema-going, Ideology and Femininity — 27
3. Feminist Spectatorship and Transformative Publics: Aspirations and Legacies of Feminist Film Festivals — 39
4. Patterns of (In)visibility: Lesbian and Queer Counterpublics — 52
5. Feminists and Porn: Protests and Campaigns — 62

Part II   Cultures of Representation: Sexuality, Race and Politics
6. Asexuality and Housework in the Anthological Comedies of the Mid-1960s — 75
7. Ines Pellegrini: Navigating (Post)colonial Representations in the 'Sexual Revolution' — 86
8. The Beginning of the End? Depoliticised Feminism in Fellini's *City of Women* — 97

Part III   Cultures of Production: Maps, Labour and Archives
9. Sexism and Women's Work: Mara Blasetti, Production Manager — 109
10. A Map of Open Questions: A Feminist Genealogy of Women Directors (1935–70) — 121

11 A Materialist Trajectory in Feminist Filmmaking: Rethinking
    Labour and Consciousness-raising   139

12 Feminist Spaces and Knowledge Exchange: Adriana Monti's
    Archive   155

Conclusion – Feminist Film Culture(s): Collectivities, Archives
and Futures   164

Works Cited   168

Index   180

Acknowledgements

Writing this book has been a long journey, and not always an easy one. There are several people who made this research possible. First of all, I want to thank Mariano Lisa, Dacia Maraini, Moira Miele, Lea Melandri, Adriana Monti, Giovanna Pala and Laura Remiddi, who shared with me their precious memories and archival materials. My gratitude also goes to the librarians and archivists I encountered in the many institutions I visited to research this project. Among them, a special mention goes to the archivists of Archivia in Rome, and the Fondazione Micheletti in Brescia. I wrote most of this book at the Bodleain Library in Oxford, a sanctuary of knowledge that has a special place in my heart: it comforted me and gave me the mental space to think during the pandemic.

Also many people in the academic community have inspired and supported me. First, I want to thank my colleagues and friends who listened, discussed and challenged my ideas, read drafts, and offered me a place to stay during my visits to the archives: Valerio Coladonato, Ilaria De Pascalis, Giuseppe Fidotta, Damiano Garofalo, Dom Holdaway, Luca Peretti, Lucia Tralli, and Francesco Sticchi. I wish also to thank Louis Bayman, Danielle Hipkins, Daniela Treveri-Gennari, and Karl Schoonover, who provided support and intellectual nourishment at different stages of the book. My gratitude also goes to my former colleagues at the University of Bologna, and in particular to Giacomo Manzoli, Claudio Bisoni, Monica Dall'Asta and Paolo Noto, who introduced me in the lands of Italian cinema and cinema history. I am also very grateful for the conversations I had with Francesco Di Chiara, Giovanna Maina, Sergio Rigoletto and Federico Zecca at the many conferences we met.

Finally, I want to thank my feminist sisters in Milan and in other parts of Italy who inspired me to pursue this project. After all, writing this book has been also a political and activist journey. My warmest thoughts go to my geographically dispersed and transatlantic family, and especially to my mother Magdalena and my father Dario, who are my biggest inspiration, and to Ben, who is always there for me. This book is for me, and the three of you.

Introduction

This book is a collection of essays investigating the role of women in cinema history, using an archival and feminist perspective to study the impact of feminism on Italian film culture from the late 1950s to the early 1980s. This period is generally associated with the 'golden age' and downturn of Italian cinema, namely with its peak and decline in domestic popularity and international appreciation. This was also a time when most of the audience was male, like almost the totality of the directors, critics, producers and film professionals. The gendered characteristic of film culture has been generally taken for granted as a 'sign of the times': this was the reaction of a senior scholar when I made this point in my PhD dissertation, which centred on the 'sexualisation' of the Italian cinema during the 1960s. In his view, it was 'obvious and self-evident' that in the Italian society of the time men and sexism were ubiquitous and endemic in film culture, and unless I was able to prove otherwise, I shouldn't emphasise that point. His words stimulated me to adjust my research and undertake a 'shadow project' that eventually kept me busy for two years following my doctoral defence in 2018. That project, which is at the basis of this book, aims to demonstrate that the dominance of men in cinema history is far from obvious.

When I started to dig into the archives and ask women about their experiences with cinema between the 1960s and 1970s, I wasn't surprised that most of them talked about a conflicting relationship with the big screen. Many of the sources and testimonies I was collecting proved that women enjoyed going to the movies, read and talked about films and stars, made films – generally with limited funding – and worked in the film industry, albeit in subsidiary positions; at the same time, this evidence was too often fragmentary, ephemeral or isolated. This ambivalence demonstrated to me that cinema represented a powerful site of cultural and social negotiation, and although it was mostly made and discussed by men, it stayed at the crossroads of wider social and cultural tensions that were inevitably part of women's everyday lives. As such, I began to work on the hypothesis that this multifaceted engagement with leisure and mass culture might have to do with women's interest and participation in public life and politics, and therefore also with second-wave feminism.

By establishing a connection between the 'ordinariness of culture' (Williams 1989) and social change, this book sees women's political participation in the light of their reinvention and redefinition of the everyday, from the perspective of their engagement with popular culture and mass media, and of course, with cinema. During the research and later in the writing process, I have sometimes struggled to balance the theoretical, empirical and political goals of this project, as the analysis of a heterogeneous array of archival materials poses diverse sets of challenges. I have explored the archives of both film and feminist institutions, watched feature films, experimental Super 8s and television programmes; I have studied popular magazines, self-help manuals, activist leaflets and the alternative press; and I have interviewed activists and directors in person, via Skype and email. Retrieving, gathering and analysing these sources has encouraged me to follow unconventional research paths that have required me to explore new theoretical and interpretative grounds, which I realised were often at odds with the most consolidated narratives about Italian cinema, in which women's cinematic experience generally consists of a handful of famous actresses and a couple of directors. In other words, this variety of sources called for a theoretical and interpretative framework capable of explaining the reasons behind the eccentricity of women in cinema history, one that couldn't simply rely on notions such as 'marginality' and 'absence', because the sources were actually proving the contrary: women were everywhere.

Researching Women in Italian Cinema

The scattered nature of the sources about women is somehow reflected in the existent studies on women in Italian cinema, which delineate a quite fragmentary line of investigation. To some extent, the most comprehensive source for Italian feminist historiography is still a book published in 1988, *Off Screen: Women and Film in Italy* by Giuliana Bruno and Maria Nadotti. The volume, stemming from a conference held at New York University in 1984, collects a group of essays by Italian feminist theorists, directors and film critics who took part in the second wave moment, and puts them in dialogue with the work of Anglo-American scholars in feminist film theory. The seed planted on that occasion led to no systematic transatlantic exchanges in the subsequent decades, but more recently the research of Monica Dall'Asta on the Italian film pioneers (2008) and the publication of Veronica Pravadelli's *Le donne del cinema. Dive, registe, spettatrici* (2014) have signalled a renewed interaction between the Italian studies on women and cinema and the international scholarship in the field. A new wave of research about contemporary filmmakers (Cantini 2013; Luciano and Scarparo 2013), film genres (Fullwood 2015; Günsberg 2004) and specific topics, like femininity, motherhood and prostitution (Faleschini-Lerner and D'Amelio 2017; Hipkins 2016; Cottino-Jones 2010), has flourished, especially in Anglo-American academia, while in Italy studies on popular film magazines by Lucia Cardone (2004, 2009) and more recently by Giovanna Maina (2018) have inaugurated a line of research that sheds light on a variety of gendered intermedial film cultures, also recently explored by Paola Bonifazio in her study of photoromances (2020). A handful of edited collections have also reawakened interest in feminist film and media production (Cardone and Filippelli 2015; Buffoni 2018; Buonanno and Faccioli 2020), though these examples cover a very broad range of case studies from different contributors, without resulting in an organic methodological conclusion. To sum up, this heterogenous body of work signals the existence of a consistent and productive interest in women's film cultures; however, it is very difficult to identify a holistic approach that challenges the marginalisation and suppression of women from cinema history with a methodological intervention. Specifically, this scholarship hasn't explicitly engaged with the current debate in cinema history, namely with the 'archival turn' in feminist film history and with the studies in New Cinema History. This book aims to fill precisely this gap by concentrating on the archive as a theoretical gendered and methodological tool that produces new narratives and provides a multifaceted and layered portrayal of women's participation in cinema history. To do so, I have equipped my study with a set of theories and methodologies that enable me to go beyond the merely documental value of archival sources, to illustrate their productive function as political, affective and narrative devices. My ultimate goal is to address the intertwining levels of politics, affect and materiality characterising women's positionality in Italian cinema, by putting into dialogue feminist film theory and historiography.

Recuperating the Feminist Film Cultures of the Past

The book adopts the notion of 'feminist film culture' to indicate its focus on a wide set of cinematic practices in which women circulated and made meaning beyond the realm of representation, to focus on experience and storytelling. Indeed, as Silvia Federici points out, the degradation of women's knowledge and creative production has been historically functional to their exclusion 'from many places where decisions are taken, [and has] deprived

[them] of the possibility of defining their own experience, [forcing them] to cope with men's misogynous or idealised portraits' (2018, 42).

As a minority in the film audience and the industry, women have been generally excluded from activities that are traditionally deemed to be part of cinema history, such as film criticism, film direction and production. However, as we anticipated, this doesn't mean that they haven't consistently engaged with these and other cinematic practices, by adopting different approaches, which were often intermedial, non-theatrical and extra-textual. For this reason, I have found in New Cinema History a rich set of theoretical and methodological tools that have allowed me to reconstruct different sets of cinematic practices. The studies in New Cinema History call for a socio-cultural understanding of the cinema as a commercial institution and a popular form of entertainment, and as such it calls for a specific attention to the formation of the film audiences, the practices of exhibition and the interconnections between the micro/local and the macro/global (Maltby 2011). This means rejecting a totalising historical project to encourage the investigation of a wide range of socio-cultural and extra-textual practices, an approach that productively dialogues with the recent 'archival turn' in women's cinema and television history.[1]

The affinity of this book with this scholarly work goes hand in hand with the interest and reflection on historiographies produced by the feminist movement during the 1970s. Activist filmmakers and film critics counteracted the exclusion of women from art and culture by rewriting and subverting the canon as a 'discourse [that] fundamentally [promotes] the worship of the artist, as a product of male narcissism' (Pollock 1999, 3). Since the 1970s, Italian feminist film collectives, directors and critics such as Maria Adelaide Frabotta, Rony Daopoulo and Annabella Miscuglio have explored figures like Alice Guy-Blanche and Elvira Notari, and screened their films at festivals, planting the seeds for a gendered historiography that challenged the hegemonic notions of authorship and artistic value.

This combined attention to contemporary film scholarship and feminist historiographies of the past enables me to understand women's cinematic experiences as interconnected responses to patriarchy, but at the same time as practices that are inherently linked with local, national and transnational cinematic cultures. As such, the book studies a wide range of cinematic practices and focuses on a group of case studies that are representative of a lively and complex historical period. The notion of 'feminist film culture', then, includes a set of experiences in which the cinema became a means to enhance social change, create gendered communities and encourage women's self-expression, prompting the development of a collective consciousness. This approach goes hand in hand with the discussion of three questions that are in fact fully fledged methodological perspectives: the recuperation of feminist genealogies, the assessment of nostalgia and the rejection of institutional rigour.

FEMINIST GENEALOGIES: *DESPITE GRAMSCI*

In the essay 'Feminist Genealogies' (1993), Teresa de Lauretis describes women's place in history in terms of contradiction, as a site that is characterised by a precarious bond between knowledge and confinement. Speaking from the emblematic 'room of one's own', women create a discursive space in which their isolation and singularity creates a genealogical history that is always 'in process, here and now, and based in practice, contradiction, heterogeneity' (1993, 9). The reconstruction of a 'feminist film culture' is the recuperation of such genealogies, balancing questions of singularity with the material and collective dimensions of women's knowledge. It therefore means collecting, gathering and analysing the traces and fragments from the past, acknowledging the material constraints, the precariousness and ephemerality of women's history as an opportunity to challenge the absoluteness of a totalising historical account. But how can we articulate these scattered and dispersed genealogies in a coherent narrative without neglecting the political importance of considering women as a collective? My answer to this question is inspired by another essay by de Lauretis, 'Gramsci Notwithstanding', which discusses the 1974 theatre play *Despite Gramsci*, written and performed by a group of feminist activists of the Roman collective La Maddalena, Adele Cambria, Lù Leone, Francesca Pansa and Laura di Nola. The play consists of a feminist reading of Antonio Gramsci's private correspondence with his wife and sisters-in-law, Giulia, Tatiana and Eugenia Schucht. Like the Schucht sisters, the experimental and militant theatre of La Maddalena has been mostly forgotten, yet it has established, through performance, a political genealogy that has subsequently been continued by Teresa de Lauretis with her essay.[2] Drawing on this example of feminist recuperation, de Lauretis calls for a theory of culture in which women are subjects, 'not commodities, but social beings producing and reproducing cultural products, transmitting and transforming cultural values' (1987, 93). The connection between scattered feminist genealogies resides in the material and cultural practices of transmission and circulation of knowledge that women had enacted throughout time. Among them, there are the many 'archiving women' (Eichhorn 2010) who assembled, put together, preserved and donated their papers and documents to feminist and film institutions. Following Kate Eichhorn's suggestion, the project approaches these archives as sites of knowledge production and transmission in which women are agents, instead of subjects, of the archival collection. This approach is not too distant from Raymond Williams' notion of 'structures of feeling', which identifies the meanings and the makings of culture in the materiality of doing and the temporality of the everyday (1978). The feminist genealogies, combined to Williams' structures of feeling, provide a necessary gendered perspective and temporality to historical inquiry, one that is rooted in the materiality of women's cultural and film practices, as well as in the affective and empirical experience of archival research.

(Un)Doing Archives: Feminist Nostalgia

However, my approach to feminist genealogies rejects an essentialist notion of gender and women, to engage with a series of cultural practices that acknowledge the intersecting experiences of patriarchal oppression faced by women and queer people. These intersections are not only part of the history of feminism but are also fundamental to understand today's intersectional struggles. Indeed, despite my generational distance, many of the genealogies emerging from the archives of the 1960s and 1970s resonate with both my personal engagement with feminism and with film scholarship.

As a woman born in the late 1980s, I have direct experience of a recent wave of feminism that has gained momentum since 2016 in Italy with the birth of the transnational network, Non Una di Meno.[3] As Daniela Chironi explains, generational conflicts are constantly at play in the Italian movement, but 'even though plurality remains a movement's value, generational replacement has led to a final predominance of intersectional feminism and growing diffusion of queer perspectives' (2019, 1491). This replacement has coincided with a gradual marginalisation of the tradition of 'feminism of difference' (femminismo della differenza),[4] which is rooted in the political experience of the Italian second-wave movement, but has ultimately become a minority – although still very vital – in the contemporary debate. In a recent article, I criticised the nostalgia for the second-wave movement that emerged in some recent Italian films about feminism and in the mainstream feminist debates (Holdaway and Missero 2020). When I was writing that piece, I felt I was in the right position to make that critique despite working on a scholarly project – this book, whose historiographic urgency can easily risk being read as a recuperative work motivated by a vague sentiment of 'postmodern nostalgia'. So, how can I reconcile my political rejection of nostalgia with my longing for women's archives, and especially for those belonging to the activists and political groups of the 1970s? Kate Eichhorn describes her own sentiment of postness and feminist nostalgia as a 'longing for the very possibility of living in a landscape where the past held little promise, little revolutionary potential, and the future was the only place where possibility dwelled' (Eichhorn 2015, 259).

Like Eichhorn, in the process of recuperating the stories and memories of the feminist activists and filmmakers of the 1970s, I felt that being present at that time was 'not only eventful, but also transformational in ways that appear to exceed representation' (Eichhorn 2015, 260). This sentiment resonates with an 'impossibility of historical re-feeling' that Jane Gaines (2009) experienced in her research on women film pioneers of the early twentieth century, reminding me that my 'post-ness' is also a powerful standpoint, which sees in the urgency of reconstructing the past a possibility of engaging with the present and a means of reinventing the future. In other words, the recuperation and reimagination of that past offers an alternative to the 'exhaustion of the future' described by Mark Fisher as a foundational feature of our contemporary times (2014).

Taking Care of the Feminist Archive, against Institutional Rigour

Given its complex relationship with the past, feminist historiography has struggled with notions of rigour and objectivity centred on the materiality of the archive. In the 1990s, a debate on the so-called 'revisionist histories' in Anglo-American film studies assigned to archival research the role of counterbalancing the 'excessive' abstraction that had apparently affected the field since the late 1980s (Kuhn and Stacey 1998). This call for empirical research urged feminist scholars to counteract a new narrative that was 'implying that feminists working in film theory have had relatively little to say about questions of film history' (Petro 1990, 9). As such, feminist scholars rejected an artificial separation between theory and history by questioning the power dynamics reproduced by the use of empirical historical sources. This call resonates with the problematisation of the 'ideology of rigour' by queer theorist José Esteban Muñoz, who argues that empiricism naturalises the dismissal of queer, race and feminist scholarship, as 'merely passing intellectual fancies, modes of inquiry that are too much in the "now", lacking historical grounding and conceptual staying power' (1996, 7). As Muñoz explains, 'rigor is owned, made, and deployed through institutional ideology' (1996, 7) and in order to respond to its exclusionary power, we should make visible its ideological mechanisms. To paraphrase again feminist scholar Patrice Petro, 'reconstituting film history from a feminist perspective is not merely a matter of making the invisible "visible". It also involves submitting regimes of visibility to a general critique of objectivity and subjectivity in the writing of film history' (1990, 10). Indeed, feminist theorists and researchers have developed multiple strategies to unveil the ideological opacity of institutional rigour. At the beginning of the 1980s, Nancy Hartsock introduced the notion of 'standpoint theory', which assigns to women's experiences a privileged position in knowledge production and academic research (1983). The adoption of a standpoint methodology, as Sandra Harding explains, leads to a 'strong objectivity' (1992), resulting from the incorporation of a wider range of experiences and subjects in scientific inquiry. To paraphrase Helen E. Longino, 'doing science as a feminist' means understanding research as a process and not as a product, admitting that 'political considerations [are] relevant constraints on reasoning' (Longino 1990, 193), and precisely for this reason, feminist scholarship is accountable and not lacking in rigour. The institutional ideology that assigns objectivity to studies that claim themselves to be 'apolitical' and 'a-ideological' because of their empirical use of archival evidence, actually incorporate bias in research without making scholars accountable for their methodological and interpretative choices. It is in the spirit of 'strong objectivity' and standpoint methodology that this study adopts a politics of citation that privileges feminist sources and materials written by women, to build a cinematic archive that aims to challenge established regimes of visibility. As Sarah Ahmed suggests, feminist citation strategies are powerful tools that reveal the limits of institutional knowledge while promoting a form of writing that welcomes affective and emotional investment, by recognising that feminism is 'a fragile archive, a body assembled from shattering, from splattering, an archive whose fragility gives us responsibility: to take care' (Ahmed 2017, 17). As a political and epistemological stance, care provides a response to a world in which 'carelessness reigns' (Care Collective 2020): disseminating and quoting but also addressing questions of archival accessibility are ways to call for a more sustainable and solidary approach to research that not only encourages researchers to share and collaborate, but also indicates the institutional pitfalls and problems in reaching and studying women's sources.

That said, how does the rejection of institutional rigour and the politics of citation translate in this study about feminist film cultures in Italy? First of all, this book does not follow a conventional periodisation. The years between the late 1950s and 1970s are often seen through the lens of the peak and decline of Italian cinema. However, from the point of view of women, the access to films and filmmaking was consistently more difficult than for men, and for this reason, a gendered approach to Italian cinema calls for an accurate reconstruction of the dynamics of this hampered access and an understanding of the ways in which women overcame them. Women's struggle to participate in the cinematic culture was linked to their struggle to participate in public life; at the same time, cinema was a space to negotiate and build alternative and imagined public spheres, building new communities and experiencing joy. From the point of view of institutional rigour, this complexity translates into invisibility, but from a feminist standpoint it is an inevitable consequence of cultural segregation, which is eminently a political question. The adoption of a standpoint methodology, then, gives us the opportunity to valorise women's diverse experiences and build new situated knowledges about Italian cinema as a multifaceted socio-cultural phenomenon.

By privileging, where possible, documents and resources produced, collected and/or consumed by women, many films and authors that are generally considered canonical to this period won't be discussed. This applies, for instance, to figures like Lina Wertmüller and Liliana Cavani, who have achieved critical recognition and have also been under the spotlight of academic research. Their compliance with authorial canons has enabled the study and preservation of their work, so my decision is to focus more closely on the women, films and experiences that occupy a more liminal space.

Finally, and most importantly, abdicating from institutional rigour and embracing a standpoint methodology doesn't mean avoiding the triangulation of the sources, or a proper work of reconstruction and contextualisation. Archival documents won't be presented here as part of a definitive, totalising project but rather in a processual and dialogical discourse aiming to establish new connections and knowledge about women's experiences with cinema. I am aware that the material and contextual aspects in which I have conducted this study and wrote this book – including a global pandemic – have prevented me from studying and visiting all the archives I wanted to, or to interview all the women and activists that I wished. However, this research remains open: in other words, the chapters in this book represent a first step in an uncharted territory that still has many stories to tell.

THE STRUCTURE OF THE BOOK

The volume splits into three parts, each exploring a specific aspect of women's cinematic culture: film consumption, representation and production. The chapters in each section follow a chronological order, and the structure aims to prompt a thematic dialogue between the different parts of the book. All sections have in common the adoption of an archive-based and empirical methodology that includes a discussion of the challenges and specificities of the sources analysed, and specific attention is given to issues and questions in feminist and film theory.

The section on film consumption, 'Cultures of Film Consumption: Affective Spectators and Activist Audiences', focuses on the shifting positioning of women in Italian film audiences, from the late 1950s to the late 1970s. Chapter 1, 'Searching for Gender in the Audience: Cultural Discourses and Opinion Surveys', provides an overview of the gender composition of

Italian film audiences to explain why and how women turned to other media, such as radio, television and magazines. The analysis of quantitative sources is complemented by a reconstruction of the main cultural debates about women's relationship with popular culture, from the post-war years to second-wave feminism. Chapter 2 'The Spectator in the Magazine: Cinema-going, Ideology and Femininity' analyses the affective and emotional aspects of film spectatorship through the study of women's magazines, focusing especially on the agony and advice columns of the early 1960s. From the transgressive nature of film spectatorship to women's attempts to navigate the moral and patriarchal meanings of cinema-going, this section analyses how the cinema-theatre represented a symbolic and physical site for negotiating sexism in the everyday. With Chapter 3, 'Feminist Spectatorship and Transformative Publics: Aspirations and Legacies of the Feminist Film Festivals', our attention shifts to the 1970s with a critical reconstruction of the first experiences of feminist film festivals in Italy as activist attempts to create a gendered and politicised public. Chapter 4, 'Patterns of (In)visibility: Lesbian and Queer Counterpublics', recuperates the cinematic experiences of politicised lesbians and queers by reconstructing the trajectories of the former actress and feminist activist Giovanna Pala and the radical lesbian collective Brigate Saffo. Chapter 5, 'Feminists and Porn: Protests and Campaigns', offers a first assessment of the Italian feminist debates about pornography in the 1970s by focusing on two main case studies: the pressures of a group of Roman activists to block the film *Life Size* (Luis Berlanga, 1975) and a series of violent protests against adult-only theatres organised between 1975 and 1980. The Italian second-wave movement widely discussed issues like women's objectification and gender violence, but refused any dialogue with the film industry and didn't eventually engage in systematic debates and campaigns on this issue. However, pornography and the sexualisation of the media more broadly are key to understanding the contradictions and limitations that were affecting the movement by the end of the 1970s.

The second part of the book, 'Cultures of Representation: Sexuality, Race and Politics', focuses on questions of representation, with the analysis of three case studies that intersected with broader feminist debates: the politicisation of sexuality, intersectionality and the fragmentation of the second-wave movement. Chapter 6, 'Asexuality and Housework in the Anthological Comedies of the Mid-1960s', analyses a group of comedies from the mid '60s that represented the crisis of the bourgeois couple. These films generally employed the tropes of popular sexology to portray female characters as neurotic, unproductive and frigid. By means of an anachronistic use of feminist theories on reproductive labour, this chapter reveals the relevance of asexuality to a feminist and political critique of compulsory (hetero)sexuality. Chapter 7, 'Ines Pellegrini: Navigating (Post)colonial Representations in the "Sexual Revolution"', addresses the re-emergence of colonial narratives in the Italian media of the 1970s in the wake of the so-called 'sexual revolution' and the peak of the feminist movement's visibility. Specifically, I focus on the trajectory of Ines Pellegrini, an Italo-Eritrean actress who worked in very different Italian productions, from prime-time television to soft-core cinema and arthouse films. The variety of Pellegrini's experience allows me to interrogate, from an intersectional perspective, the conflicting political, cultural and gendered meanings associated with race in this period. Chapter 8, 'The Beginning of the End? Depoliticised Feminism in Fellini's *City of Women*', analyses the conflicts between activism and its representations in mainstream cinema in relation to the incipient fragmentation of the second-wave movement in the early 1980s.

The last part of the book, 'Cultures of Production: Maps, Labour and Archives', focuses on women's participation in the Italian film industry and on feminist film production. The first two chapters analyse the experiences of women professionals and their individual strategies for negotiating the patriarchal structures of the industry; the last three focus on feminist experimental film production and its dialogues with mainstream cinema and television. Chapter 9, 'Sexism and Women's Work: Mara Blasetti, Production Manager', retraces the affective and material consequences of sexism in the career trajectory of Mara Blasetti, to discuss the trans-historical impact of gender inequality, and specifically sexual harassment, in the film industry. Chapter 10, 'A Map of Open Questions: A Feminist Genealogy of Women Directors (1935–70)' reconstructs the paths of a group of students of the Centro Sperimentale di Cinematografia (CSC) from the 1930s to the 1960s. These trajectories intersect at different levels with the structural difficulties encountered by women in the film industry, at the crossroads with politics, sexism and strategies of resistance. Chapter 11, 'A Materialist Trajectory in Feminist Filmmaking: Rethinking Labour and Consciousness-raising', focuses on Italian feminist filmmakers' attempts to work in mainstream cinema and television, but also on radical experiments in collective filmmaking. Owing to the practical and theoretical issues posed by economic and technical constraints, Italian feminist audio-visual production was unable to fix the structural inequalities affecting the film industry. Finally, the last chapter, 'Feminist Spaces and Knowledge Exchange: Adriana Monti's archive', concentrates on issues of knowledge transmission and the transformation of feminist experiences, focusing on the case of the Milanese filmmaker, Adriana Monti.

A Note on Terminology and Periodisation

The chosen periodisation for this book goes roughly from 1958, the beginning of the 'economic boom', to the early stages of the so-called *riflusso nel privato* (1978–82),[5] which saw the decline of the social movements and the end of the season of political turmoil of the 'years of lead'. My discussion of this historical period emphasises the complexity of intertwined socio-cultural processes rather than ruptures and singularities, and the reference to specific events, figures or films is made in relation to the study of a specific archival source, theoretical problem or methodological consideration. The expressions 'economic boom', *riflusso* and 'second-wave feminism', then, are adopted as working definitions in order to provide a set of chronological coordinates. The expressions 'economic boom' and *riflusso*, indeed, are widely diffused in historiography as well as in Italian jargon to indicate two very specific, transitional phases in the history of the country. The boom has been identified mainly with a five-year-period (1958–63) of unprecedented economic growth and affluence (Crainz 2005); this definition has been repeatedly questioned for its rigid adherence to economic indicators, and doesn't consider the processes that foresaw that phase, or its lasting socio-cultural impact (Lanaro 1992). Likewise, the so-called *riflusso* has been variously associated with different time-spans between 1978 and the mid-1990s, and has also been questioned for its reductive understanding of the political and social transformations of the period. However, a cautionary use of both terms remains particularly useful to evoke certain tendencies of Italian public and cultural debates. As the concept of economic boom emphasises notions of modernisation and progress, the idea of *riflusso* engages with the history of the social movements, as well as with the shifting divide between the public and private spheres that characterised the 1980s.

Similar considerations apply to the term 'second-wave feminism', which is not used in the Italian language, and has been widely challenged by scholars and activists as it is based on the problematic conceptual framework of the 'waves of feminism'. The main issue here is the concentration of women's struggles in a handful of years, running the risk of reproducing an historical narrative of progress and loss that erases the continuities between periods (Hemmings 2011). In addition to this, the 'waves' generally stem from the timeline of white North American feminism, with the consequent erasure of other experiences. As Maud Anne Bracke has righteously observed, these issues resonate well with the history of Italian feminism, which in the 1970s was pervaded by an unquestioned sense of its own newness, and despite its multiple transnational connections, it rarely engaged with non-Western feminisms (2014: 5). For all these reasons, I use the expression second-wave feminism only when the context requires me to distinguish the movement of the 1970s from the previous 'emancipationist' phase, a season dominated by women's associationism with an institutional affiliation.[6] Otherwise, I privilege umbrella terms like women's movement and feminism.

Notes

1. I am using this expression to indicate a relatively recent turn in feminist film scholarship whose breadth and scope are well exemplified by the excellent work published in the journal *Feminist Media Histories*, founded in 2015, and showcased at the 'Doing Women's Film and Television History' conferences organised by the Women's in Film and Television History Network. These conferences have also inspired the publication of two foundational edited collections discussing methodological questions and transnational case studies in feminist cinema history: Vicki Callahan, ed., 2010, *Reclaiming the Archive. Feminism and Film History* (Detroit: Wayne State University Press); Christine Gledhill and Julia Knight, eds, 2015, *Doing Women's Film History: Reframing Cinemas, Past and Future* (Urbana: University of Illinois Press).
2. In 1976 Adele Cambria 'secured' the legacy of this play in her book *Amore e Rivoluzione* (Love and Revolution). It was Teresa de Lauretis (1987) and Renate Holub (1992) who recuperated this seminal feminist reading of Gramsci's work, bringing it to the attention of academia.
3. Non Una di Meno (NUDM) is an Italian movement, born in 2016, inspired by the protests of the Argentinian group Ni Una Menos against gender violence and femicide. In 2017, NUDM collectively wrote a feminist plan against violence on women, and every year mobilises thousands of people on International Women's Day, 8 March, for the women's strike, and on the international day against violence on women, 25 November. NUDM refuses any form of gender essentialism and supports the struggles of non-binary and trans women.
4. By endorsing a radical revision of the symbolic order through language, primarily inspired by the work of Luce Irigaray, the feminism of the difference in Italy is generally associated with the group of feminist philosophers Diotima, although it encompasses the work of numerous intellectuals and thinkers, such as Ida Dominijanni and the group of the Women's Library in Milan. Diotima's philosophy of sexual difference sees in the figure of the mother the mythological access to new forms of knowledge of the world and the self. For an in-depth analysis of Diotima's theories see Graziella Parati and Rebecca West, eds, 2002, *Italian Feminist Theory and Practice: Equality and Sexual Difference* (Madison, WI: Fairleigh Dickinson University Press).
5. The expression *riflusso nel privato* – literally 'ebb in the private' – can be translated as 'backlash' or as reflux, withdrawal, in the private sphere.
6. For a historical assessment of this terminology, see Perry Wilson, 2019, 'Confusione terminologica: "femminismo" ed "emancipazionismo" nell'Italia

liberale', *Italia Contemporanea – In Rete*, no. 290: 210–29. For an in-depth discussion of the transition from the emantipationist strategies of the women's movement of the 1950s and the early 1960s to the feminism of difference see Fiamma Lussana (2012), *Il movimento femminista italiano. Esperienze, storie, memorie* (Rome: Carocci); Graziella Parati and Rebecca West, eds, 2002, *Italian Feminist Theory and Practice: Equality and Sexual Difference* (Madison, WI: Fairleigh Dickinson University Press).

Part I

Cultures of Film Consumption: Affective Spectators and Activist Audiences

The decision to dedicate the first section of the book to film consumption and audiences reflects the conceptual and historical framework of this study, which sees in the popularity, everydayness and pervasiveness of the cinematic experience a key to understand the complexity of women's film cultures. From a numerical perspective, women represented a minority in the Italian film audience, reflecting a gender composition of the public sphere that persisted throughout the decades. Women went to the cinema less and less frequently than men, but aspects such as age, class and location are equally important to understand the complex gendered dynamics influencing the audience composition. In addition to this, women's spectatorship has been subjected to a long tradition of gendered discourses around cultural consumption, that linked women's engagement with culture to emotionality, domesticity and repetition, all notions that were at odds with the most acculturated and renown discourse about the cinema and spectatorship.

Drawing on a notion of film consumption as a gendered and contested cultural practice, this section analyses the historical evolution of women's position in the Italian film audience, to investigate the tensions between their marginalisation and their persistent engagement with the medium. To do so, the section is split in two parts, each divided in two groups of chapters. The first concentrates on the 1950s and the 1960s, from two intersecting perspectives: the cultural debates around women's cultural consumption and their reflections on the gender composition of the film audience, and women's strategies of negotiation of these discourses in their everyday life. To do so, I have worked on a heterogeneous array of sources, such as market surveys, film criticism and women's magazines. The second chapter focuses on the years of the economic boom and the discourses on cinema-going present in women's magazines with different political orientations, such as *Annabella*, *Famiglia Cristiana*, *Alba*, *Così* and *Noi Donne*, to provide a comprehensive analysis of the competing views of women's spectatorship circulating at the time. The readers' rejection and/or acceptance of the advice and recommendations published in the magazines reveal the variety of practices and understandings of cinema-going in their everyday life.

The second part concentrates on the formation of feminist and lesbian publics during the 1970s. Chapter 3 reconstructs how feminist collectives and individual activists built numerous, yet marginal, spaces for the consumption of women's cinema, while Chapter 4 focuses on the practices of counter-cultural spectatorship developed by politicised lesbians and which refused forms of cultured and middle-brow film consumption. Chapter 5 analyses the campaigns and protests against pornography organised by the Italian second-wave movement, which approached the question in relation to sexual violence and women's right to experience the urban space safely. My approach to activist and counter-cultural audiences accounts for a vast array of practices in which cinema works as a tool for resistance and rebellion, and as a form of intervention in the cultural and political debate.

As a result, this section ultimately aims to trace a genealogy between the readers of the women's magazines and the feminist publics of the 1970s, and their experience of the cinema as a space to negotiate or transgress oppressive notions of femininity. What links these publics to each other is their challenging position in confront to the male-dominated context of the Italian cinema audience, and their resistance to broader patterns of gender segregation persisting in the Italian society.

CHAPTER 1

Searching for Gender in the Audience: Cultural Discourses and Opinion Surveys

Since the end of World War II, Italy has seen an evolution and complexification of its media system, marked by a process of democratisation and the Americanisation of formats and infrastructures (Forgacs and Gundle 2007). Italian mass culture has adopted forms of intermediality that have required consumers to familiarise themselves with an increasing range of registers and products (Bonifazio 2020). While these considerations apply to the general context, gender has continued to condition access and experience of mass culture, by means of discourses about legitimacy, taste and ideology. In specific regards to cinema, several factors have led to a steady decrease of female spectators in Italian theatres, a trend that continued from the post-war years until the 1980s. Mariagrazia Fanchi reads the male-dominated composition of cinema audiences as a reflection of a domestication process that started in the late 1940s, hampering women's participation in public life and making the cinema less accessible for them (Fanchi 2010). However, considering that women continued to be a minority in Italian public life in the following decades, it is arguable that the reasons for this have changed according to transformations in Italian society and also their adaptations to the evolving media system. Moreover, as suggested by scholars of the Italian Cinema Audience project, the reasons for women to avoid the cinema-theatres varied according to geographical, class and generational factors that are equally important (Treveri Gennari et al. 2020, 4–5).

With this in mind, this chapter focuses on the connections, exchanges and contradictions between the cultural debates about women and mass culture, and the actual trends and practices of media consumption. Using a systemic approach, the chapter analyses cinema-going in relation to the consumption of other media, such as radio, television and magazines. To do this, the chapter splits into two parts: the first provides an historical overview of the cultural discourses around women and popular culture, in order to frame the trends in cinema-going in a specific socio-cultural context; the second, which is mainly based on quantitative data sets, such as market and opinion surveys, illustrates the main characteristics of women's media consumption, and their adaptation to changes in the media system. Looking at these two aspects (cultural debate and quantitative trends) allows us to locate in media and film consumption a series of contradictions that coexisted in Italian cinematic culture: on the one hand, to paraphrase the title of an essay by Andreas Huyssens (1986), women were seen as mass culture, and therefore their engagement with certain genres and narratives of popular culture was 'natural' and at the same time problematic; on the other hand, in a context of an increasingly centralised media and mass culture, this association made evident the growing importance of women in the public sphere.

THE BAD AND GOOD FORTUNES OF WOMEN'S RELATIONSHIP WITH MASS CULTURE

A persistent cultural tradition has tied together a poor opinion of women's writing and cultural production generally, and the dismissal of popular and gendered publics. These discourses have persisted despite the transformations of the media system and evolutions of mass culture, beginning with serial and popular literature and magazines, and continuing with cinema and television.

Some of the most memorable female characters in post-war Italian cinema were passionate readers of popular magazines, like Silvana in *Riso Amaro* (Bitter rice, Giuseppe De Santis, 1949) and Wanda in *Lo Sceicco Bianco* (The white Sheik, 1952), while others were directly involved in their production, like Lady Eva in Steno's *Piccola posta* (The letters page, 1955). Lady Eva (Franca Valeri), an agony aunt, embodies many of the characteristics conventionally attributed to women's writing: her work was serial and characterised by a colloquial and sentimental style, and despite the success of her column, she penned her articles with a pseudonym without claiming any authorship. The complicity between Lady Eva and her readers was based on the mystery surrounding her figure, which, contrary to any notion of the public intellectual, counted on privacy and the domestic aspects of her work. These characteristics resonate with a genealogy of female novelists and champions of Italian serial literature that trace back to the early twentieth century, with writers like Carolina Invernizio, Mura (Maria Assunta Giulia Volpi Nannipieri), Liala (Amalia Liana Negretti Odescalchi) and Alba De Céspedes. Despite their popularity, these authors struggled to be incorporated in the canon of Italian literature not only because of their sentimental and melodramatic style, but also because of their bond with mass culture, especially with the women's magazines that published their work and had a gendered readership.[1] However, the success of these writers, especially among the popular classes, didn't go completely unnoticed, as Carolina Invernizio's novels were mentioned by Antonio Gramsci as examples of national-popular culture, demonstrating the impact of her work but also its problematic reception.[2] Indeed, Gramsci didn't hide his dislike for her novels: he nicknamed Invernizio as 'the earnest hen of popular literature' (Gramsci 1975, 344). Invernizio was also targeted by other male colleagues, who named her 'la casalinga di Voghera' (the housewife from Voghera), a pejorative moniker that alluded to her provincial origin, and to her – vast – readership of northerner bourgeois women (Garofalo and Missero 2018). In the 1950s, these categories re-emerged in relation to cinema, with the so-called *neorealismo rosa* (pink neorealism), which has also been labelled *neorealismo d'appendice* (feuilletton neorealism), a genre that has only recently been approached seriously for its specificity, beyond the biased view of its gendered public.[3] The expression 'housewife from Voghera' came back into use thanks to the intellectual and writer Alberto Arbasino – also born in Voghera – who used it in a series of articles for the political weekly *Il Mondo*, in which a fictional 'housewife from Voghera' embodied the average Italian point of view. The term then regularly appeared in other debates, especially about television consumption, to describe a spectator with simple taste and with no particular interest in politics or culture. This stereotypical and gendered image would eventually be parodied by Nanni Moretti in his film *Sogni d'oro* (1981), in which the 'housewife from Voghera' was evoked by a left-wing cinephile to criticise Moretti's inaccessible, self-reflexive cinema. The juxtaposition between the 'average and uncultured' media consumer and a housewife produces a curious contradiction, as it paradoxically aligns common sense with a gendered, working-class experience of the world, but at the same time dismisses its perspective because of its domestic character and supposed cultural simplicity.

Besides this tradition, another perspective emerged in the late 1950s, one that would influence later feminist interventions in this area. This genealogy started with the work of Gabriella Parca, who in 1959 published the book *Le italiane si confessano* (Italian women confess), a paperback success that compiled extracts from over eight thousand unpublished letters originally sent to the agony columns of the illustrated magazines *Sogno* and *Luna Park*. Parca worked for these magazines and had access to the correspondence that was discarded from publication due to its scabrous content, which discussed topics like virginity, masturbation and abortion (Morris 2006, 12). The author understood that those letters were actually opportunities to access the everyday lives and experiences of sexuality and the relationships of readers, who mostly belonged to the popular classes. As such, *Le italiane si confessano* 'elevated' the agony column to a testimony of Italian women's condition, one that could be presented and discussed with the general public. In order to do so,

Parca had to explain in the introduction of her book the context in which the letters had originally been published, as well as the editing that she had performed in order to make the materials suitable for publication: her book targeted a middle-brow readership, assumed to be unfamiliar with illustrated magazines. To the same extent, Parca's book included forewords by two – male – intellectuals, Cesare Zavattini and Pier Paolo Pasolini, respectively published in the first (1959) and second (1962) editions.[4] Zavattini, in line with his emancipatory understanding of popular culture,[5] interpreted *Le italiane si confessano* as a call for social justice: in his view, Italians couldn't be good citizens unless they practised democracy and equality in their private relationships, a belief that he pushed further in his project for the collective film *Le italiane e l'amore* (1961), based on Parca's book. Conversely, Pasolini interpreted the extracts of the letters as expressions of a rampant conformism, which was caused by working-class women's partial encounter with modern capitalism (Pasolini 1962). According to Pasolini, the letters discussed sexuality and intimacy in an artificial and insincere fashion, which was also completely disconnected from other social issues, an aspect that, combined with a certain use of language, demonstrated the inherently conservative nature of women.[6] A few years later, another progressive journalist, Gioacchino Forte, affirmed that women who wrote to agony columns and consumed popular literature were responsible for their own condition: these magazines accommodated women's 'natural inclination to lock themselves in their shell' and withdraw from public life (Forte 1966, 119–20).

Although Pasolini and Forte confirmed the persistence of negative views on women's magazines and their readers, especially in relation to their political and social engagement, Parca's book actually opened up a new understanding of women's relationship with popular culture – one that acknowledged its complexity and political relevance. Even though this approach resonates with the Gramscian notion of the national-popular, its main innovation resides in a feminist interest in women's experiences and their problems. This is quite a distinct attitude compared with Betty Friedan's classic *The Feminine Mystique* (1963), in which media (serial novels and advertising) are considered responsible for perpetuating women's unhappiness and their segregation in the domestic sphere. As Joanne Meyerowitz (1993) has pointed out, Friedan's analysis didn't allow the reader to reject or negotiate those contents, a question that is actually crucial in Parca's book, which focuses on the readers' columns as a space primarily devoted to interaction, and an opportunity to hear women's voices and opinions.

Also, for this reason, other Italian feminist authors such as Laura Lilli and Milly Buonanno saw in these magazines an opportunity to understand women's everyday condition, rather than a means for their oppression. Although

Lilli considered these publications responsible for the dissemination of an Italian brand of the 'feminine mystique', which was nurtured by a 'Cinderella-complex of Catholic matrix' (Lilli 1976, 285), Milly Buonanno, who similarly cautions against the conformism characterising these magazines, admits that 'it is not the case to grant [mass culture] a monopoly in the control of women's minds, nor powers of total and immediate impact [on society]' (1978, 20). From this perspective, it is unsurprising that the Italian feminist movement approached and reappropriated the format of the women's magazine to connect with a broader, non-activist audience. The case of the feminist magazine *Effe*, whose brief life (1973–82) coincided with the peak and decline of the Italian second-wave movement, is emblematic of a wider attempt to establish dedicated spaces of communication and (counter)cultural production that embodied and represented the identity of this political community, so much so that in a brief scene of the film *Io sono mia* (I belong to me, 1978) by Sofia Scandurra, a young feminist activist is portrayed with a copy of it. Activists and collectives also used women's magazines to survey the public debate, as demonstrated by the numerous do-it-yourself press reviews consisting of clippings from newspapers and magazines that are preserved in the feminist archive 'Archivia' in Rome. These collections, organised in thematic folders on topics such as divorce, abortion, religion and sexual health, present the traces of a collective and reflexive work around mass culture, with minutes, highlights and notes. Another interesting example in this genealogy is Lea Melandri's agony column in the girls' magazine *Ragazza In* during the 1980s, an experience that resonates with the author's engagement with the feminist practice of *autocoscienza* (consciousness-raising).[7] As such, Gabriella Parca's seminal book continued to inspire the activist practices of the following decades, proving once again the central role played by popular culture in women's lives as well as in their politicisation. It is also in light of this complex role of mass culture that my research consistently relies on these sources to investigate the evolution of women's film cultures and political engagement.

Picturing a Male-dominated Cinema Audience

As illustrated in the previous section, the debates around women and popular culture have focused mainly on women's literature and magazines, as these publications had an explicit focus on femininity and were associated with a gendered readership. But in what context and to what extent did the formation of a political and gendered approach to mass culture intersect with the practices of media and film consumption? And why was cinema so resistant to these counter-discourses? Since the second half of the 1950s women have been increasingly oriented towards the consumption of television, radio and, of course, magazines, and such trends are clear in market and opinion surveys conducted by the Servizio Opinioni RAI and the Doxa Institute from 1954.[8] A feminist reading of these quantitative data sets calls for a preliminary assessment of their original purpose and the way they championed gender.[9] These surveys were interested in women as a consumer group, and set out to understand their willingness to buy and spend in a context of a rapid consolidation of consumer capitalism. Some of these studies also surveyed the subgroup 'housewives' (*donne di casa*), a definition that didn't refer to their occupational status but indicated women who were in charge of managing the family budget. For this reason, these surveys, while attributing a crucial role in the economy to women, also incidentally documented inequalities reproduced by capitalism, at the intersection of questions of gender, class and location. Drawing on the accidental meanings of these data sets, this section offers an intersectional overview of women's media consumption in respect to the composition of Italian film audiences. Indeed, regardless of their education and economic condition, Italian women's media consumption habits were very similar to those of the less educated and poorer class, given their preference for illustrated magazines and the radio, two media whose consumption was generally solitary, domestic and relatively cheap. Until 1966, TV sets were mostly present in middle- and upper-class households, while the radio remained particularly favourable among the popular classes. In 1964, 47 per cent of the women interviewed by the Servizio Opinioni RAI had never watched television, while the habit of watching television in public places, such as bars and clubs, was prevalently practised by lone adult men, sometimes as an alternative to the more expensive admission to the cinema-theatre (RAI Servizio Opinioni 1965). By contrast, women were more likely to watch it at a neighbour's apartment, though this percentage remained significantly low, confirming women's tendency to consume media at home, especially during the daytime, while men tended to watch TV after dinner and attend film screenings in the evenings. As such, this picture confirms women's tie to domesticity, an aspect that didn't change during the economic boom, when more women began to work outside the home. These trends are further confirmed by the evolution of the market in women's magazines, which was monitored by the Istituto Accertamento Diffusioni (IAD), an independent agency that controlled the circulation and sales of the products of publishing companies on their behalf.[10] In 1964, two Catholic weeklies alone, *Alba* and *Così*, sold more than half a million copies per week,[11] while more established magazines like *Annabella*, *Grazia* and *Gioia*[12] had an average weekly circulation of 450,000 copies each. These figures only account for middle-end publications, as the circulation of low-cost illustrated magazines, such as *Bolero Film*,

Bella, Confidenze, Grand Hotel and *Novella*, per week was over 4 million (IAD 1964). Considering that each copy could be read by others, we can assume that there were at least twice as many weekly readers of these magazines. The IAD bulletins released in 1972 confirm the tenure of this market, while new publications debuted in 1973, when *Cosmopolitan* and the feminist monthly *Effe* appeared for the first time in Italian newsagents, reflecting the formation of new tastes and interests.

Going back to the years 1958–63, the data sets on cinema audiences reveal that cinema-going played a very different role in women's experience of media and culture. Although the cinema intercepted a heterogeneous and vast public, the consumption of specific genres and certain modes of exhibition were strongly tied to aspects of class, gender and location.[13] Although the highest number of tickets sold was in 1955, with 819.4 million admissions, cinema remained a very popular form of entertainment at least until the early 1970s, when a deep crisis hit the sector. Although the introduction of television in 1954 had an impact on cinema revenues only two years later, in 1956, causing the loss of 29 million spectators, the sale of tickets increased again during the economic boom, between 1958 and 1963, only to decrease more steadily in the following years (SIAE 1968). Throughout this period, the audience continued to be predominantly male. The surveys conducted by Doxa between 1958 and 1960 reveal that among the 48 million admissions sold on average on the peninsula each month, at least two-thirds were purchased by men (32 million) and only one-third by women (16 million). Moreover, 80 per cent of male respondents aged between 18 and 34 went to the cinema at least once per month, compared with 47 per cent of women (Luzzatto-Fegiz 1966, 242). To sum up, women attended film screenings less and less frequently, anticipating a general trend established in the second half of the 1960s. Indeed, if we observe the decade from 1958 to 1968, cinemas suffered a total loss of 171 million spectators, a process concentrated mostly between 1964 and 1968. In the same period, ticket prices doubled, and numerous peripheral cinemas began to shut down, with significantly fewer showing days (SIAE 1968).

In other words, movie-going became a more planned and eminently urban activity, with peripheral and rural publics becoming increasingly marginal, while the gender composition remained similar, yet with some relevant differences between the north and the south. A survey conducted by Doxa in 1965 indicates that in Northern Italy 38 per cent of the audience was constituted by lone men, and only 5 per cent of lone women; groups of two or more males represented 25 per cent of the spectators, as opposed to 6 per cent represented by groups of two or more females; 20 per cent was represented by couples of opposite sexes and 6 per cent by groups of three or more people of different sexes. In the south, the percentage of female spectators was even lower: 56 per cent of the audience were lone men, as against 1 per cent of lone women; groups of two or more men represented 25 per cent of the total, and groups of two or more women represented 2 per cent; couples of different sexes 5 per cent, and 11 per cent were groups of three or more people of different sexes (Doxa 1966). In other words, women went to the cinema mostly with other people, especially with men, who might be a partner or a sibling, and the man was usually the person in charge who picked the film (Garofalo and Missero 2018; CoDiS 1962). The Doxa data sets also illustrate that women's attendance at the cinema, decreased especially in the older age cohorts, while 81 per cent of girls aged between sixteen and twenty went to the theatre at least once a month (Luzzatto-Fegiz 1966, 394). As revealed by the Italian Cinema Audiences (ICA) project, this can be explained by the fact that many women ceased to attend films after marriage and especially after they had children (Treveri Gennari et al. 2020).

At the same time, the high percentage of men who went to the cinema alone, especially in the south, suggests that the theatre represented a site for male socialisation, and the relatively low number of couples who attended screenings together reduces the importance of the theatre as a site for heterosexual dating, although an association with courtship recurs in many accounts and memories of post-war cinema-going (Treveri Gennari et al. 2020, 180–97). Such narratives, which usually emphasised heterosexual desire, enabled to disrupt what Eve Kosowsky Sedgwick has called the 'continuum between the homosocial and the homosexual' (1985). According to Sedgwick, homosociality, which dominated the cinema-theatre, excluded women in order to allow men to retain their privilege; at the same time, homosocial relations are haunted by the possibility of homosexual desire, a threat that is constantly exorcised by forms of homosexual panic, as testified by some accounts of male spectators of the 1950s (Treveri Gennari et al. 2020). The queer potential of the theatre space is confirmed by theatres' historical role as cruising sites for gay men (Pini 2011) and the very late incorporation of this counter-narrative in the history of Italian cinema confirms the bond between homosocial spaces and heteronormativity, and their repercussions on the processes of history-writing.

Conclusions

The late 1950s saw the emergence of a new perspective on women and mass culture that complicated the established derogatory assumptions about the frivolousness and lack of taste of women's cultural production and consumption. Gabriella Parca added to the Gramscian approach to popular culture a specific interest in women's social condition that foresaw forms of feminist intervention in the field of popular and mass media. At the same time, overall patterns of media consumption suggest that the evolution and complexification of the media system shaped and nurtured, but didn't revert, the process of domestication that began in the post-war years, to which women adapted by buying more magazines and watching more television than radio – when television became more affordable. At the same time, an increasing number of them, especially married women, avoided the cinema theatre. These consumption patterns coincided with those of the lower classes, although women's management of the family budget increased the attention given to their habits of cultural consumption. In other words, the evolution of the media system consolidated pre-existent trends in the gender composition of the publics, while the new centrality of women in consumer capitalism didn't challenge the gendered divisions of the public and the private spheres.

At the same time, recognising the complexity of women's relationship with popular culture had no impact on the practices of media consumption more broadly. This means that reappropriating the formats of popular culture, such as those performed by Parca and later by the feminist movement, couldn't and didn't influence women's access to mass culture, yet prompted a political and collective response to cultural segregation that passed through the formation of gendered and affective counterpublics.

Notes

1. For an introduction to the work of these writers see Anna Laura Lepschy, 2003, 'Are there rules of the game? Invernizio, Vivanti, Liala, and the popular novel', *The Italianist* 23, no. 2: 321–35. For Alba De Cespedes see Penny Morris, 2004, 'From private to public: Alba de Céspedes' agony column in 1950s Italy', *Modern Italy* 9, no. 1: 11–20; Carole C. Gallucci and Ellen Nerenberg, eds, 2000, *Writing Beyond Fascism: Cultural Resistance in the Life and Works of Alba de Céspedes* (Madison: Fairleigh Dickinson University Press).
2. For an introduction to Gramsci's notion of 'national-popular' see Forgacs 1988, 363–78.
3. As recently demonstrated by Louis Bayman (2014), the melodramatic and the realist sensibilities are inextricable aspects of the Italian culture, and this is particularly evident in post-war cinema. Similar considerations had been made by Adriano Aprà and Claudio Carabba (1976) yet these two authors, who introduced the label 'neorealismo d'appendice' (feuilletton neorealism), didn't engage with questions of gender.
4. *Le italiane si confessano* appeared with three different forewords (1959, 1962, 1973), written respectively by Cesare Zavattini, Pier Paolo Pasolini and the author herself. In the 1973 edition, Parca suppresses Zavattini and Pasolini's contributions, archiving them as 'dated'. It is no coincidence that this new introduction came

at a time when the feminist movement was at its peak and Parca was actively involved in it. In this edition, she also eliminated the 'methodological' introduction in which she frames the reader's columns in the panorama of media consumption of the time. In this way the volume is updated and has taken a new meaning in the editorial and cultural landscape of the 1970s, which also fits with a new political phase.

5. This attitude could be explained by Zavattini's experience as editor for the weekly women's magazine *Piccola* during the 1930s, and later, in 1954, his collaboration with *Noi Donne* (Cardone 2009, 104–5).
6. Pasolini's consideration of the linguistic choices were clearly based on a misunderstanding, as Gabriella Parca points out in the 1973 edition of the book, where she explains that her editing of the letters included the removal of possible mistakes and dialectal expressions.
7. Some extracts and reflections about this experience are in Lea Melandri, 1992, *La mappa del cuore. Lettere di adolescenti ad un giornale femminile* (Soveria-Mannelli: Rubbettino).
8. The Servizio Opinioni was an agency founded by the public broadcaster RAI to survey television and radio ratings, as well as the opinions of subscribers to the service; Doxa is a private agency, established in 1946, that specialises in market surveys, including a few on film audiences, commissioned by private clients such as the advertising agency Opus-Sipra.
9. For a feminist perspective on the use of quantitative methodologies and data sets see Joey Sprague and Mary K. Zimmerman, 1989, 'Quality and quantity: Reconstructing feminist methodology', *American Sociology*, no. 20: 71–86; Ann Oakley, 1998, 'Gender, Methodology and People's Ways of Knowing: Some Problems with Feminism and the Paradigm Debate in Social Science', *Sociology* 32, no. 4: 707–31.
10. The editions of the bulletins that I could access cover the time span 1962–73.
11. *Così* had an average circulation per issue of 151,060 copies, compared to 190,269 of *Alba* and 280,953 of *Gioia*. Both cost 100 lire, while *Così* had just gone up to 80 lire in mid 1963.
12. These three magazines were founded during the Fascist regime, introducing into the Italian publishing market middle-end publications that adapted and popularised the formats of high-end French fashion magazines and American magazines for a wider public of unmarried working women. See Silvia Cassamagnaghi, 2007, *Immagini dall'America. Mass media e modelli femminili nell'Italia del secondo dopoguerra, 1945–1960* (Milan: Franco Angeli).
13. See in particular the association between popular classes, popular genres and peripheral circuits of exhibition, which was the result of well-established production and distribution policies that both shaped and reproduced inequalities of access to entertainment. See Vittorio Spinazzola, 1985, *Cinema e pubblico. Lo spettacolo filmico in Italia 1945–1965* (Rome: Bulzoni); L. Bayman and S. Rigoletto, eds, 2014, *Popular Italian Cinema* (Basingstoke: Palgrave Macmillan).

CHAPTER 2

The Spectator in the Magazine: Cinema-going, Ideology and Femininity

The five years that conventionally coincide with the economic boom (1958–63) witnessed a series of relatively rapid socio-cultural transformations, prompted by the industrialisation of the economy and the introduction of new consumer cultures (Ginsborg 2003). These changes impacted on the understandings and experiences of the private and public realms, primarily through the diffusion of the model of the nuclear family, the expansion of the middle class and the assignment to women of a primary role in household consumer choices (Saraceno 1993; De Grazia 2005).

In this context, women's cultural consumption and experiences of leisure became a synecdoche of major changes in the public and private spheres, and their gendered meanings. As the data sets analysed in the previous chapter suggest, cinema-going was a leisure activity that women experienced mostly with other people, as it entailed leaving the house to go to a public space, the theatre, that was usually occupied by men. Despite this, cinema remained a very popular form of entertainment that was at the centre of the public debate and was constantly under the spotlight of the popular press, including illustrated magazines and women's weeklies. The market for these publications, indeed, saw a boom in this period, with the inclusion of articles and advice columns about housekeeping, fashion, family relationships, beauty and budgeting becoming a sort of 'guide to modernity' (Arvidsson 2003). Women's magazines worked as fully fledged emotional texts that encouraged reflexivity and self-scrutiny, while disseminating forms of sentimental education in line with the ideological views and projects of renovation of society pursued by the main political formations of the time, the Catholics and the Communists, who used popular culture as means to reach wider publics (Tonelli 2003). For many women, then, the purchase of a magazine represented both a form of self-care and a key to accessing the outside world, while the presence of agony and advice columns opened up opportunities of interaction and identification with other readers that formed a – gendered – community, an 'intimate public', which offered 'a porous, affective scene of identification among strangers, that promise[d] a certain experience of belonging and provide[d] a complex of consolation, confirmation, discipline, and discussion about how to live as [a woman]' (Berlant 2008, viii).

As suggested in the previous chapter, cinema-going and magazines had distinct yet complementary roles and meanings in women's everyday lives and their experiences of the public and domestic sphere. Given their function of 'guides to modernity', the magazines offered advice about cinema-going as well, and their readers wanted to discuss this experience, which sometimes caused them trouble. These 'conversations' illustrate well the meanings commonly associated with the cinema as a gendered public space, and its role in the socio-cultural transformations brought on by the economic boom. They also allow the recuperation of the perspectives of readers, and their attempts to negotiate the conflicting pressures about femininity characterising the period, in which traditional values coexisted, converged and sometimes clashed with those of consumer capitalism.

As such, this chapter is based on the study of discourses on cinema-going present in a heterogeneous group of women's magazines, *Annabella*, *Famiglia Cristiana*, *Alba*, *Così* and *Noi Donne*, focusing on the years 1958–63, with a particular attention to the advice columns as discursive spaces, in which authenticity and ideology blurred. As noted by Penelope Morris, although it is very likely that most of the letters sent to agony aunts were authentic, they were certainly subjected to substantial editing and some of them were possibly fabricated by the magazines as well (2007). However, instead of invalidating their documental value, the interplay of 'authenticity' and 'manipulation' typical of agony columns enables the recuperation of both the readers' expectations and the gendered discourses produced by the magazines, including those about cinema-going. This aspect, combined with the diverse ideological orientations of the many publications considered in this chapter, allows me to survey competing discourses around cinema-going that reflected divergent views on gender and society, addressing a vast and mixed range of publics and a variety of experiences.

THE CINEMA-THEATRE AND THE CITY

Annabella was one of the first and most popular women's weeklies in Italy. Founded in 1933 by the major Italian publishing company Rizzoli, during the post-war years it increased its circulation as well as its foliation, and adjusted its editorial line to offer a cautious negotiation of American consumer culture for a readership of Italian middle-class women (Harris 2017). In 1960, *Annabella* published a series of articles about the 'modern woman and the city' penned by the regular contributor and writer of popular crime novels,

Giorgio Scerbanenco.[1] The opening of department stores and supermarkets, and the diffusion of cars and scooters among the working class, were relatively rapid in the main industrial cities of the north such as Milan, Genoa and Turin, and the idea that young women might or want to take part in these changes and enjoy them ruptured with consolidated notions of gender and the public space.[2] These articles aimed to offer practical solutions to the challenges that the urban space might pose to a young woman who wished to go shopping, or simply stroll around and drive a car. An article of the series titled 'A delicate problem for the modern woman: Living with others' portrays the young diva Claudia Cardinale walking in the crowded streets of a city, asking a policeman for directions, going to a repair shop to retrieve her car, stopping at a newsagent to buy a magazine, and drinking an aperitif at the bar (Scerbanenco 1960a). Cardinale plays the part of a stylish young girl who is learning to navigate on her own the chaotic and stimulating opportunities offered by the city, showing the readers how to handle every situation in the appropriate manner. Very interestingly, the pictures show Cardinale interacting only with men, suggesting that the urban space was still prevalently male, and it was men that she had to learn how to deal with. As Beverley Skeggs (1997) points out, respectability is an essential trait of middle-class femininity, conditioning not only social interactions but also self-perception. Cardinale's behaviour precisely illustrates a gendered and classed form of respectability based on the control of the body and the choice of an appropriate and elegant outfit that aimed to prevent equivocal moments with men.

In another article focusing on catcalling, sexual harassment and the so-called *pappagalli* – literally parrots, a nickname coined at the time for sexually aggressive men in public spaces – Giorgio Scerbanenco suggests that women avoid cinema-theatres in the daytime on working days, when the *pappagalli* were more likely to be there to molest young women (Scerbanenco 1960b). The *pappagalli* were recurring characters in the Italian public debate and popular culture of the time, representing stereotypical figures of Mediterranean masculinity whose uncontrollable sexual appetites made them unsuitable for modern social life (Reich 2004). Interestingly, according to the article, they were more likely to go to the cinema at a time of the day when people are generally at work and children are at school, an aspect that emphasises their unproductiveness and alienation from the nuclear family. A modern woman, therefore, should avoid going to the cinema alone when the 'pappagalli' are there, and exposing herself to the risk of sexual harassment; rather, she should attend film screenings with her family, as suggested by the *Enciclopedia della donna*, a popular domestic guide aimed at middle-class women. The *Enciclopedia*, indeed, gives detailed instructions about how to go to the theatre with husband and children, emphasising the importance of good manners (avoid coughing or talking during the film) and wearing appropriate outfits (1964, 226).

It is impossible to measure the impact of these instructions on everyday practices; however, sexual harassment undoubtedly influenced women's experience of cinema-going. As the oral history project ICA confirms, the cinema-goers of the 1950s associated their memories of movie-going with the possibility of unsolicited sexual contact. However, while male participants tend to minimise episodes of harassment of women, linking them with courtship, or minimising them as *ragazzate*, the testimonies from women express anger and frustration, and some of them even resorted to self-defence, or wished they had reacted more promptly (Treveri Gennari et al. 2020, 189–97). These reactions reveal that women struggled to cope with sexual harassment, reminding me of what Rachele Borghi has written about women and self-defence: as women we are educated to reject violence and avoid using our bodies to act against injustice and oppression, yet self-defence assumes a political meaning when practised by an oppressed and subaltern group (2020). Although the advice to avoid cinemas sounds sensible, asking women to remove their bodies from the theatre, or policing their behaviours in terms of respectability is actually a way to delegitimise their presence in the audience and prevent an autonomous experience of this space. The normalisation of sexual harassment as 'a woman's problem' has certainly contributed to make cinema theatres homosocial and male-dominated spaces, while insistence on good manners and outfits has shifted women's focus from engagement with the film and leisure to class distinction and respectability.

THE CATHOLIC GIRL AT THE MOVIE THEATRE

While *Annabella* suggested avoiding cinema theatres specifically at certain times of the day, a magazine like *Famiglia Cristiana* (FC) was way more restrictive, reflecting the Catholic preoccupations with morality in the cinema. Since the post-war years, the Church and many Catholic lay organisations promoted systematic interventions in the areas of film production, censorship, distribution and exhibition, both nationally and locally.[3] Founded in 1931, FC aimed at a readership of married mothers of lower economic status, and was conceived as a publication that could potentially reach the entire family, with sections dedicated to children and current affairs. Considering its diffusion – it sold over 1 million copies per week, at least until the early 1970s – FC was particularly suitable for translating, in simpler terms and with everyday examples, the policies and actions developed by Catholic institutions and activist organisations.[4] For instance, FC regularly published the ratings of the Centro

Cattolico Cinematografico (Catholic Cinema Centre), a moral classification of films that oriented parish cinema programmes, and advised believers who wished to attend screenings at commercial theatres.[5] FC also gave space to longer articles discussing educational cinema and the morality of television, reporting the debates and actions of the Christian associations that monitored the media at the time. Between the 1950s and the 1960s, the number of articles about film and television increased dramatically in contrast to the early post-war years, suggesting not only the growing importance of this medium in everyday life, but also that Catholic mothers were in charge of surveying and monitoring the cultural consumption of the family. In addition to this sort of educational content, the magazine also made few concessions to entertainment, publishing news about films or interviews with film and television personalities whose private life could give a good example to the reader. Other recreational content was about fashion, beauty, home furnishing and domestic economy, and was introduced in the mid-1950s following a renovation of the editorial line (Cullen 2013). However, the tone and style of these articles were distant from those of the glossy, middle-end commercial weeklies like *Annabella*, as FC's approach was based on sobriety and moderation, which were considered the governing principles of the Catholic household. In this framework, cinema-going was depicted as a dangerous distraction from religious and family duties, which could also lead to moral corruption. The illustrated article 'Il cristiano e il cinema' (The Christian and the cinema), published in November 1960, well summarises the prescriptions that the believer had to consider before attending a screening. It is interesting to notice that a few recommendations were directed explicitly at girls and mothers, such as: 'A nice young lady never goes to the cinema alone, nor will her parents let her go alone with her boyfriend'; or 'Before enjoying the fun of cinema, the good Christian must have fulfilled all the duties of her state, for example, a mother must not leave small children at home alone or the kitchen in disarray'. In another section, an illustration portrays a mother who takes her children to the theatre despite their bad financial situation, a behaviour that is explicitly condemned in the caption, which reminds readers that it is better to give money to the Church or to the poor than to spend it on entertainment. However, such prescriptions weren't easily negotiated in everyday life, as testified by the letters on the topic sent to the advice column 'Colloqui con il padre' (Conversations with the Father), penned by Father Atanasio Lamera. In 1960, an anonymous female reader wrote: 'I'm over 20, and I'd like to know if it's true that a girl who never goes to the movies is not a girl. In this case, someone like me, who stays years without attending a screening, is not a girl?' Atanasio reassured her by saying that avoiding cinemas was actually the best way to find a husband, which is the highest reward for a 'good' girl:

> The cinema is not really indispensable to train good, smart girls ... worthy of a man's trust for a family. Not at all! If anything, given what is all too often modern cinema today, namely obscene, mundane, frivolous and corrupting, and given the promiscuity of the dark theatre, it must be said that the more a girl stays away from the cinema, the more she deserves esteem, praise and consideration. (Una lettrice 1960)[6]

The publication of letters penned by young readers had the double function of providing guidance to mothers concerned about the education of their daughters, and addressing the doubts of girls who might approach the magazine, as in this case:

> I'm a thirteen-year-old girl and I am unhappy because my parents and brothers don't let me go to the cinema, because they think I would fool with the boys. I say that it is not true, and this is really the sincere truth . . . . In the evening, when I see that my friends go to the theatre, I get a knot in my throat and I burst into tears. My dad says that it is okay if I go with him or my brothers, but not on my own. (Una tredicenne lombarda 1959)

In his reply, Atanasio suggests that she continues to avoid the theatre, to suppress her tears with prayers and to swear 'the cinematic promise'. The 'cinematic promise' was a formula that the believer had to pronounce in front of a member of the clergy, and consisted of swearing that one would never attend film screenings and would refrain even from the desire to do so. To better understand the sense of this promise, we should read Atanasio's reply to the letter of a fifteen-year-old girl, Adelina, who asks if it is a mortal sin to see films forbidden to the underage:

> at your age you need to begin to guard your heart and senses. The most generous and good girls go even further; they deprive themselves from seeing certain shows for various reasons: they want to pay homage to the good God, offended by so many spectators and actors, and make amends, and obtain grace for these sinners more in general. (Adelina 1960)

The way Atanasio describes the 'cinematic promise' suggests that young girls especially were encouraged to take this vow, which was presented as a sacrifice that would not only atone for one's personal sins but also make amends for the moral corruption of the cinema and society more broadly. In sum, Father Atanasio and FC left no doubt about what it was right or wrong to do, and the variety of content about cinema and television published in the magazine helped the reader to form a comprehensive opinion about media, which corresponded with the Church's initiatives in this area.

The rigidity that emerges from FC, however, does not correspond with the totality of Catholic positions and practices on women's spectatorship and cinema-going. In Catholic publications aimed at a middle-class urban readership, such as *Alba* and *Così*, these discourses are way more nuanced. For instance, *Alba* regularly published a two-page review section, the 'Cine Guida' (Cine Guide), which began to appear in 1963 and was edited by the Catholic writer and journalist Natal Mario Lugario, with the help of an anonymous 'Vice', who it is fair to assume was a junior member of *Alba*'s editorial staff, possibly a woman. The section covered especially the latest releases distributed in the elegant 'prime visione' venues,[7] with special attention given to the 'artistic, technical and moral aspects' of the films. To begin with its title, 'Cine Guida', the intent of the column was to provide guidance and information to the female spectator who was interested in films not only as a form of entertainment, but also as a source of cultural nourishment. The section published reviews of films like Federico Fellini's *8½*, but also morally ambiguous features, such as the collective film *Ro.Go.Pa.G.*, which included Pier Paolo Pasolini's episode *La Ricotta*, Antonio Pietrangeli's *La Parmigiana* (1963) and *Violenza Segreta* (Secret violence, 1963) by Giorgio Moser. Despite recommendations to avoid these films, the reviews offered an informed opinion that enabled the reader to fully understand the reason for their immorality so that they could explain it to others.

A similar approach to women's film consumption is shared by *Così*, founded in 1956 by a branch of the Edizioni San Paolo, the same publisher as FC. *Così* was directed by a nun, Suor Lorenzina Guidetti, and had an editorial staff of mostly nuns and religious women, with a targeted readership of unmarried, lower-middle-class women who, as Catholics, Guidetti pictured as 'beautiful, more beautiful than the others . . ., well dressed, fashionable, and able to keep the house well'.[8] In 1959, the magazine launched a survey to learn more about its readers, asking about their views on religion, culture and family. The results, based on 'several thousands of participants', revealed that almost 70 per cent of the respondents were under 21, lived in Northern Italian cities and came from blue- and white-collar families (Maccari 1959a). Only 17.1 per cent of the total affirmed that they had never been to the cinema, against 61.9 per cent who never attended a play in a theatre. All of them had been to the movies at least once in their life, while 16.2 per cent attended film screenings at least twice a week, with a clear preference for sentimental films (Maccari 1959b). The author of the article, Dino Maccari, interpreted the reader's high interest in cinema as a confirmation of young women's 'dubious taste and approximative approach to culture and art', but other than this, he didn't comment on the immorality of cinema-going per se (1959b: 9). Moreover, the survey reveals that young *Così* readers were avid film consumers who went to the movies alone or accompanied by a girlfriend, suggesting that this particular demographic didn't consider cinema-going as a contradiction of their faith. And this seems to have been the position of the magazine, as the article emblematically opens with a big picture of two girls in front of a cinema theatre who, according to the caption, met after work to attend a screening. Although this survey seems to suggest that the moral recommendations of FC didn't correspond with the practice of many Catholic girls, it is important to keep in mind the differences between the readership of these two magazines. They differed not only by age – FC was directed mainly at married women with children – but also by class and geographical distribution. All these aspects concurred to articulate distinct discourses about entertainment and consumption, including clear reflections about the cinema in the discussions. The fact that *Così* was read especially by young women from northern cities confirms what is suggested by quantitative data sets and the ICA project, that going to the cinema with girlfriends was much more common before marriage and at a young age, and was less diffused in the southern regions (Treveri Gennari et al. 2020, 126–34). However, despite the demographic of its targeted readership, the editorial line of *Così* was considered too liberal by some of its most observant readers. An anonymous letter sent to Lorenzina Guidetti's column in 1959 explicitly criticised the magazine for its coverage of the failed marriages of VIPs and stars:

> I despair at times thinking how hurtful are the overly casual articles about actors, singers, sportsmen [in your magazine], which minimise their conjugal failures. I think that, if in a house of good people, you don't let in individuals of dubious morality, [. . .] the same thing should be done by our [Catholic] magazines. (A.M. 1959)

However, Guidetti replies that a Catholic magazine can't overlook what happens in the world and avoid saying how things are, and continues:

> How is it possible to ignore the author of *Rome, Open City*, the actress who played *S. Giovanna d'arco* [. . .] and other leading figures? Ignoring is not always the most constructive system; guiding, instead, to make a judgement, positive or negative [. . .] helps to form the personality and one's ideas.

This brief exchange demonstrates the coexistence of two different approaches to women's social role among Catholics: one represented by FC and this reader, that believed that simple exposure to immoral behaviours could cause damage; and one represented by Lorenzina Guidetti and her magazine, who believed it was important for girls to be aware of what happens in the world in which they live, and develop their personality.

As Stefania Portaccio (1982) noted, in the post-war years the Catholic press had to admit the possibility that its female readership could make choices, and this change reflected the advent of democracy. It also meant acknowledging that women had a 'right to happiness', which ultimately corresponded with the fulfilment of specific expectations about femininity, a 'conditional happiness' (2010), to borrow an expression from Sarah Ahmed, that meant, for women, being happy because others were (a husband, a child, a parent). In the pages of FC and *Così*, going to the cinema or not had much to do with this, so much so that it could lead to discussions with the family, compromise the possibility of a happy marriage or distract from religion. As cinema-going could be potentially so disruptive, some of the readers' letters and the responses to Maccari's survey express a misalignment from those discourses exclusively based on renunciation. In the everyday, many Catholic girls experienced the cinema alone with their girlfriends, finding their own way to happiness and a place in the film audience as spectators and fans.

POLITICALLY ENGAGED SPECTATORSHIP IN *NOI DONNE*

The origins of the left-wing magazine *Noi Donne* are rooted in the history of women's political engagement, as its first edition was clandestinely published in Paris by a group of exiled anti-fascists between 1937 and 1939. Publication was resumed during the war of resistance, in 1944, by clandestine regional committees. With the end of the conflict, *Noi Donne* became a monthly publication of the women's political organisation UDI – Unione Donne d'Italia – which was close to the Italian Communist Party.[9] The magazine aimed to reach a vast public of working-class women, in line with the Italian Communist Party's commitment to the project of a 'new universal culture in which the historic division between the culture of the elite and the common people would be overcome' (Gundle 2000, 36). Later changes in the UDI's political strategies inevitably impacted on *Noi Donne*'s editorial line, thus during the economic boom, it mirrored the UDI's emancipationist agenda and campaigns calling for legislative changes in the fields of labour and welfare. In this framework, cinema represented first and foremost an instrument for cultural and political engagement, yet this project had to be translated in accessible terms to a working-class readership that was familiar with the formats and topics of popular women's and illustrated magazines. This meant including fashion articles and photoromances, or personality tests like the one titled 'What kind of spectator are you?', published by *Noi Donne* in May 1962, which invited readers to express an opinion on sixteen female characters played by famous actresses in films or TV dramas, and to reflect on topics such as marriage, politics, fashion and consumerism. The final score would reveal whether you were 'a modern spectator with a critical spirit, or if you passively absorb everything that the big and small screen present to you' (*Noi Donne* 1962, 38). Among the characters selected, there was Rosalia played by Daniela Rocca in *Divorce Italian Style*, Marlene Dietrich in *Judgement in Nuremberg*, Audrey Hepburn in *Breakfast at Tiffany's*, and depending on the score obtained, there were three possible results: the lowest referred to a 'passive spectator, with an old-fashioned mentality, outdated by modern life'. At an intermediate level there was:

> the easily influenced spectator; [. . .] who condemns or forgives on the basis of the first impulses of her feelings. Don't forget that cinema and television are often conditioned by commercial interests, and it is precisely in the calculation of the producers to leverage the feelings of the spectators in order to make success. You must [. . .] analyse well the substance of the show and see if it does not contradict your opinions, and if it [. . .] contradicts the reality of life.

Finally, the highest score corresponds to

> [the] intelligent and modern spectator, who is equipped with a good critical sense. [. . .] You have shown that you know how to distinguish between stereotypical and false models and the characters inspired by today's reality. [. . .] You have expressed an opinion, which reveals your personality and shows that you know how to choose.

These distinctions reveal that, for the magazine, the intelligent viewer was a woman who understands that individual actions are conditioned by broader systems of oppression, and who distinguishes between stereotyped representations and those based on real life. Although presented in a playful fashion, this personality test is a fully fledged exercise in film analysis, which stimulates the spectator's identification with the female characters on screen in order to enhance social and political criticism. In other words, we see in essence some discourses developed by Italian feminist film criticism later in the 1970s, and its attention to the study of stereotypes and its critique of the film industry. Overall, *Noi Donne* promotes a form of spectatorship based on awareness and reflexivity, which encourages women's engagement with films, warns against passivity, conformism and sentimentality: all negative characteristics generally associated with female spectatorship. This aspect is symptomatic of the difficulty faced by the magazine (and the UDI) in developing an autonomous approach to film spectatorship to confront the model present in other left-wing magazines of the time, like *Vie Nuove*, which was mainly directed at male militants. However, in *Noi Donne*, watching films and going to the cinema are presented as positive activities, if undertaken with the right degree of awareness. Indeed, girls should be encouraged to go to the theatre, either alone or with a boyfriend. In 1959 the reader 'A Concerned Mother' asked the magazine if it was the right decision to give her twenty-one-year-old daughter permission to go to the cinema with a boy. Giuliana Del Pozzo, who was responsible for the readers' column, approved this decision, emphasising the positive fact that the reader took it autonomously, without waiting for her husband's opinion (Una mamma preoccupata 1959). As such, this letter confirms that *Noi Donne* readers also had concerns about cinema-going, especially in relation to the promiscuous character of the theatre. However, Del Pozzo's reply, as opposed to the recommendations found in *Annabella* and FC, encouraged the reader to trust herself and her daughter's good judgement, and to enjoy the big screen.

Conclusions

The competing discourses about cinema-going present in some of the most diffused women's magazines during the economic boom reveal the existence of competing discourses and meanings assigned to femininity, mass culture and leisure time. They ecompassed burning ideological questions in relation to consumer capitalism, morality and political engagement that dominated different areas of the contemporary public debate. This demonstrates that such ideas circulated and were negotiated by women in their everyday lives, and as such they actively participated in the transformation of Italian social life. Indeed, women's presence at the cinema-theatre perturbed the hegemonic conceptions of gender and the public space, to the extent that Catholics especially attempted to monitor women's attendance or even dissuade women from attending film screenings. Respectability, the moral implications of taking the right decision, being a politically engaged spectator: all these discourses charged affectively and ideologically women's relationship with the cinema, and would have a decisive impact on the ways in which feminist groups elaborated their reflections and practices around spectatorship. However, despite these pressures, the letters sent to FC and *Noi Donne* reveal that many girls and women went to the cinema just because they liked it. Women's presence at the cinema-theatre, then, especially alone or with other women, represented a physical and symbolic contradiction of consumer capitalism's values of domesticity, and a threat to traditional and patriarchal values, because of its implications for cultural engagement and leisure.

Notes

1. Scerbanenco also penned an agony column that he signed with the pseudonym Adrian. This column was particularly popular precisely because it was a man replying and readers were interested to get relationship advice from someone of the opposite sex who wasn't a priest – another recurrent advice column in most Italian women's magazines.
2. Natalie Fullwood (2015) has analysed the ways in which Italian comedies of the 1960s represented the changes brought on not only by the sites of consumerism in urban space, but also by the impact of consumer goods and appliances in shaping the domestic space.
3. It is also noteworthy that despite the preoccupations for the morality of cinema, the Church developed an extensive and competitive circuit of parish cinemas, that in many parts of Italy represented the only supplier of films. For a detailed reconstruction of the scale and objectives of Catholic intervention in post-war cinema, please see Daniela Treveri Gennari, 2008, 'Endemic Propaganda: Catholic Production, Exhibition and Criticism', in *Post-War Italian Cinema: American Intervention, Vatican Interests* (London: Routledge), 62–88.
4. Silvia Cassamagnaghi divides the Catholic press for women into two main categories: publications of 'opinion and orientation', which included all the weeklies, monthlies and periodicals for women involved in lay activist organisations like Azione Cattolica (Catholic Action); and those of popular dissemination, directed to a wider public, like *Famiglia Cristiana*, and the middle-end women's magazines *Gioia*, *Alba* and *Così* (Cassamagnaghi 2007, 46). In both cases, the purchase of these magazines, whose main point of distribution was churches and parishes, was clearly linked to identification with the Catholic community.
5. The ratings published in *Famiglia Cristiana* were reduced versions of the more elaborated reviews published in the *Segnalazioni Cinematografiche*, a sort of handbook published each year by the Catholic Cinema Centre.
6. All translations from Italian-language sources are my own.
7. The 'cinema di prima visione', literally 'first vision cinemas', were generally located in the main urban centres, where films were released first, and for this reason represented the most expensive circuit of film theatres in Italy.
8. FSP sicom, 'Testimonianza di Suor Lorenzina Guidetti, fsp' YouTube 2016. Last access, 12 June 2020, available at https://www.youtube.com/watch?v=Ya3iVPalkio, accessed 5 May 2021.
9. In 1944, in the same spirit as the UDI, the CIF – Centro Italiano Femminile (Italian Women's Centre), a Catholic women's organisation that brought together twenty-six local associations – was founded. The CIF practices and campaigns often overlapped with those of the UDI, despite their different political inspirations. The CIF also had its own publication, *Cronache*, which, unlike *Noi Donne*, was aimed specifically at activists.

CHAPTER 3

Feminist Spectatorship and Transformative Publics: Aspirations and Legacies of Feminist Film Festivals

In her analysis of the reception of *Personal Best* (Robert Towne, 1982), Elizabeth Ellsworth argues that the many reviews of the film that appeared in the American feminist press articulated a form of discursive self-production (1990). Indeed, the movie portrayed a love story between two women in an unprecedented way for mainstream cinema, and for this reason it opened a debate in politicised lesbian communities that, in the act of rejecting or negotiating the film, recognise themselves as a collective subject. Italian feminist film critics did something very similar when in the 1970s they began to use feminist 'spaces' like activist magazines, film festivals and political collectives to build a community of politicised spectators. Such fragments of 'discursive self-production' are characterised by an emotional tension – anxiety, loneliness, anger, hope and desire – that reflected women's difficult position in Italian film culture more broadly. Activists worked hard to create the material conditions that allowed women to meet and discuss films together, and this, in itself, is a transformative political project, that is remarkably different from the isolated and individualist acts of rebellion analysed in the previous chapter. By means of collective film readings and festival programmes, feminist activists built a community of spectators that replaced institutional knowledge with new epistemologies and interpretative frameworks based on their individual and collective experience as women.

CONCEPTUALISING FEMINIST HISTORICAL PUBLICS

In order to reconstruct the variety of these practices, feminist film publics should be approached as the combination of public cultures and lived experiences, whose existence emerges from a wide 'range of texts and artifacts [which] enable attention to how publics are formed, in and through cultural archives' (Cvetkovich 2003, 9). As Catherine Russell explains in her study of early cinema, women have historically represented a part of the audience that was more 'fluid, mobile, unstable and heterogeneous than the limited position of "mastery" that has been theorised as both masculinist and bourgeois' (Russell 2002, 533). Drawing on Russell's intuition, I am interested in the fluidity and instability of the feminist film publics of the 1970s, as part of the complex history of women's film audiences.

The traces of the feminist film publics emerge in a heterogeneus array of sources such as pamphlets, feminist press and festival booklets that are preserved in different institutions, like the documentation centre Archivia in Rome and the Fondazione Badaracco in Milan. I also conducted complementary research on feminist magazines such as *Effe*, *Quotidiano Donna* and *Noi Donne*.[1] All these materials are accessible in libraries and public archives, but despite this, they haven't been systematically studied in relation to what they say about Italian film cultures of the 1970s. In order to understand the insider perspective of the women who organised and participated in these events, I interviewed the activists Silvana Campese/Medea, a member of the collective Le Nemesiache of Naples, and Moira Miele, a collaborator with *Effe*, a member of a feminist film collective in Bologna and the organiser of an itinerant series of screenings with the feminist film critic and filmmaker Maricla Tagliaferri. These perspectives are particularly important because they add to our historical reconstruction the affective quality of memory, that, paraphrasing Jackey Stacey, is crucial 'if we are seriously concerned with the history of cinema audiences' (Stacey 1994, 63). These personal stories dialogue with the archival sources illuminating a diversity of positions in the collective narratives of the past, complicating our understanding of feminist experiences of film programming, spectatorship and community organising.

As Giuliana Bruno and Maria Naidotti have explained, 'Italian feminism has vacillated between separatist opposition to dominant culture and attempts at insertion' (Bruno and Nadotti 1988, 10): feminist film festivals, film clubs and film reviews were clear attempts to reach a broader public and break the small circle of the militants, a goal that had sometimes entailed a strategic alliance with public institutions as well as a constant dialogue with existent circuits of film distribution and exhibition. These collaborations reflected a specific characteristic of the Italian film culture of the time, which was experiencing a process of fragmentation and an acculturation of its audience, brought by a new collective demand for non-commercial cinema (Bisoni 2009). In the 1970s, cinema-going was becoming more and more planned and occasional, and film choice was increasingly associated with a specific taste for a genre or a director. A national survey on the habits of cinema-going published in 1977 confirms that most of the participants decided to attend a film screening several days in advance, and the choice of the film was generally conditioned by the reviews published in newspapers and specialised magazines (Doxa 1977, 13). The same report reveals that young adults and the urban, educated middle class constituted most of the spectators of the many cine-clubs flourishing at the time, and this same demographic group showed a clear preference for politically engaged films (Doxa 1977, 26). Moreover, the overall percentage of female cinema-goers dropped from the 38.9 per cent of 1972 to the 34.4 per cent of 1977 (Doxa 1977, 15), meaning that feminist film festivals and the cine-clubs had a limited impact, in quantitative terms, on the overall habits of cinema-going, and therefore represented a niche practice in a context of general contraction of film consumption.

FEMINIST FILM FESTIVALS: THE MAKING OF AN AUDIENCE, IN THEORY AND PRACTICE

The case of feminist film festivals provides a good example of the contradictions inherent in the activist project of creating a space for women's cinema and feminist spectatorship in Italy, a context marked by a steady decrease of women spectators in the theatres and a contraction of the audience more broadly. Anglo-American scholarship on early feminist film festivals of the 1970s emphasised the importance of these initiatives for the formation of gendered and politicised counterpublics that contributed to the foundation of new creative and intellectual spaces for women (Heath 2018). Moreover, as B. Ruby Rich (1998) points out, feminist film exhibitions weren't ghettos for women's cinema, but political laboratories and 'research projects' based on activist and volunteer work that challenged the competitiveness and market-oriented character of the mainstream festivals. All these characteristics resonate with some of the Italian experiences, yet the archival sources I surveyed reveal that programmatic goals and enthusiasm were often frustrated by a persistent lack of economic support and infrastructure, and most importantly by the difficulty of reaching a non-activist and non-cinephile audience. Although these preoccupations were also present among the organisers of Anglo-American festivals (White 2006), exhibitions like the Edinburgh International Film Festival and the Alternative Cinema Conference in New York established a bond between intellectual labour and feminist activism that would continue in subsequent decades (Damiens 2020), suggesting that these events had more impact on the local film cultures than Italian events.

However, like the exhibitions overseas, the Italian festivals reflected a combination of creative, theoretical and activist concerns that appealed to a very specific community of spectators who were also attracted by the opportunity to see a selection of international and avant-garde films that it was otherwise impossible to see in the regular exhibition circuits. This latter aspect is in line with the cinephile practices of engaged spectatorship prompted by other organisations, like the Federazione Italiana Cineclub (FIC, Italian

Cineclub Federation) and the ARCI.² At the same time, the collective experience of watching women's films together nurtured a sense of belonging to a transnational feminist film community, an aspect that is further testified by the translation into Italian of several writings of Anglo-American feminist film theorists and the publication of reports from feminist film festivals. For instance, the essays of Claire Johnston, Laura Mulvey and Julia Lesange were translated and discussed in *Effe* and other collective publications like *Lessico Politico delle donne* (Women's political vocabulary)³ and *Kinomata* (Daopoulo and Miscuglio 1980). The assimilation of international feminist film theory dialogued intensely with the practice of the consciousness-raising groups, establishing a sort of protocol for the collective textual analysis sessions that often took place after the screenings. The dialogue between praxis and theory was essential to the festivals' design, which combined a militant approach to the medium with the theoretical aim of rewriting cinema history from a feminist and collective standpoint. To paraphrase the feminist critic Lina Ossi, 'Films about women, or created by women, have their most radical meaning in the "invention" of a wider female audience' (Ossi 1979, 27). For all these reasons, the experience of the feminist film festivals gives us the opportunity to understand the multifaceted material and political implications of feminist film spectatorship, in their practice and their limitations. In this chapter I focus on three exhibitions, *Kinomata* (1976), *Le Rassegne del Cinema Femminista* (1976), and *L'Occhio Negato* (1980) as attempts to establish a space and practice of feminist spectatorship, in which the circulation of women's cinema prompted new ideas and forms of film knowledge, but at the same time revealed the limits of these feminist cinematic and cultural projects.

Kinomata

The festival Kinomata – which literally means 'cinematic mother' – took place in Rome at the Filmstudio 70 cine club between 15 and 30 November 1976. It was the first fully fledged feminist film festival organised in Italy, although other programmes of feminist film screenings have already taken place previously. Kinomata was an idea of the Feminist Cinema Collective (Collettivo Femminista di Cinema, FCC), which involved activists from the Roman Feminist Movement (Movimento Femminista Romano) and the group Lotta Femminista (LF). One of the founders of the FCC, Rony Daopoulo, explained in an interview with *Effe* that the Collective was born in 1971 from a consciousness-raising group, and the organisation of the festival represented just one of their many interventions in this field (Tagliaferri 1977). Since its foundation, the group sought to combine politics and theory with film practice, including the organisation of programmes of screenings.

The FCC manifesto, titled *Per un cinema clitorideo vaginale* (For a Clito-Vaginal Cinema, 1971) defines cinema as an 'authoritarian' medium, and film spectatorship as an inherently passive activity, and for this reason, the group aimed to open new collective spaces where women could experiment and practise forms of active spectatorship, outside of the existing male-dominated film clubs. In their view, debates and discussions are not enough to enhance women's political action, and therefore 'it is necessary for the female spectator to take a different perspective' by rejecting masculinist film expertise. Indeed, the FCC is not 'interested in speaking to those who go to the movies for entertainment or distraction, or to deal with those who are simply seeking for cultural orgasms. We appeal for a form of critique that translates into action' (Collettivo Femminista di Cinema in *Almanacco* 1978, 134–5). We can see these words in practice in one early film exhibition that the FCC opened to a women-only audience, which took place at the Filmstudio, presumably in 1973.[4] The document that presented the programme mentioned the issue of the stereotypes in the cinema and called for a new type of film culture, in which women wrote and directed films that could really express an image of femininity in line with their experiences. The idea of a separatist audience was later abandoned by the Kinomata festival, which despite being advertised as a collective effort of the FCC has been prevailingly attributed to Roni Daopoulo and Annabella Miscuglio as curators. Indeed, in the catalogues of the shorter itinerant editions of Kinomata held in Milan (1–18 December) and Verona (5–10 March 1977), there is no explicit reference to the collective.[5]

The exhibition consisted of two programmes of screenings: the first, titled 'The woman with the camera', was a selection of films directed by women from the silent era to the 1970s aiming to recuperate and discuss women's contribution to cinema history. The programme put together pioneers like Elvira Notari and Esfir Schub, and contemporary directors like Elda Tattoli and Liliana Cavani. The second programme, titled 'The eternal feminine', focused on the representation of femininity in the history of Italian and international cinema, aiming to analyse the 'subjective and affective relationship of the female spectator with national cinema' (Rassegna Kinomata 1976). Specifically, it consisted of a series of thematic screenings with films starring divas like Silvana Mangano, Gina Lollobrigida and Sophia Loren, to stimulate a collective reflection on the impact of their characters on the female spectator. This programme was evidently inspired by Laura Mulvey's Gaze Theory, yet the invitation to rethink the gendered experience of cinema, both collectively and individually, resonates with the practice of the consciousness-raising groups. In a short essay, the artist Giulia (Bundi) Alberti describes the Kinomata festival as 'a collective shock', because it emphasised the woman's role as a spectator ahead of her countless other ways of being a woman

(Alberti 1980, 37). The Roman edition also scheduled a series of debates with feminist film critics, directors, actresses and activists to address the pragmatic issues of the production and distribution of women's films. These meetings aimed to open a debate about the opportunities for production and circulation of women's cinema in Italy as an independent project, led and designed by women, that was completely autonomous from capitalist and patriarchal infrastructures.

This curatorial approach resonates with the work of Claire Johnstone, Lynda Myles and Laura Mulvey at the Edinburgh International Film Festival, which became a hub for women's cinema and feminist film theory (Stanfield 2008; Kamleitner 2018). However, it is difficult to find other similarities between these two experiences. Kinomata was an independent initiative that relied on infrastructures for alternative film distribution and exhibition operating in Italy, such as film cooperatives and independent cine-clubs. Albeit it benefitted from the support of a network of national and international institutions, such as the Cineteca Nazionale, the British Film Institute, the associations Musidora – Femme/Media and the Danish Embassy (Rassegna Kinomata 1976), which facilitated the recuperation of the films and the permits to show them – it is evident that the festival had less resonance outside of its specialised publics, and its legacy has struggled to find a proper space in the histories and theories of Italian cinema.[6]

Le Rassegne del Cinema Femminista of Naples and Sorrento[7]

A couple of months before Kinomata, on 28–30 September 1976, the Neapolitan feminist collective Le Nemesiache inaugurated La Rassegna del Cinema Femminista (Reviews of Feminist Cinema): *L'altro sguardo* (The other gaze). La Rassegna continued until 1995, subjected to the alternating fortunes of the hosting festival, the International Film Meetings of Sorrento. The first Rassegna was scheduled in three matinées (10am to 2pm) at the cinema Filangeri in Naples, in parallel with the International Film Meetings, working as a sort of counter-programme.[8] The idea of this festival came from the charismatic artist, performer, filmmaker and activist Lina Mangiacapre/Nemesi, who involved the rest of the collective Le Nemesiache in the organisation.[9] The exhibition became an important hub for women's cinema in Europe, promoting the formation of independent circuits for the distribution and production of feminist cinema. Silvana Campese/Medea told me that a consistent proportion of the public were activists, but many people, both men and women, showed up just out of curiosity. There was no separate programme for women, although Le Nemesiache had excluded men from their events in the past. Silvana recalls that men were not admitted to the first showing of Lina Mangiacapre's theatrical performance *Cenerella* in May 1973, but those who wanted access had to come with a woman who vouched for them. This initial call for separatism was perhaps motivated by the particular nature of the play, which Lina Mangiacapre called *psicofavola* (literally 'psycho-fairytale'); it was a performance that encouraged female spectators to identify with the atavistic character of Cenerella, and engage with the rest of the audience in a group of *autocoscienza* (consciousness-raising). The format, aims and scopes of the Rassegne were very different from this theatrical performance, and in regards to public participation, Campese recalls that the discussions were spontaneous and required no particular moderation, while the press conferences and debates with the directors required a great deal of preparation and work. At the conclusion of the first edition, the organisers published a collective resolution asking for the introduction of a mandatory quota for female professionals on every film set, and the request to the city council of Naples to open a creative and cultural centre for women in the neighbourhood where Le Nemesiache lived, Posillipo (Le Nemesiache in *Almanacco* 1978, 139). The document is emblematic of Le Nemesiache's approach to the exclusion of women from the arts, which they understood as a systemic issue that should be faced with and, to some extent, within, the institutions. According to Campese, the main goal of the group 'was the practice of utopia through art, culture and creativity', and she admits that some of their creative work was financially supported by public funding (Silvana Campese, Correspondence with the author, 28 October 2019). This is also true of the Rassegna, which was sponsored by the Campania regional government's department of tourism, and by the municipalities of Naples and Sorrento.

As a witness and someone involved in the organisation, Silvana Campese/Medea admits that her interest in women's cinema was inextricably linked to her activism:

> the discovery of women's cinema was certainly related to my involvement in Le Nemesiache. Despite this, I remember that I was impressed by seeing *La moglie più bella* (The Most Beautiful Wife, 1970), by Damiano Damiani, which was about the kidnapping of Franca Viola. (Silvana Campese, Correspondence with the author, 28 October 2019)[10]

The specification of Damiani's film suggests that 'commercial' movies not directed by women, but somehow related to contemporary feminist struggles by reason of their topics or message, had a different role in the activist's memory. Asked about the changes in the practices of the feminist movement between the 1970s and 1980s, Campese links that phase to the escalation of violence that characterised the 'years of lead', and then notes:

> the expression 'years of lead' (*anni di piombo*) comes from the film directed by Margharete Von Trotta with the same title. We, Le Nemesiache, invited her to Sorrento for the presentation of her film at the Reviews, before she was famous in Italy. (Silvana Campese, Correspondence with the author, 28 October 2019)

L'Occhio Negato and Sherazade in Florence

The cultural association Sherazade was founded by a group of students who attended a seminar about women's cinema at the University of Florence, and in 1979 decided to organise a film exhibition, *L'Occhio Negato*. The festival consisted of a series of lectures, debates and sessions of collective analysis of women's films, whose meanings otherwise 'would disappear and be absorbed [by the hegemonic film culture]' (Pallotta 1981, 14). The positive response to these moments of collective reflection was surprising:

> [At the beginning] we believed that a very specialist and niche program, with screenings of avant-garde films and stuff like that, would create a very limited space for discussion . . . Instead, they stimulated a very lively participation, and everybody was happy to stay for the discussions after the screenings . . .; for instance, at a debate about film distribution, we were expecting to see only female film professionals, but it ended up similar to a big assembly. It was a very social atmosphere, with people who met, stayed and remained, interested not just in seeing the movies, but also in taking part in a sort of permanent seminar. (Pallotta 1981, 15)

Like the Rassegne of Naples/Sorrento, this exhibition was aided by the city council and the Tuscany Region to include also a programme of women's films at the Festival dei Popoli, one of the most renowned film exhibitions dedicated to documentary and ethnographic filmmaking in Italy. The Florence exhibitions had an educational vocation, and although the idea came from an academic environment, no such dialogue continued at later editions of the festival, which is still in place today under the name 'Cinema e donne', but handled by a different organisation.

Negotiating a Radical Vision

These three examples of feminist film festivals are the result of years of grass-roots initiatives, which gradually took the shape of institutionalised cultural events. Despite this, these exhibitions didn't succeed in their project of creating solid infrastructures for the circulation and distribution of women's cinema and feminist film culture more broadly. To understand the reasons for this apparently missed opportunity it is necessary to take a step back and look at other examples of grass-roots feminist film exhibitions that lacked means and institutional support.

In 1977, a feminist collective of students of the faculty of communication at the University of Bologna questioned the format of the film club by introducing the use of a video camera in the debates that followed the screenings they had organised on campus. The participants recorded the discussions by means of a participative practice that involved the entire audience. This collaborative and empirical approach also entailed the sharing of technical skills within the rest of the group:

> some of us already knew how [the camera] works, so we teach others... We use [the camera] in a playful manner and enjoy the interchangeability of our roles... As a result, our debates are half discussions and half lessons in videomaking..., in spite of the wordiness... and rigidity typical of male cultural events! (Barina et al. 1977, 27)

In this way, the collective called for an active form of political spectatorship that was eminently inclusive and participatory, and like the manifesto of the FCC, openly challenged the hierarchical structure of male-dominated cine-clubs.

Self-organisation and mutual support were key to such grass-roots experiments in community making through cinema. Feminist magazines and bulletins promoted these initiatives by publishing practical information on renting films (i.e. contact details of distributors and costs) and the technical information needed to screen them. These lists of films appeared in magazines such as *Effe* and *Noi Donne* and publications like the *Almanacco*, resulting in 'catalogues' that supported independent and DIY channels of distribution. Activists and collectives had to contact companies and venues directly, collect money to rent the copies of the films and find the film projection equipment.

Along with formats such as the 35mm, 16mm and Super 8, these alternative forms of distribution also circulated videos and types of audio-visual artefacts specifically conceived for political training and activist propaganda, which aimed to enhance audience participation. Activists brought feminist films wherever they thought it was important to bring them, as the feminist filmmaker Adriana Monti, activist of the Milanese group of the Wages for Housework campaign, recalls:

> We made this audiovisual show[11][in 1974] titled *We are Women, We are Many, We are Sick and Tired*, that was for the campaign for the referendum on divorce [...].

> In 1976 it was dismantled after being screened all over Italy. [. . .] I remember that once I went with Grazia [Zerman] to show it to the workers of the Alfa Romeo car factory [. . .] and the atmosphere became very festive . . . there were all those men who talked about emotions and love stories . . .! (Adriana Monti, Interview with the author, 4 June 2019)

Monti saw the emotional response of the male crowd as a success, as the process of consciousness raising, enabled by the screening, disrupted the conventional ideas of masculinity associated with factory workers.

Another interesting example of itinerant screenings involved two activists and contributors of the magazine *Effe*, Moira Miele – who was also among the organisers of the screenings at the University of Bologna – and Maricla Tagliaferri. After a first event organised in Rome, at the feminist theatre La Maddalena and at the Cineclub Roma in 1978, the two travelled with a selection of films to Caserta, Messina, Genoa, Turin and Ancona. They advertised the initiative on *Effe*, asking 150,000 lire for renting and travel costs. Pointing to material and economic constraints, this initiative would support the circulation of feminist films, with activists personally organising their distribution and supply to the detriment of the existent infrastructures. Tagliaferri describes the purpose of these itinerant screenings with these words:

> Not all women . . .[can] afford to leave their town and travel to watch films [at the festivals]. For this reason, the many festivals organised so far couldn't fulfil this [diffused] need for cinema . . . Moreover, it is difficult and expensive to find films, the equipment and the theatre for the screenings if you do it by yourself, without the support of male institutions . . . A women's film exhibition must be a moment of communication and reflection about definite [women's] experiences. (Tagliaferri 1978, 35)

In her view, this effort would eventually build a solid audience that would support the production of new films directed by women. When I asked Moira Miele about her memories of this experience, she commented: 'the only thing I remember is the tiredness. It was just me and Maricla, and I was exhausted. We carried the film reels around in local trains, up and down stairs, etc. and those reels were very, very heavy' (Moria Miele, Interview with the author, 16 September 2018). Moira's memories reveal the emotional and physical burden of activism, which she also linked to her experience as editor of *Effe* that relied similarly on voluntary work. Miele told me that at the time she was already aware that those efforts couldn't last, as many other activists like her were wondering if that type of unpaid work could ever lead to a career. Indeed, the ultimate goal of overturning patriarchal cultural structures eventually faded throughout the 1980s with a change of strategies and goals in the feminist movement more broadly, which inspired new forms of feminist activism in professional contexts, such as personal services, social care and education (Bracke 2014, 189–90). Campese/Medea described this phase with a line of disappointment:

> An increasing number of feminists [. . .] the most inserted and integrated [. . .] in the patriarchal organisations of institutional and political power, were just a little bit more than emancipated and emancipationists. For this reason, their presence [in the institutions], despite few exceptions, was if not useless, from a feminist point of view, at least complicit to the reaffirmation of a form of equality that didn't express parity in diversity, but rather a form of advocacy of theoretical notions for the sake of male power. (Silvana Campese, Correspondence with the author, 28 October 2019)

THE END OF UTOPIA

In her consideration of the legacy of feminist film theory and the women's movement of the 1970s, Laura Mulvey remembers that in that period 'cinema was . . . a symptom and symbol of utopian political teleology. Not only could cinema articulate the desire for a better world, its complex way of interpreting and representing could also produce both critique and new ways of seeing' (Mulvey 2004, 1287). As in Italy, these hopes eventually foundered in the 1980s in the face of changes in the political landscape and the evolution of the cinema as a medium, which opened a deep fracture between the 'now' and 'then' (Mulvey 2004, 1290). From the vantage point of posterity, Mulvey's considerations also resonate with the Italian experience, yet with a significant difference. While Anglo-American feminist film theory found a place in academia, in Italy the legacy of the festivals and their organisers remained confined to the alternative and cinephile circuits that they sought to transform, which gradually reduced their relevance in the evolving context of film consumption and production of the 1980s and 1990s. The episodic support from public institutions didn't translate into policies that enhanced the production, consumption and circulation of women's cinema any further. As such, although the movement renounced its early radical agenda to prioritise the democratisation and opening of films to a wider public, these exhibitions were eventually confronted with the lack of networks and infrastructures, including a difficult dialogue with the film industry. The project of a feminist film community changed, along with the idea of women's cinema and spectatorship at its basis, to fit the new priorities and practices of feminism in the 1980s. The utopia of a feminist spectatorship, as a transformative experience for the individual and the community, clashed with the reality of intense (voluntary) labour for the activists, and the difficulty of transforming the spaces opened in the 1980s into something that could last beyond the contingency.

Notes

1. Specifically, I conducted a detailed analysis of the complete collection of *Effe* (1972–82), *Quotidiano Donna* (1978–1981) and *Noi Donne* (1977). *Quotidiano Donna* was founded in 1978, and until 1979 was a supplement of the *Quotidiano dei Lavoratori*, a weekly edited by the leftist extra-parliamentary organisation Autonomia Operaia. The complete collections of these feminist periodicals are available at the feminist archive Archivia, based at the Casa Internazionale delle Donne in Rome.
2. These two organisations are rooted respectively in the Catholic and Communist experiences of cultural associationism stemmed in post-war Italy. In the 1970s both the FIC and ARCI intersected with groups and promoted activities that were not necessarily tied with Catholic and Communist institutional policies.
3. This publication consisted of a series of six volumes focusing on different areas: Women and Law; Women and Health; Theories of Feminism; Sociology of the Family; Emancipation; Cinema, Literature and Visual Arts (Fraire 1978–9).
4. The document that presents this exhibition is undated, yet the chronological organisation of the documents in the folder suggests 1973 as a possible year of publication. Archivio Fondazione Elvira Badaracco Milano, Fondo Movimento Femminista, Folder 105, Collettivo Femminista Cinema, 12, 1, MF 1863.
5. Daopoulo and Miscuglio, indeed, already had several contacts with local and national film institutions, since Miscuglio was among the founders of the Filmstudio, Daopoulo graduated in film direction at the Centro Sperimentale di Cinematografia and both were working on projects funded by the RAI broadcaster. Daopoulo and Miscuglio's experience as filmmakers will be discussed in detail in Chapter 11.
6. Indeed, besides the itinerant exhibitions already mentioned, the Kinomata festival had only one edition.
7. The reconstruction of the history of this festival is based on pamphlets, documents and festival catalogues in the folder Le Nemesiache no. 23, Archivio del Femminismo Fondazione Badaracco, Classificazione 1, busta 4, fascicolo 6.
8. The document announcing the exhibition is dated 30 August 1976 (Archivio del Femminismo, Fondazione Badaracco, Le Nemesiache, Classificazione 1, busta 4, fascicolo 6). It is also published in *Almanacco* 1978, 138–9, with a programme of the screenings, which consisted mainly of 16mm, Super 8 and 8mm films.
9. The collective was founded in Naples in 1970 and members adopted a nickname, usually taken from Greek mythology, to sign and perform their artistic creations and political documents.
10. In 1966 Franca Viola, a Sicilian woman, refused a 'rehabilitating marriage' (matrimonio riparatore) with the man who kidnapped her, held her hostage and

raped her. At the time, it was customary that a woman who lost her virginity (even when raped) could 'rehabilitate the honour' of her family with marriage. Instead, Franca and her family successfully prosecuted her rapist, and Viola became a symbol of women's emancipation in post-war Italy.

11. Monti calls 'the audiovisual' *audiovisivo* in Italian a screening of diapositives made with a projector connected to a set of speakers. It was a very cheap and effective form of political communication that Monti learned via her involvement in the Wages for Housework group. I will discuss Monti's experiences in the last chapter of the book, on filmmaking.

CHAPTER 4

Patterns of (In)visibility: Lesbian and Queer Counterpublics

The previous section reconstructed the experience of the feminist film festivals and their attempt to build new forms of spectatorship and a feminist audience. Specifically, we saw the coexistence of radical experiments and attempts to negotiate these political projects with the opportunities to obtain funding and support from cultural institutions and the difficulties brought by the lack of infrastructure. Between the 1980s and the 1990s, feminist film theory enageged in a debate about lesbian spectatorship in relation to the so-called 'lesbian film'. The main concerns of scholars participating in these conversations gravitated around questions of identification and representation, and the possibilities of developing oppositional and resistant readings of popular films.[1] With these experiences and debates in mind, this chapter focuses on lesbian counterpublics, as experiences that were linked to the formation of autonomous lesbian political groups in the late 1970s and the gradual disgregation of the second-wave movement. My reconstruction is based mainly on an analysis of the DIY leaflet of the lesbian collective Brigate Saffo (Sappho Brigades), which was published for two years (1978–9) as an insert of the gay activist magazine *Lambda*, edited in Turin. These sources are complemented with personal testimonies and other contextual archival materials.

OPACITIES AND IN/VISIBILITIES: INDIVIDUAL PATHS OF LESBIAN POLITICAL ACTIVISM AND THE CINEMA

The writings of the Brigate Saffo are mostly about representation in mainstream culture, and their activism is intertwined with the first manifestations of queer subcultures in Italy. These experiences can be interpreted as those of a politicised counterpublic in conflict with the dominant discourses about culture and cinema, but at the same time aware of its subordinate status (Warner 2002). The Brigate explicitly opposed 'compulsory heterosexuality' (Rich 1980), and contested some aspects of the feminist movement, especially in regards to class, but also discussed their marginality in the gay and the women's movement.

Along with collectives like the Brigate, the 1970s saw also individual lesbian activists intersecting their political experience of homosexuality with the discourses developed within the women's movement. An emblematic example in this respect is Rony Daopoulo, the founder of the Collettivo Femminista di Cinema and organiser of the festival Kinomata, who in May 1972 went with Giovanna Pala, an activist of the Roman collective of Pompeo Magno, to the *Journées de dénonciation des crimes contre les femmes* (Days for the denunciation of crimes against women) organised by the MLF (Mouvement de libération de la femme/Women's Liberation Movement) in Paris. Among the crimes against women publicly condemned by the activists at the meeting there was the oppression of homosexuality: several women, including Daopoulo and Pala, went on to the stage to 'come out' as lesbian (Biagini 2018, 88–9).[2] The Daopoulo–Pala duo is an interesting one, as not only was the former engaged with cinema, but also the latter had first-hand experience in the Italian film industry. Giovanna Pala, indeed, was a former actress. Like Lucia Bosé, Sophia Loren and other divas of the post-war period, Pala began her career as actress after a producer noticed her at the Miss Europe beauty contest in 1950.[3] Between 1951 and 1956 Pala took part in ten films with actors like Alberto Sordi, Nino Manfredi and Claudio Villa, and she eventually quit acting in 1957, just before the shooting of the film *Racconti d'Estate* (Gianni Franciolini, 1958). In a 2008 interview, Pala 'explains her trajectory from 'objectified' film star to committed feminist by highlighting the importance of her discovery and acceptance of her lesbianism (Gildea et al. 2013). Her experience in Italian cinema, indeed, was incompatible with her sexual orientation, as the Italian film industry of the 1950s was unapologetically sexist and homophobic, a space in which lesbians couldn't exist outside the restrict horizons of patriarchal imagination. In this respect she remembers:

> In regards to [male] homosexuals, there were certainly some of them, but in such environment, they stayed well concealed, whereas the so-called *checche* [sissies], who were so visibly extravagant, were tolerated because they made people laugh. For [the men in the film industry], lesbians were those prostitutes who consented to erotic games with other women for the use and consumption [of men]. (Giovanna Pala, Correspondence with the author, 27 October 2019)

In such context, only a foreign diva like Maria Felix could dare to be bisexual, while it seemed virtually impossible a space for lesbian existence: 'it was a real scandal when Maria Felix shot a movie in Italy and came to Cinecittà with her partner. Locked in their caravan during the breaks from acting, the two ladies triggered the frenzy and obscene jokes of the crowd of men' (Giovanna Pala, Correspondence with the author, 27 October 2019). It was the political climate that led to the formation of the student and workers' movement in 1968/9 and it was in the subsequent encounter with feminism that Pala developed a political consciousness of her sexuality. In a round table with Teresa de Lauretis that discussed the influence of American feminism on the lesbian movement in Italy, Pala affirms that 'for many women, it wouldn't even been possible to be lesbians without feminism' (CLI 1992, 21). In other words, Pala believed that feminism had made lesbianism a possibility, an idea that she had already expressed in occasion of the National Conference of Lesbian Women held in Bologna in 1983, when she distributed, with Rina Macrelli, a programmatic document about the centrality of feminism in the history and agenda of the lesbian movement (Cavarocchi 2010, 86–7). Macrelli had worked in television and the film industry too, initially as an on-set interpreter and subsequently as a scriptwriter and as assistant and assistant director for Liliana Cavani (Women of the Resistance, Galileo) and Michelangelo Antonioni (Zabriskie Point). Her career lasted almost twenty years (her last job in television was for the mini-series *Il passatore* in 1978), which possibly overlapped with the first period of activism. Unfortunately, since Macrelli has recently passed away, it is not possible to ask her about the intersections between her professional life and her militancy.

With all the due differences, these apparently casual encounters between cinema and politicised lesbianism suggest that there is something particularly complex behind the 'invisibility' of lesbians in Italian cinema. Indeed, though the gay and feminist movements were practising political forms of 'being out', lesbianism remained quite 'invisible' in Italian feminist films, including in a mainstream example like *Io sono mia* (I belong to me, 1978) by Sofia Scandurra, in which the single – brief – scene hinting at a sexual and intimate relationship between two women alludes only to the fact that they had spent the night together.

To some extent, this opacity of representation persists in Italian cinema today, in both mainstream and independent productions. Drawing on Nicholas De Villiers' reflections on the 'opacity of the closet' (2012), Sergio Rigoletto reads the absence of the 'coming out' in many Italian contemporary films as the enactment of a queer strategy that rejects both the teleological transparency of 'being out' and its individualistic dimension (2017). However, while Rigoletto's argument works in relation to some contemporary examples, if we look retrospectively at the experiences of Daopoulo, Pala and Macrelli, the contrast between their 'being out' and the absence of a lesbian discourse in Italian cinema, at least during the 1970s, suggests another possible path of interpretation, which similarly draws on the concept of 'opacity' as a queer strategy. These activists, indeed, had embraced feminism and lesbianism politically and had opted and fought for visibility, but they didn't choose the cinema as the place to do it. At least for Daopulo, we can imagine that the reason lies in the different theoretical and political priorities that the theory of feminist filmmaking was addressing at the time, mirroring also the struggles of the women's movement more broadly. For Pala, the personal experience of the cinema industry as a deeply misogynistic and homophobic environment made it incompatible with any manifestation of lesbian visibility. As such, the 'opacity' of the lesbian experience in Italian cinema can't be read without considering these activists' political experience of 'being out'. Indeed, it is from this position of visibility that Pala reads and speaks about her trajectory as an actress today, to point out the oppressive and exploitative character of the cinema in relation to lesbian and queer subjects. In other words, her political and activist life builds a situated perspective on the lesbian experience that opens up a series of opportunities to rewrite a past that would otherwise have been eclipsed by a 'taken-for-granted' and supposedly self-evident heterosexuality in Italian cinema history. This means that in our consideration of the regimes of in/visibility of lesbian and queer existence in cinema, we must consider the interplay and interdependence between the levels of representation and those of historical and political subjectivisation that make it possible, today, to recuperate these experiences.

THE BRIGATE SAFFO AND THE FORMATION OF A LESBIAN COUNTERPUBLIC

In relation to the examples of Daopoulo, Pala and Macrelli, the case of the Brigate Saffo stands out as a subcultural and collective experience of lesbian politicisation, which was linked to a specific experience of activism. The sources available to reconstruct the political activity of the Brigate are particularly scattered, based on a form of 'anecdotal and ephemeral evidence' that resonates with many other archives of queerness, which are 'randomly organized, due to the restraints historically shackled upon minoritarian cultural workers' (Muñoz 1996, 7). Despite these limitations, the leaflets of the Brigate Saffo 'grant entrance and access to [the experiences of] those who have been locked out of official histories and "material reality"' (Muñoz 1996, 9). This particular nature of the queer archive resonates with a fragmented experience that according to Chris Staayer characterises lesbian lives, which vacillated between two worlds: one in which they are included by reason of their humanness and assumed heterosexuality, and a second one, a lesbian-created world centred on the practices of the lesbian subculture (Staayer 1984).[4] The Brigate Saffo, with their political actions and their subcultural production, created a lesbian-centred world that aimed to subvert the strategies of silencing and invisibilisation enabled by heteronormativity, which was also present in the Italian social movements of the time.

Though the formation of feminist and the gay movements during the 1970s had been crucial to the existence of a 'lesbian-centred world', a radical lesbian political agenda became autonomous only by the end of the decade, but this doesn't mean that lesbian activists hadn't expressed a specific political standpoint earlier. The first ground-breaking manifestation of lesbian political visibility is associated with a picture of the activist Mariasilvia Spolato holding a sign with the words 'Liberazione Omosessuale' (Homosexual Liberation) at a feminist demonstration in Rome on 8 March 1972.[5] While the photo cost Spolato her teaching job, marking the beginning of a precarious life, the moment and place where the picture was taken are emblematic of the political journey of many Italian lesbians, who oscillated between participation in the gay-led organisation FUORI (and later the formation of a lesbian section, FUORI Donna), and the militancy in feminist collectives with heterosexual women. This situation was particularly diffused among members of the Roman group via Pompeo Magno (to which both Pala and Daopoulo belonged), but also in the feminist groups based in Turin, where the FUORI was founded and was also particularly active. These experiences, along with the practices of lesbian separatism brought on by French and American activists, eventually led to the formation of lesbian collectives in Italy (Biagini 2018). The Brigate Saffo was one of the first experiments in this direction, and the group was founded in Turin in 1977 by Matilde Bona and Rossana Pittatore, two former members of the local section of FUORI (Biagini 2018, 51–5). In line with the counter-cultural practices of the radical left, the Brigate adopted a provocative and radical form of activism, beginning with their name, which echoed that of the terrorist organisation Brigate Rosse (Red Brigades). The group contested the elitism of the feminist practice of consciousness raising, privileging direct action, and the subversion of the urban space, in continuity with the counter-cultural practices of the Italian Movement of 1977. Their creations and initiatives included graffiti, frequenting lesbian bars and discotheques where it was possible 'to meet other lesbian proletariats' (Biagini 2018, 55), a radio programme and the publication of a DIY sheet that, as we have seen, became part of *Lambda*, a militant gay magazine also based in Turin. The Brigate wished to constitute a permanent editorial committee to publish a lesbian edition of *Lambda*, but with the 1980s approaching, their space in the magazine became increasingly precarious, and the destiny of the gay periodical itself was on thin ice. Indeed, the first series of *Lambda* ended in 1980, and the magazine resurfaced more than a year later, with a reduced foliation. The beginning of the 1980s brought significant changes within the homosexual and feminist movement that also somehow sanctioned the end of the Brigate's political experience. For this chapter, I have surveyed the traces of politicised gay and lesbian film spectatorship in the first edition of *Lambda*, which was published from 1976 to 1980. The structure of the magazine itself reveals implicit 'power relations' between the gay male and the lesbian communities: the Brigate's leaflet was just three to four pages long, and was also poorer in terms of design and editorial composition than the rest of the magazine, yet both included drawings, pictures, poems, personal messages, interviews, articles about politics, music and personal stories. Unlike the sources about cinema and feminist publics, which were generally concerned with theory and cultural policy, the Brigate's ideas about cinema, television and leisure were more spontaneous, and often marked by sentiments of frustration, anger and distress, making this activist publication a powerful space for collectively managing forms of 'minority stress' (Staayer 1984).

Subcultural Practices against Heteronormativity: The Brigate and the Gay Cruising Guides

In the second issue of the Brigate Saffo leaflet, which appeared on January 1979, there is a short piece titled 'Dear father, dear hetero' that powerfully addresses questions of representation and identification (Matilde 1979). The author, Matilde (Bona?), describes a typical family lunch with some of her relatives 'who have accepted that [she is] a *dyke* [frocia]'. Such a domestic and familial setting is where patriarchal oppression reveals its casual and ordinary presence in the everyday life of the activist:

> as usual, we had the same old discussion [about homosexuality]. This time it started because of my sister and her husband have watched one of those stupid porn films starring so-called lesbians [. . .]; all this because my eminent father asked: 'Are there any films with homosexuals?' Nauseated, I tried to explain why I can't and I will never accept that those mercenary, heterosexual women try to pass off as lesbian something that represents just the ramblings of the morbid and distorted fantasies of shitty hetero-policemen who don't know what else invent for their daily masturbation. My father then said: 'But you [lesbians] only talk about sex, you always show off . . .'. Well no, dear father, dear hetero-policeman, [. . .] we don't talk about sex, we talk about free sexuality, in other words, in the state of the norm, we want to live our diversity freely. (Matilde 1979, 3)

In this brief and fierce piece about the incomprehension in her family, Matilde rejects not only the images of lesbianism circulating in the mainstream media, but also the idea that heterosexual women could 'pass off' as lesbians.

The same reprimand applies to the show girls who claimed to support the feminist movement but then 'sold out' to the heterosexual male spectator. In a little piece on the actress and singer Ombretta Colli, the wife of the praised left-wing songwriter Giorgio Gaber, the author criticises the show girl for chanting on the second national TV channel 'with naked butt cheeks and tits to the wind' the famous feminist slogan 'Tremate tremate, le streghe son tornate!' [Tremble, tremble, the witches are back!]. The anonymous contributor condemns such performance for being enacted by 'a self-proclaimed "comrade" and "feminist"', and adds: 'Women [like Colli] . . . want to replace the bras they burnt at the demonstrations with the crowd, with veils and frills, to become even more yours, dear drooling little men' (Brigate Saffo 1978, 3).

With respect to the rest of the writings published in *Lambda*, the Brigate used a very direct, anti-intellectual tone to privilege spontaneity and the discussion of everyday aspects of activism and lesbianism. A very good example is an article penned by Polina and other members of the Brigate titled 'A proposito di locali gay!' [About gay clubs!] (Polina 1978). The piece is structured as a collective conversation about the pros and cons of going to lesbian and gay bars. Most of the discussion is about the iconic gay club KB in Turin, which Polina describes as

> [a] mix of lives and metamorphic sexes, like the *balún*, the flea market of Porta Palazzo [in Turin], a place where you can find everything: fags [*froci*], lesbians, lesbian-whores, male hookers [. . .], lesbian-males [*sic*] namely lesbians who dress up as thugs and wear suits and ties. (Polina 1978, 10)

The picture is completed by heterosexual couples looking for threesomes, drug dealers, undercover policemen and groups of transgender women, including some who have had gender reassignment surgery. Polina likes the KB because it is distant from the bourgeois respectability that you can find everywhere else. She loves it, not just because it is a gay club, but because it is 'real', a place that expresses the real harshness of life. Another contributor, Anna, likes gay clubs because she can be herself in those places, even if sometimes, she admits, they are quite boring, always attracting the same people. This is also why heterosexual clubs are better if you are looking for a hook-up.

Unlike Polina, Anna no longer likes the KB, and prefers instead to go to the movies or dance at the FIRE, a new dance event organised by the local FUORI activists. Polina wonders if gay clubs are actually ghettos for the lesbian and gay community, but another girl, Cristina, claims that there is still a need for such spaces:

> it is a matter of fact that lesbians tend to lock themselves in the private, but there will be a day when we will have our own space. Look at Maria Schneider,

she can say publicly what she is, but someone like me needs to remain silent, because I risk my job or being bullied.

Maria Schneider came out as bisexual in 1974, and in a famous interview with Roger Ebert affirmed: 'Most of the members of my generation are gay, or bisexual, they have more open minds about sexuality, about what a woman's role can be, or what the potentials are'.[6] Cristina accorded to the film star the privilege of *being out*, in a way that is very distant from her everyday experience of homophobia. This is particularly interesting to read today, since Maria Schneider is now remembered mainly for her traumatic experience on the set of *Ultimo tango a Parigi* (Last tango in Paris, Bernardo Bertolucci 1972), and her incompatibility, as a rebellious and independent young woman, with the entertainment system. In other words, she is now the symbol of someone who has paid the consequences for challenging patriarchy and bigotry. However, at the time Cristina was writing, Maria Schneider's open bisexuality – she had a relationship with Joan Townsend – sounded not just unprecedented, but a sign of her hard-won goals, which were beyond the reach of most people. This idea resonates with Pala's words on Maria Felix, in which the *queerness* of the film star not only represents an imaginative space for possibilities but also reminds one how difficult it is to be/come *out*. From the description of the KB to these few words about Maria Schneider, this article is a powerful sketch of the lesbian subculture of the late 1970s. It was a world that shared many spaces with the gay and trans community, where discontent and conflict were always around the corner, but it was also characterised by solidarity and mutual support.[7]

In this context, the gay cruising guides published in *Lambda* highlight the striking difference between the lesbian experience of the public and urban space, as described by the Brigate Saffo, and that of gay men. In the two cruising guides of Milan and Rome published in *Lambda* in 1980, the question of safety emerges as the main priority of the reviewers, who offer several recommendations about the kind of people that can be found in each place, including in the many film theatres used as meeting places (Teobaldelli et al. 1980; Giordiani 1980). These guides shaped a new geography of the city, modelled on desire and pleasure, which was also highly conditioned by the segregation of the gay community in a society widely dominated by homophobia. Cinemas represented a relatively safe (and warm) alternative to other cruising spaces, such as parks and public toilets. However, they still present many dangers and obstacles, like police stings, ushers and, of course, the people who went there just to see the films. For this reason, readers were particularly discouraged from attending screenings at arthouse films, or at weekends when more families went to the movies. Another interesting aspect to note in these cruising guides is that many places, including bars, clubs and cinemas are described as sad and boring, echoing the sentiments in the collective piece penned by the Brigate. On the back cover of an issue of *Lambda*, there is a poem titled 'Nel cinema' (In the cinema), which describes a cruising experience at a film theatre.[8] It begins with the description of a peripheral cinema in the early afternoon, full of military and old people, and this situation is described as 'a dreariness'.

Conclusion: A Matter of Space and Possibility

A comparison between articles aimed at the gay male readership and the Brigate Saffo leaflet reveals very different experiences of the urban space, which reflected broader gendered notions of the public sphere. Despite this, both communities shared a sense of marginality and a clandestine condition that reverberate in the use of an affective, and sometimes aggressive, vocabulary to describe their experiences, confirming that the space of the magazine was created for and addressed by a counterpublic. As Micheal Warner argues, although nobody is in the closet within a gay or queer counterpublic, individual struggle with stigma is transposed into a conflict between modes of publicness (2002, 424). There is no trace of this conflict in the writings and manifestos of the feminist groups analysed in the previous chapter. The reason resides not just in the different nature of the documents surveyed, but also in the different ways in which the feminist movement and the gay and lesbian communities perceived themselves in relation to the mainstream and public cultures, including the cinema. Most feminist groups sought forms of institutional insertion, attempting to infiltrate the cultural industries on the basis of gender difference. Lesbian feminists and politicised gays were immersed in a subcultural world that refused insertion and rejected compulsory heterosexuality, measuring the constraints of the present while their words expressed a longing for a future of possibilities.

Notes

1. A reconstruction of this debate can be found in Karen Hollinger, 1998, 'Theorizing Mainstream Female Spectatorship: The Case of the Popular Lesbian Film', *Cinema Journal* 37, no. 2 (Winter): 3–17.
2. At the event many women went as far as to say publicly that they had had an abortion, performing a strategy of 'coming out' that has been central in many political struggles for its legalisation. For an assessment of feminist strategic narratives about abortion see Kelly Suzanne O'Donnell, 2017, 'Reproducing Jane: Abortion Stories and Women's Political Histories', *Signs: Journal of Women*

in Culture and Society 43, no. 1: 77–96. Some of these strategies were also adopted in feminist filmmaking see: Julia Lesage, 1978, 'The political aesthetics of the feminist documentary film', *Quarterly Review of Film & Video* 3, no. 4: 507–23.
3. Pala obtained second place at the beauty pageant.
4. The article 'Personal Best, Feminist/Lesbian Audience' originally appeared in the journal *Jump Cut*, no. 29, February 1984: 40–4, available at https://www.ejumpcut.org/archive/onlinessays/JC29folder/PersBestStraayer.html, accessed 5 May 2021.
5. Mariasilvia Spolato also authored the book *I movimenti omosessuali di liberazione* (The movements of homosexual liberation), published in 1972. This foundational text for the Italian LGBTQ+ movement collects extracts from the political documents of gay and lesbian activist groups from all over the world, and also reproduces the picture discussed in this section.
6. Roger Ebert, Interview with Maria Schneider, appeared originally in the *Chicago Sun-Times*, 14 September 1975, available at https://www.rogerebert.com/interviews/interview-with-maria-schneider, accessed 5 May 2021.
7. An incredibly lively reconstruction of this world can be found in the recent memoir/essay by trans activist Porpora Marcasciano, 2018, *L'aurora delle trans cattive* (Rome: Alegre).
8. 'Nel cinema di periferia/nel primo pomeriggio, che squallore/con le nuche dei militari offerte/alla decollazione e la bocca sfiatata d'un pensionato./Ma l'arrivo del ragazzo aveva tutto/ cancellato./In piedi, contro la parete,/si lascia andare sulle ginocchia/al ritmo distratto del chwengum [sic!]./Il film di certo non lo interessava/se così spesso abbandonava lo schermo/ per naufragare in sala la noia/dello sguardo./Ancora non s'erano incontrati/e l'uomo prese a girarsi silenziosamente/per fare volare la sua voglia dritta al/sesso./Un fotogramma più luminoso subito glielo scoprì tenero e rigonfio/ che attraversava i jeans,/e come la sua vestige l'avesse accompagnato/una mano scese ad accarezzarlo,/segnandone i confini./Ora gli beveva tutta l'anima/ e fu così che il giovane lo sorprese/ cogli occhi scintillanti e la gola/lastricata dal batticuore./Non servirono cenni./Sdraiandosi pesantemente sul sedile di fianco,/il ragazzo aprì le gambe/allo schiaffo della certezza'. Extract from the collection of poems by Ivan Teobaldelli and Massimo Quinto, 1978, *Nel ghetto. Frammenti di omosessualità* (In the ghetto: fragments of homosexuality), (Milan: Ottaviano). Published in *Lambda* 3, nos. 16–17 (September–October), back cover.

CHAPTER 5

Feminists and Porn: Protests and Campaigns

This last section about feminist spectatorship concentrates on the reactions and debates about pornography in the Italian feminist movement. Although in a context that was foreign to the so-called 'sex wars', local activists organised anti-porn campaigns, but most of these feminist interventions approached pornography as one aspect of a broader process of commodification of women's sexuality in the media. Specifically, Italian feminists believed that pornography affected women at the level of representation (pornography promoted the objectification of women) and everyday life (sexualised images were often violent, and therefore instigated sexual violence and violent gender relations). This latter approach translated into grass-roots campaigns that targeted specific films and cinema theatres as threatening for women, as they contribute to making the urban and the public space unsafe. Although many of these actions raised a heated debate at the time, they inspired no structured reflection on pornography or theoretical production on the subject in the following years.

In this chapter, I analyse two case studies that exemplify the movement's approach to the circulation of sexualised films and the diffusion of pornographic theatres, to the extent of providing a preliminary systematisation of Italian feminist debates about porn. The first case is the requisition request of the film *Life Size* (Luis Berlanga, 1974), promoted by Laura Remiddi, a lawyer and activist of the Roman feminist group Pompeo Magno. Remiddi and her supporters attempted to raise a public debate about sexual violence by comparing a few scenes of the film, considered pornographic, with the infamous Circeo Massacre.[1] The episode is emblematic of the ways in which Italian second-wave feminists linked pornography with patriarchal violence. This case study is based on the analysis of the documents that Laura Remiddi has generously shared with me, and her personal memories of the events that we have discussed.[2] The second case study consists of a reconstruction of the series of attacks against cinema theatres that groups of feminist activists attempted in several Italian cities during 1976, in the wake of the international campaigns of the US-based organisation Take Back the Night. These episodes escalated in 1979, when an anonymous group called 'Compagne Organizzate per il Contropotere Femminista' (Organised Comrades for the Feminist Counterpower) set explosives in four porn theatres in Rome. This part of the research is based on the study of the feminist weekly *Quotidiano Donna* and the general press.

The archival approach underlying this section responds to the call of feminist scholars such as Linda Williams (1989) and Susanna Paasonen (2007) to overcome the polarisation between pro- and anti-pornography, to engage critically, analytically and affectively with porn as a complex socio-cultural and historical phenomenon with specific material and political meanings. In other words, pornography can represent a key to understanding the past, including the history of the women's movement, while challenging our position as scholars and feminists.

THE ADVENT OF MASS-MARKETED PORNOGRAPHY IN ITALY

The Italian feminist movement's protests against pornography coincided with a period of expansion and liberalisation of sexually explicit media products, which saw for the first time, at the beginning of the 1970s, the introduction of hardcore images in low-end magazines and comics. These publications presented an unprecedented level of sexual explicitness and violence that was generally excluded from up-market glossy magazines such as *Playmen* – and later *Playboy* – which were oriented towards lifestyle contents and high-quality pictorials, and have been sold by Italian newsagents since the mid-1960s (Maina 2018, 2019). Audio-visual pornography had a much slower and contested diffusion, and its 'liberalisation' is generally dated with the opening of the first porn cinema theatres between 1978 and 1979. However, in the Italian case we can't properly talk about a process of legalisation, as there was no specific legislation regulating pornography, whose circulation, in both print and audio-visual form, was actually subjected to the general practices and regulations of censorship. Press censorship was abolished in the aftermath of World War II with the advent of democracy, yet many Italian Catholic associations in support of morality appealed to the existing laws for the preservation of 'public decency' to stop the circulation of 'obscene' materials. These laws gave judges case-by-case discretion in the requisition of obscene magazines and pictures from newsstands and book sellers. A principle of discretion applied to film censorship too, as despite reforms to the dedicated legislation in 1962, films needed clearance from a special commission in order to be screened legally. Despite this, individuals or associations of private citizens could report to the authorities any film that they considered obscene, leading to its requisition until a judge took a final decision. This situation made the circulation and consumption of sexually explicit materials particularly fluid and subject to a high degree of discrection. At the level of production, many Italian film producers have become well established in the international market of hardcore porn since the beginning of the 1970s, releasing multiple versions of the same film: one with hardcore inserts for foreign markets where pornography was already legalised, and a 'softer' one for Italian theatres (Maina and Zecca 2012). However, screenings of hardcore versions have been recorded in Italy too, as some theatre owners arranged clandestine projections with the complicity of the audience (Grattarola and Napoli 2014, 46–50). Meanwhile, since the deregulation of the broadcasting sector in 1974, television gradually became an outlet for pornographic films, especially thanks to private TV channels, which transmitted porn films at night (Grattarola and Napoli 2014, 56–61). In other words, hardcore pornography was produced and available in Italy well before 1978, and some of these products could be found at regular newsagents, in comic shops, on television and even at the cinema. These semi-clandestine practices contributed to a general process of 'sexualisation' of the Italian mainstream media in which debates about obscenity, pornography, art and freedom of speech were particularly blurred. Indeed, it was in this context that the release of arthouse films like *The Decameron* by Pasolini (1971) and *Last Tango in Paris* (Bernardo Bertolucci, 1974) were confiscated by the judiciary for their explicit sex scenes, raising heated debates about the distinctions between pornography and art, and the repressive function of censorship.

Initiatives of the feminist movement responded to this very specific context of pornography circulation, and were also influenced by the debates on the censorship, and the distinctions between pornography and artistic expression. At the same time, they also produced an autonomous discourse and approach to the circulation of explicit images and films that was rooted in wider feminist reflections on sexuality, patriarchal violence and the urban space.

Feminist Protests against *Life Size*

On 4 October 1975, the Roman Feminist Movement organised a sit-in at Piazza Navona in solidarity with Donatella Colasanti, the survivor of the infamous Circeo Massacre that took place few days earlier, on the night of 29–30 September. At the sit-in, Laura Remiddi, a lawyer and activist, took the microphone to share with the crowd her impressions of a film she saw the night before at the cinema Quirinale: the film *Life Size*. She evoked two scenes in particular that she believed were particularly close to the tortures that Colasanti and her friend Rosaria Lopez suffered on the night of the massacre. In the first, the main character, played by Michel Piccoli, penetrates a doll in a bathtub with a sharp object; in the second, the same doll is repeatedly raped by a group of men. Remiddi didn't know whether the Circeo killers had seen the film, but she had no doubt that violent and sexualised films like *Life Size* could instigate men to rape and torture women. Many people at the sit-in agreed with this point, and supported Remiddi's idea of writing a statement asking the judiciary to arrange the requisition of *Life Size* from theatres. The document was eventually signed by 166 people, including the feminist writer Dacia Maraini,[3] and ended with an annotation:

> The reasons that have pushed the feminist movement to denounce [this film] are not moralistic or repressive. None of us believes that censorship has a positive effect on the public mores. It is only a demonstrative action, which will be extended to other spectacles that insult and offend women and incite violence against them.[4]

Life Size was directed by an estimated arthouse Spanish director, Luis Berlanga, who wrote the script in collaboration with Rafael Azcona, a regular collaborator with Italian politically engaged director Marco Ferreri. The role of Azcona and the stylistic proximity of *Life Size* with Ferreri's work resonates with the practice of European arthouse cinema of sharing similar aesthetic and narrative models, as well as identical production and creative know-how, in order to intercept the taste and sensibility of a transnational audience of cultured spectators (Elsaesser 2005). The authorial status of this film gave immediate visibility to Remiddi's initiative, stimulating a harsh response from a wide coalition of film critics and journalists, but also from the feminist collectives that deprecated the appeal to censorship of their fellow activists. Indeed, besides of the accusations of being moralistic and naive, the document prepared by Remiddi was considered an apology to censorship, aggravated by the fact that it put an arthouse film on the same level as a low-end pornographic film. Needless to say, the fact that feminists appealed to a judge to take a film out of circulation was considered proof of the illiberal character of the movement and its moralism.

As such, the entire debate appears mostly counterproductive for Remiddi and the others, as even many feminist groups dissociated from the campaign; however, looking at the initiative from the vantage point of the present, its main weakness resides in its evident reference to the sociological theory of media effects, which at the time circulated not only in academia, but also worked as an easy means of social commentary in tabloids and newspapers.[5] Indeed, as Karen Boyle has pointed out, the media effects theory is a media-blaming explanation for anti-social behaviour that ultimately exonerates individuals from responsibility, as it calls into question society as a whole (Boyle 2005). As such, Remiddi's argument was particularly slippery: while she clearly pointed at the suspects of the Circeo Massacre, it also assigned part of the responsibility for their actions to a film that had been seen by many others, men and women – herself included – who had commited no crime. Remiddi certainly made a good point about the pervasiveness of sexual violence in Italian society, yet its ambivalence also erases the specificity of what had happened to the victims of the Circeo.

INTERLUDE – A FEMINIST FILM ABOUT PORNOGRAPHY: A MONTHLY RATION OF ATROCITY

Whereas in the Anglo-Americna context of the 'sex wars', documentaries like *Not a Love Story: A Film About Pornography* by Bonnie Sherr Klein (1981) participated in the feminist anti-porn debates, in Italy the only case of a feminist film released in the 1970s on this topic is *Una razione mensile di atrocità* (A monthly ration of atrocity, 1977), a short investigative documentary by Vanna Paoli, Nieves Zenteno, Gianluigi Bruni and Serenella Isidori. The authors were students of the national film school Centro Sperimentale di Cinematografia (CSC), who presented this 16mm short as their graduation essay.

Despite being a production of the school and therefore not intended for commercial distribution, *Una razione mensile di atrocità* found a circulation in the activist circles, thanks to Paoli and Zenteno's frequent presence in the feminist movement (*Effe* 1978).[6] The film's approach to pornography, indeed, reflects the feminist and political leanings of the authors, who focused specifically on the circulation of violent hardcore comics among children and adolescents. Quite remarkably, the documentary approaches porn as a mass industry, and not as a cultural, abstract phenomenon, presenting interviews with comic artists, typographers and owners of comic shops and newsagents. The authors also interviewed different groups of consumers, alternating this footage with images taken from the comics, in which a voice-over reads the dialogues in the balloons while replicating the moaning of sexual intercourse. These sections evidently aimed to stimulate a sense of embarrassment and disgust, but also underlined the exaggerated and unrealistic character of these publications. Hardcore and violent comics are presented as distorted representations of sexuality that instigate sexual violence, and whose success is tied to the lack of sexual education programmes in Italian schools and in families. This reading resonates with ideas diffused in the Italian student movement since the 1960s, which demanded the introduction of sex education programmes in schools, and advocated for new forms of liberated sexuality inspired by the writings of Wilhelm Reich and Herbert Marcuse.[7]

The coexistence of these claims confirms that the film understood pornography as a complex socio-cultural phenomenon, but at the same time highlights the directors' difficulty in articulating a specific feminist reflection on the topic, beyond the issue of sexual violence. Moreover, the insistence on discussing porn as a collective and systemic question opens up possible solutions that go beyond the stigmatisation of the consumer, and the creative reuse of pornographic images stimulates a playful and subversive interpretation of mass culture that is typical of the counterculture.

FEMINIST ATTACKS ON FILM THEATRES

During the autumn of 1976, many groups of the extra-parliamentary left promoted a series of initiatives called *autoriduzione* (self-reduction) in many Italian cities. The actions of self-reduction usually saw activists gathering at a cultural event (a concert, a theatrical play or a film screening) with the intent of forcing the ticket seller to sell admissions at a discounted price (500 lire for films, instead of the cost of a regular ticket, which was around 2,000 lire). Taking a clear anti-capitalist stance, the activists claimed more affordable entertainment, especially for students and workers, while making a critique of the commodification of culture. On a few occasions, these actions interrupted shows and film screenings, substituting the projections with a reading of a political document, and also mentioning the rejection of films that objectify women (Grattarola and Napoli 2014, 89). Such demonstrations often caused damage and provoked the arrest of several activists (Europa 1976). It is in the wake of these actions that a group of feminists destroyed the windows of the cinema Fiammetta in Milan, which displayed the posters of *Deadly Weapons* (Doris Wishman, 1974), a German exploitation film about a woman who kills men with her disproportionately big breasts. Similar episodes followed a few months later in Bologna and Turin, provoking a violent reaction in the press that accused feminists of being violent moralists and censors (Carrano 1977, 181–3). The facts of 21 January 1977 in Turin are particularly interesting, because they coincided with a night-time rally inspired by the international campaigns of Take Back the Night.[8] A lesbian activist from Turin, Daniela Mezzano, interviewed by Elena Biagini, recalls that during the rally her group destroyed several windows of pornographic theatres, and assaulted the *Moulin Rouge*, the only night club in the city (Mezzano in Biagini 2018, 105). The first Italian Take Back the Night (*Riprendiamoci la notte*) demonstration was organised in Rome on 28 November 1976, and was replicated a week later.[9] The rally began at the main train station, Termini, with a huge crowd of women walking through the demi-monde and populating the area carrying candles and torches: 'transvestites and prostitutes, bullies from the borgate (suburbs), pimps ... and mobsters' (Madeo 1976). Then demonstrators stopped in front of the Volturno cinema, a renowned location for strip-tease shows and erotic films. Alarmed by the chants of the crowd, the venue closed and turned off the lights, but the protesters burned and vandalised the film posters hanging outside the building. After arriving in the centre, the rally was attacked by a violent group of far-right militants, and a few shootings were heard on the street; the organisers dispersed the crowd into small groups, taking care that nobody had to walk home alone (Madeo 1976).

The Take Back the Night rallies aimed to challenge the geography of the city, and reclaim the public space for women. They targeted cinemas as homosocial spaces, which displayed sexualised posters that made the streets unsafe for women. A campaign launched by the Paduan feminist movement in May 1976 further confirms the relevance of this question. During the night between 21 and 22 May, a group of activists put stickers with the slogan 'this film offends and exploits women' on film posters in the windows the local cinemas that 'shamelessly offended the dignity of women in the streets of all the Italian cities' (Centro di Documentazione Donna di Padova 1976a).[10] Almost three years later, between the nights of 7 and 8 December 1979, the group Compagne organizzate per il contropotere femminista (Organised Comrades for the Feminist Counterpower, hereafter COCF) placed an explosive device among the seats of four porn cinemas in Rome: the Ambasciatori, the Majestic, the Jolly and the Blue Moon. No victims were reported, yet they provoked considerable damage to buildings and goods. The night before, the COCF had put a bomb in the studio of Giorgio Zeppieri, the lawyer of the defendants at the trial for the Circeo Massacre, whose chauvinism has been already exposed in the feminist film *Trial for Rape*. The COCF claimed responsibility for the attacks in a public statement sent to the news agency ANSA, in which they accused cinema owners of being responsible for the epidemic of violence against women, and making money by their exploitation of the female body.[11]

These episodes coincided with a very delicate period for the feminist movement. The escalation of violence and social anxiety was reaching an unprecedented level after the kidnapping and killing of prime minister Aldo Moro by the terrorist organisation, the Red Brigades. Also, for this reason, the bombs of the COCF opened a debate in the feminist press about opportunities for violent action. Between December 1979 and January 1980, the feminist weekly *Quotidiano Donna* published an animated discussion on the COCF opened by the journalist and activist Adele Cambria, followed by a series of opinions and statements from readers (Cambria 1979a). Some of them considered these incendiary attacks as timely, symbolic gestures that expressed a diffused sentiment of anger and frustration. The porn industry was considered responsible for a form of violence that ultimately represented a mode of capitalist accumulation by means of the commodification of women's sexuality. An anonymous reader linked the attacks of the COCF with Take Back the Night demonstrations: 'I was waiting for something like this for a long time... I don't understand why... in '76–'77 we restrained ourselves to more symbolic and ineffective actions, like dirtying with sprays the windows with the film posters' (*Quotidiano Donna* 1980). In another extract, a reader named Maria Clara believed that violence was necessary to avoid feminism turning into a mere cultural movement, without a real engagement in class struggle (Maria Clara 1980). As such, the economic damage caused to cinema owners was seen as an attack on the material structures that capitalism and patriarchy employed to subjugate women, and violence represented the only weapon that women had to change a society that silenced and exploited them. Supporters of the attacks expressed anger and frustration, as they wanted to subvert patriarchy with clamorous gestures. However, such positions were opposed by those who believed in the use of peaceful and non-violent strategies of dissent and expressed evident concern about the potential for criminalisation of the movement. Aligned with these positions were the editors of *Effe*, whose December 1979 issue opened with a collective piece announcing the renewal of the magazine and a reflection on this delicate political phase. The group explicitly condemned the attacks on the cinemas, defining them as futile and excessively violent, and therefore a wrong approach to the issue of pornography. According to the *Effe* group, 'the movement's reaction to pornography is entirely on another level', as they believed that the only effective way to counteract pornography was the transformation of sexuality, and that violence was useless (*Effe* 1979, 2).

This debate sees at play two opposite political views and understandings of feminism, revealing a profound division in the movement. On the one hand, supporters of the attacks favoured a strategy that opposed patriarchy by striking and violent action, on the other, the 'pacifists' proposed a wider project of cultural and sexual reform that the others felt would take much too long. The calls for non-violence also expressed fears that the movement would be criminalised, somehow anticipating the imminent backlash of the 1980s (Bracke 2014, 196–211).

Conclusions

As shown by these anti-porn demonstrations, from Remiddi's sit-in to the attacks of the COCF group, the Italian feminist movement carried out a series of protests against pornography based more on direct action than on theoretical arguments. This is a substantial difference from the American debate, in which the arguments pro and against pornography became a synecdoche of wider political questions and occasions for theoretical and academic debates. In Italy, the main issues at stake were those of sexual violence, the capitalist exploitation of female sexuality and the experience of the public space, yet pornography was perceived as an aspect, maybe the most visible, but not the most emblematic, of broader ideological and political questions. Despite this, pornography still raised questions of method and approaches to activism that reflected the evolution of the movement and the historical context of the time. Looking back, the political and historical limitations of these actions reveal that feminist responses to porn and mass culture are mediated and influenced by the ways in which these images were circulated and consumed. In Italy, during the 1970s, the conditions of dissemination and consumption of pornographic content were imbricated in the existent circuits of distribution and exhibition of mass culture. As such, the feminist movement approached porn as a degeneration of problems they had already noticed in the media in regards to sex and gender.

From an archival perspective, which brings together the affective, the material and the political, pornography reveals its ability to move people through and beyond their desires, feelings and political passions. As an historical object and interpretative key, pornography gives us the opportunity to understand Italian feminism as a movement that occupied the political and the urban space, which borrowed and elaborated from the strategies of other radical groups and borrowed from counterculture. Without approaching pornography for its complex socio-cultural meanings, most of these complexities would have been kept in the archives, limiting our understanding of the past and our knowledge of the inevitably complex positions that feminism has taken in regards to sexual representations.

Notes

1. Angelo Izzo, Gianni Guifo and Andrea Ghira were neofascist militants belonging to renowned upper-class families. On the night of the massacre, they kidnapped and raped two girls who were out on a date with them – Rosaria Lopez, 19 years old, and Donatella Colasanti, 17 – in a villa at San Felice del Circeo, a town outside Rome. After many hours of torture and sexual violence, Rosaria drowned in a bathtub, while Donatella, faking death, actually survived, and was found naked and covered in blood in the trunk of the car that the three men used to go back to Rome on the following morning.
2. I interviewed Laura Remiddi in Rome on 7 September 2018. I am very grateful for her help and collaboration. A more extensive reconstruction of the '*Life Size* case' is in Dalila Missero, 2021, 'Note sul femminismo italiano e la 'crisi della mascolinità'. Il 'caso Life Size', in Angela Bianca Saponari and Federico Zecca, eds,

Oltre l'inetto. Rappresentazioni plurali della mascolinità nel cinema italiano (Milan, Udine: Meltemi).
3. At the time, Maraini was part of a collective of the Pompeo Magno group who founded La Maddalena, a feminist book store and theatre collective based in Rome. Maraini also had brief experience of filmmaking, which is discussed in Chapter 11. Very interestingly, Maraini's partner, the writer Alberto Moravia, was responsible for adapting the dialogues of the Italian version of *Life Size*.
4. Remiddi gave me a copy of the original document, which is part of her personal archive.
5. One of the few scholarly studies conducted on pornography in Italy in this period was based entirely on the theory of media effects and was commissioned by the Italian national broadcaster RAI and published in 1976 (Ferracuti and Solivetti 1976).
6. The film was screened in 1978 in a programme of feminist films compiled by Maricla Tagliaferri on the occasion of the Manifestazioni del Cinema non Professionale (Manifestation of the Non-Professional Cinema) organised by the Fedic (the Italian Cineclub Federation).
7. On the demands for sexual education and the influence of Reich's thought on Italian and European counterculture, see Wanrooij 2008 and Herzog 2005.
8. The first demonstrations of Take Back the Night were organised in the United States in the early 1970s. Similar initiatives were repeated in many cities of North America and Europe (Germany, UK), often targeting pornography and exploitation films. In 1982 the activist Laura Lederer published *Take Back the Night – Women on Pornography* (London: Bentam Books), a collection of essays about pornography that would soon become a staple of anti-porn feminism. For a detailed reconstruction of these campaigns, see Bronstein 2011.
9. Footage of the 4 December demonstration is available on the AAMOD Archive's YouTube channel. In the short film we see a militant holding a poster saying 'Riprendiamoci la notte'. Available at https://www.youtube.com/watch?v=NbwGm5xAXWo, accessed 5 May 2021.
10. The initiative was replicated in the autumn, also targeting newsagents and theatres (Centro di Documentazione Donna di Padova 1976b).
11. A detailed reconstruction of the events as reported in the newspapers is in Grattarola and Napoli 2014, 88–90.

Part II

Cultures of Representation: Sexuality, Race and Politics

This part of the book consists of three chapters focusing on aspects of the representation of sexuality, race and gender. Specifically, I have focused on three case studies (comedy Italian style, the actress Ines Pellegrini, and Federico Fellini's film *La città delle donne*, 1980) that are representative of three different aspects of the Italian film culture: genre, stardom and arthouse cinema. They also address three distinct historical moments: post-economic boom Italy, the so-called 'sexual revolution' and the early stages of the *riflusso*/ backlash. The goal of this section is illustrating the complex socio-cultural meanings of the film text by approaching its analysis through different sets of archival materials, and addressing intersecting complementary historical and contemporary feminist debates about cinematic representations, social reproduction, sexual objectification, intersectionality and activism.

Chapter 6 focuses on a group of anthological comedies that were released between 1964 and 1966 and part of the Comedy, Italian-style genre. My analysis concentrates on a recurrent character in these films, the figure of the middle-class, frigid housewife, which is based on the tropes of popular sexology disseminated in magazines and other middle-brow publications circulating in Italy since the early 1960s. Despite their frequent misogynist traits, these characters provide an opportunity to engage in an anachronistic discussion of the political meanings of asexuality in the framework of feminist theories of social reproduction and reproductive labour. Chapter 7 discusses the interplay of colonial imageries and soft-core pornography in the years of the post-1968 'sexual revolution', by focusing on the experience of Ines (Macia) Pellegrini, an Italo-Eritrean actress who worked in Italian films and television programmes during the 1970s. Chapter 8 offers a feminist analysis of the production history and representational agenda of Federico Fellini's

La città delle donne (City of women, 1980), a film that offers a mainstream representation of the Italian feminist movement. In particular, I consider the 'cinematic contract' (de Lauretis 1987) that the director establishes with the female (and particularly the feminist) spectator, proposing a counter-reading of Fellini's approach to filmmaking and representation. In conclusion, I look at this film as a cinematic device aiming to erase the political dimension of feminism, and as an early manifestation of the cultural climate characterising the dispersion of the second-wave movement in the 1980s.

CHAPTER 6

Asexuality and Housework in the Anthological Comedies of the Mid-1960s

> They say it is love. We say it is unwaged work.
> They call it frigidity. We call it absenteeism.
>
> Silvia Federici, *Wages Against Housework*

'Italians have known years of prosperity, in which they have travelled around, and ultimately ended up with housing problems and unemployment. All this was enough to change their morality, and that's why, in my next movies, I will keep just one aspect of the typical Italian comedic character: his need for escape, and his incontrollable erotic lust' (Viola 1964). These words of the actor Alberto Sordi well summarise the characteristics of a group of successful comedies produced in Italy since the end of the economic boom. Between 1964 and 1966, the acclaimed genre 'comedy, Italian style' shifted its focus from the social mobility stories of the early 1960s to concentrate on the emergent middle class. These films, generally structured in five or six short episodes by renowned directors and starring popular actors, were centred on the problems of the nuclear family and particularly of the married couple, with an emphasis on sex as 'a complicating factor in modern man's attempts to get by in a modernising Italy' (Fullwood 2015, 3). It was especially women's lack or excess of sexual desire that prompted the comedic situations, framed in a middle- or upper-middle-class environment in which women are relegated to the 'unproductive' domestic sphere and men are lazy and foolish professionals.

My interest in these comedies resides in their representations of the 'sexuo-economic relations'[1] dominating the domestic sphere, a topic that has, crucially, been at the centre of the theoretical and political reflections of Italian feminism. The gendered dynamics portrayed in these films, indeed, are similar to those analysed by Silvia Federici in her pamphlet *Wages Against Housework* (1975), where she observes that the normalisation of women's unpaid housework prevents them 'from struggling against it, except in the privatised kitchen-bedroom quarrel that all society agrees to ridicule' (Federici 1975, 2). There is no better way to describe the gender dynamics in these comedies: they make fun of the problems in the bedroom to criticise the middle-class lifestyle and the changes that have occurred in Italian society, but they ultimately put women in a passive, subjugated position by trivialising their domestic role as 'unproductive' and their unhappiness as a private and individual matter. This characterisation becomes particularly notable in those episodes in which unproductive housewives are depicted as 'frigid' or disinterested in sex. As well summarised by Ela Przybylo, in the heteronormative context of a 'sexuosociety' – like the one portrayed in these comedies – those performing heterosexual and coital sex define what is 'natural' and 'normal', leading to the pathologising of the celibacy and asexuality of 'those who are not sexual enough, or who do not repeat sexuality faithfully to "the norm"' (Przybylo 2011, 449).[2] Women's lack of sexual desire, then, seems to contradict the hypersexualised and hedonistic culture of consumer capitalism, yet in these films, as well as in Italian feminist theory, it becomes symptomatic of broader capitalist contradictions. In both these contexts, the reason resides in the connection between the sexuality of the married couple and the realm of the economic, but while in the comedies women's rejection of conjugal sex is seen as a neurosis caused by their condition of 'unproductive' housewives, in feminist theory, 'frigidity' means refusing to engage in unpaid reproductive labour. In other words, from a feminist perspective, strategic celibacy and asexuality are symptoms of women's discontent, and as such they represent solitary acts of rebellion against the sexuo-economic pact of the household.

By focusing on a group of episodes in which women reject their partners, this chapter adopts an archival and textual-based methodology to offer an historical contextualisation and at the same time an anachronistic feminist approach to asexuality in the 'comedy, Italian style' genre. My goal is to complicate the political dimension of women's sexuality in the films of the 1960s by rejecting any pathologising or moralising view of the refusal of sex and the lack of sexual desire. In particular I am interested in a feminist approach to asexuality that problematises the rhetoric of sex as liberation (Cerankowski and Milks 2010), to reflect on the cultural and political meanings of women's withdrawal from sex in a political and historical dimension. To do this, the chapter is split into two main parts, respectively centred on the representational agendas of these comedies and their adoption of a sexological discourse and their take on female asexuality and class.

Portraying Sex: Sexology, Anti-Americanism and Capitalism in Anthological Comedies

To give a sense of the popularity of these comedies, but also their positioning within the Italian film production, I start by paraphrasing an article published in the popular tabloid *Epoca* and emblematically titled 'Pornographic Italy', which affirmed that 'from 1948 to 1963, the sketch formula has been used in 37 films, [while] it has been exploited as a gold mine for 25 titles in 1964 only' (Livi 1965, 29). Directed by champions of the Italian comedy like Mario Monicelli, Dino Risi and Luciano Salce, they also count on the participation of popular actors such as Marcello Mastroianni, Ugo Tognazzi, Catherine Spaak, Gina Lollobrigida and Vittorio Gassman. Despite these credentials, critical reception was generally lukewarm as film critics saw in the use of dirty humour and the emphasis on the sex appeal of the stars, a call to the 'lower instincts' of the public.[3] Indeed, the indulgence in sex, and especially in extramarital sex, was the main reason for the negative reception of these films, as well explained by Tullio Kezich, who defined them as a series of 'scripted jokes' [barzellette sceneggiate]' lacking of satire, but full of smug obscenity (1979, 216–17). The explicit and transgressive character of the plots created legal issues for the cast, producers and directors of *Le bambole* (The dolls: Dino Risi, Luigi Comencini, Franco Rossi, Mauro Bolognini, 1965), in a case that became emblematic of debates about the supposed immorality of Italian cinema (Missero 2017).[4] To some extent, these controversies are in line with the general reception of comedy, Italian style, which had been praised for its realism and social criticism, but blamed for its indulgent characterisation of Italian vices (Comand 2010). At the same time, debates about the anthological films went well beyond mere discussions of their quality and morality, as they made evident that sexuality was a popular means of social commentary in modern Italy. As suggested by titles like *Alta infedeltà* (High infidelity, Franco Rossi, Elio Petri, Luciano Salce, Mario Monicelli, 1964) *Controsesso* (Countersex, Franco Rossi, Marco Ferreri e Renato Castellani, 1964) *Questa volta parliamo di uomini* (Let's talk about men) (Lina Wertmüller, 1965), *Tre notti d'amore* (Three nights of love, Renato Castellani, Luigi Comencini e Franco Rossi, 1964) and *Extraconiugale* (Extramarital, Massimo Franciosa, Mino Guerrini, Giuliano Montaldo, 1964), the focus of these comedies was explicitly on the married couple and its participation in a supposed 'battle of the sexes'. As explained by Mary Jo Buhle, the discursive framework of the 'battle of the sexes', so ubiquitous in post-war American and West European culture, relies on the use of sexological and psychoanalytic tropes as means of social commentary (1998). In line with this tendency, sexology and sex therapy offered a set of flexible and repeatable plot devices that put together social criticism – satire of the middle class – with a cutting-edge representation of modern sexuality. Thanks to their location in the realm of scientific production as well as in the twin realms of elite and popular culture, sexology and therapeutic discourse offered collective diagnosis and marketable cures to the relational problems affecting the household of modern capitalism (Illouz 2007, 6–7).

In these films, sexology and sex therapy are presented as bizarre – American – practices that Italian men ultimately don't need, while women, who are generally at the root of the sexual problems of the couple, seemed naturally more inclined to trust specialists. For instance, in the episode *The Group Therapy* of *Marcia Nuziale* (The wedding march, 1965) by Marco Ferreri, an American woman forces her Italian husband, Frank (Ugo Tognazzi), to attend sex therapy sessions led by a priest. Despite Frank's initial willingness to please his wife, he eventually leaves the meeting to have sex with another woman from the group. In an episode of *Tre notti d'amore* (Three nights of love, 1964), Giacinto, a middle-aged engineer, can't have sex with his young spouse, Cirilla (Catherine Spaak), because of his sense of inferiority. A psychologist, a friend of the couple, recommends Giacinto commit adultery in order to regain his self-esteem, but following this advice he ends up in bed with another young girl.

Such characterisations mirrored the reception of popular sexology in Italy more broadly, which, since the translation of the Kinsey Reports (1953 and 1955), had raised conflicting opinions in the public. On the one hand, the supposed vigour of Italians in bed was counterposed to the coldness of their American counterparts, echoing the anti-modernist myth of virilism popularised by the Fascist regime (Bellassai 2011, 73–89; Morris 2013); on the other, some areas of the Catholic Church became manifestly open towards sexology as a scientific protocol that aimed to increase the solidity of marriage and contributed to its popularisation in the popular press.[5] The Americanisation of popular culture, and especially of the publishing sector, favoured the circulation of sexology especially among a middle-class readership, and particularly among women, who became recipients of articles about frigidity and fertility, while sexological studies about men and couples were generally presented in opinion pieces or in reports from the US in progressive tabloids like *L'Espresso*.[6] In this context, Hollywood also contributed to popularising sexology on both sides of the Atlantic, introducing experts and therapy in the plots of the many 'comedies of the sexes' produced by the end of the 1950s (Krutnik and Neale 1990). In films like *The Tender Trap* (Charles Walters 1955), *Pillow Talk* (Michael Gordon 1959), *It Started with a Kiss* (George Marshall 1959), *How to Murder Your Wife* (Richard Quine 1965) and *What's New Pussycat?* (Clive Donner 1965) marriage represents an end to male fantasies of sexual freedom, while women are generally disinterested in sex but obsessed with money and social status. As in Italian comedies, then, men's aversion to marriage is treated condescendingly, while women's dislike of conjugal sex is presented as pathological, and a manifestation of a repressed and perverse character

(Krutnik and Neale 1990, 171–2). As noted by Steve Neale and Frank Krutnik, these comedies reflected the public debates of post-Kinsey American society, in which the sexuality of the average American became a thermometer for the well-being of the nation. In line with the latest discoveries of sexology, combined with a Freudian vulgate, women's lack of sexual desire was a proof of their 'emasculation', brought about by consumer capitalism, which gave them an unprecedented agency in the family, creating a tension in the traditional role of wife and mother centred on self-sacrifice and passivity (Ehrenreich and English 1978). In popular culture this tension translated into the diffusion of two opposing types of female characters, the sexually exuberant and career-obsessed 'single girl' and the frigid, hysteric housewife.[7]

The use of sexology in Italian anthological comedies assimilated and articulated all these cultural tensions, but the characterisation of sex therapy as a foreign, middle-class and modern protocol calls into question the relationship between comedy, Italian style and the national character. According to Silvana Patriarca, the national character is a collective, self-reflexive image of the national community based on a set of mostly negative dispositions that constitute the moral and mental traits of the Italian people, perceived as immutable and ahistorical (Patriarca 2010, vii–xv). These characters generally resurface in public debate in periods of profound socio-historical changes that test the unity of the national community, providing a reassuring image of Italians as stable in the face of wider transnational transformations. Notably, comedy, Italian style and its stardom had made profitable and paradigmatic use of the national character (Patriarca 2010, 242–51), which in the case of the anthological films is also explicitly gendered: the male characters are played by renowned Italian actors like Ugo Tognazzi and Marcello Mastroianni, while female roles are often assigned to foreign performers, like Catherine Spaak and Claire Bloom. Despite this, the comedic reference to sexology can't be reduced to a form of anti-Americanism, or to a defence of Italian virilism, as they primarily represent a reaction to the intrusion of capitalism in the private and relational sphere. As noted by Eva Illouz (2007), the popularisation of sexology and therapy had been central to the rationalisation and economisation of relationships that was typical of post-war capitalism, and therefore its circulation and reception in Italy are symptomatic of a difficult negotiation of the values and lifestyles introduced by consumerist capitalism more broadly, calling for a series of local responses rooted in Italian idiosyncrasies.

STRATEGIC CELIBACY, FRIGIDITY AND CLASS CRITIQUE

Considering the complex relationship between sexology, capitalism and the national, what are the meanings assigned to women's lack of sexual desire in these films? As we explore in this section, these representations gravitated around different strategies of class critique, which are directed mostly against the urban, professional middle class, who are perceived as a socio-cultural product of the economic boom. In the episode 'L'Uccellino', directed by Tinto Brass, and part of the film *La mia signora* (My wife, Mauro Bolognini, Tinto Brass, Luigi Comencini), a middle-class lady (Silvana Mangano) pays no attention to her husband's sexual approaches because she has eyes only for her canary, a pet that is emblematically trapped in a cage. Similarly, in 'La telefonata' (The phone call) – an episode of *Le bambole* (The dolls) by Dino Risi – the main female character, Luisa (Virna Lisi), is indifferent to the sexual advances of her husband Giorgio (Marcello Mastroianni), because she is too busy talking on the phone with her mother. After being rejected multiple times, Giorgio runs to the neighbour and has sex with her, while the wife continues to talk on the phone. The camera emphasises Luisa's relaxed pose on the sofa, making her an erotic spectacle who is indifferent to both the husband and the spectator, making clear her complete control of the domestic space as well as of the spectator's gaze. Her comfortable position in the living room, a distinctive space in the middle-class household, makes explicit the link between class privilege, economic affluence and troubled sexuality. The rejection of the partner, then, frustrates the 'norm' that commands married women to fulfil their husbands' sexual appetites, and her disinterest in sex therefore leads the sly, sexually vigorous Italian men to violate the moral imperative of monogamy. Men's behaviour is generally portrayed condescendingly, in line with the idea that marriage is a constraint on men's sexual appetites; conversely, their asexual wives are depicted as distracted women obsessed with frivolous objects and with social status. These characteristics are schematically counterposed to the accommodating character of working-class women: in an episode in *Se permettete parliamo di donne* (Let's talk about women, 1964) by Ettore Scola, an underage middle-class girl asks her older partner (Vittorio Gassman) for a safe and discreet place to lose her virginity; after spending the entire afternoon driving around Rome to find a location that would satisfy his young partner, he decides to have sex with a waitress instead. Unlike the pretentious middle-class girl, then, the working woman is immediately willing to accept his approaches and engage in intercourse without complications.

The link between the unproductivity of troubled middle-class sex is also central to the anthological films directed by politically engaged authors like Elio Petri and Marco Ferreri. In Petri's episode 'Peccato nel pomeriggio' (Sin in the afternoon), part of *High Infedelity*, Laura (Claire Bloom) is a troubled affluent woman who is incapable of having satisfactory sex with her husband. One day, she forces him to act like a stranger, and fake a date that simulates adultery. The husband, an unscrupulous contractor, tries to fulfil Laura's desires, but inevitably fails. At the end of the episode, tired of the situation, he suggests she seek psychotherapy or, even better, get a job instead of bother him with her false problems. The explicit connection between her lack of sexual pleasure with her unproductivity resonates with other well-known characters portrayed in contemporary *auteur* cinema. Indeed, similar figures appeared in the same years in 'Il lavoro', an episode of the anthological film *Boccaccio '70* (1962) directed by Luchino Visconti, in *Deserto rosso* (Red desert, 1964) by Michelangelo Antonioni, in *Giulietta degli spiriti* (Juliet of the spirits, 1964) by Federico Fellini, and later in Pier Paolo Pasolini's *Teorema* (1968). Petri himself described *Sin in the Afternoon* as 'a little, affectionate satire of the antonionism that was in great fashion at the time', and in order to justify the direction of a banal, apparently non-politically-engaged short film, he affirmed that he agreed to do it because he 'needed to work' (Petri in Faldini and Fofi 1981, 366). Ferreri sets a similar narrative in the context of the lower middle class in the episode of his film *The Wedding March* emblematically called 'Conjugal duty'. Here, the main character, Michele (Ugo Tognazzi), is a white-collar employee who comes home and wants desperately to have sex with his spouse, Laura (Shirley Anne Field), who repeatedly rejects him. Laura is a housewife obsessed by summer vacations and house cleaning, and Ferreri indulges on her passion for photo-romances and women's magazines to indicate her light-headed character. One night, when Michele becomes too forceful in bed, Laura eventually cries out: 'You are a beast, a man who still believes that a woman could find pleasure without any preparation!' She obviously means 'without foreplay', as we see Michele grabbing her without acknowledging her requests to stop. After a brief focus on the brutality of his approaches, the film concentrates on Michele's unhappiness and sense of inadequacy caused by Laura's demands for better sex – namely for pleasure. Michele can't understand the reasons for her dissatisfaction and reacts with anger to her refusal to have sex whenever he wants. In a monologue, he 'diagnoses' Laura as a hysteric, using these words:

> this is a question of nerves, you are not frigid, quite the opposite, the fact is that you don't care. You are selfish and self-centred. You, the house, the kid, the grandmother, the holidays 300 miles distant, and then who is the dick who pays?

Michele thus explicitly connects Laura's refusal to have sex as something related to her egoism and pretentious bourgeois lifestyle. In the framework of Ferreri's leftist class critique, the fact that Michele is the only waged worker in the family appeals to the spectator's empathy, leading to the – perhaps involuntary – conclusion that if a man works to pay for his wife's lifestyle, he should expect, at least, to have sex in exchange. The problem, indeed, seems to be that he can't understand the sexual demands of a bored and spoiled wife, who stays at home and is always demanding more.

As these two examples demonstrate, Marxist/left-wing authors mocked the sexual problems of the middle class by identifying them with marriage, but also with the 'unproductive' housewife, as the embodiment of neurotic capitalism. This portrayal problematically combines elements of popular sexology and its obsession with 'frigidity' with well-engrained Marxist theories on the economic dimension of bourgeois sexuality. The unproductive wives in the comedies resonate with Michel Foucault's description of the 'idle' woman, a figure that 'inhabited the outer edges of the "world" in which she always had to appear as a value of the family, where she was assigned a new destiny charged with conjugal and parental obligations' (Foucault 1980, 120–1). In these films, the identification of the bourgeois wife with 'value' is presented as an unstoppable and disruptive force brought about by consumer capitalism. In *Prison Notebooks*, specifically in the essay 'Americanism and Fordism', Antonio Gramsci discusses sexuality and addresses gender in relation to theoretical and economic questions. As Nelson Moe pointed out, Gramsci, in a 'unusual moment of productionism', cleanses the realm of reproduction from sexuality and the feminine to become a 'neutral' function related to economic production and labour. In the same essay, Gramsci pairs sexuality with words like 'sport', leisure and excess, making clear that 'only the parasitic upper classes can afford . . . sexuality and, indeed, can afford unconsciousness. And it is the figure of the woman that is loaded with these functions, with representing this excessive complex' (Moe 1990, 140). With this move, Gramsci somehow erases women and sexuality from the realm of production, and accidentally excludes them from the political sphere. In discussing Gramsci's relationship with feminism, Renate Holub notices that although Gramsci 'insists on the centrality of sexuality, [he] ties the woman's inalienable rights of control over her sexuality and her body to the processes of rationalization of production' (Holub 1992, 191). In other words, he believes that new and liberated forms of sexuality for women are contingent on the sphere of production and the possibility of restraining the impetus of the body. In a simplified and vulgarised version of Gramsci's thought, Petri and Ferreri's episodes portray women's sexual demands as middle-class commodities, as products of the minds of women who are excluded from the realm of production, while the spheres of social reproduction are completely ignored, despite being absolutely pivotal to their representations of the dynamics of the middle-class couple.

A Place in (Her)story: The 'Frigid' Housewives from Carla Lonzi to the Wages for Housework Movement

As 'frigidity' and celibacy have a long history in international feminist thought (Cryle and Moore 2011), Italian second-wave feminism has adopted a critical approach to mainstream discourses about women's lack of desire, which considers the specificity of the local socio-cultural context. In her essay *Women and the Subversion of the Community* (1972), Mariarosa Dalla Costa explains that her political reflections were inspired by the condition of Italian women, as they were particularly subjected, for historical and cultural reasons, to an ideology of domestic labour as 'a personal service outside of the capital' (Dalla Costa 1972, 28). The observation and reflection on personal experience was also crucial for Silvia Federici, who, as the daughter of an Italian housewife, saw at first hand the weight of domestic labour in her mother's condition of oppression (Federici 2012, 2). Such a personal and political impulse to valorise and politicise the experience of the housewife contrasts with the invisibilisation of women's domestic labour in the anthological comedies which, by insisting on women's unproductivity, reduce them, to borrow an expression from Federici, to 'nagging bitches, not workers in struggle' (Federici 1975).

At the same time, Italian feminists assimilated the vocabulary of popular sexology to overturn Marxist productionism and refuse patriarchal discourse. To begin with Carla Lonzi and her subversion of sexological discourse in *The Clitoral Woman and the Vaginal Woman*, Italian feminism has provided powerful examples of politicisation of the female orgasm, connecting its erasure from history to multi-layered patterns of patriarchal dominance. In the opening quote of this chapter, when Silvia Federici writes 'They call it frigidity. We call it absenteeism', she equates celibacy with the desertion of the workplace, stressing the economic nature assigned by capitalism to conjugal sex. Similarly, Dalla Costa observes: 'capital, while it elevates heterosexuality to a religion, at the same time ... makes it impossible for men and women to be in touch with each other, physically or emotionally. It undermines heterosexuality except as a sexual, economic and social discipline' (Dalla Costa 1972, 30). The link between sexual alienation and work alienation, while resonating with the ideas of Willhelm Reich and Herber Marcuse, and therefore, to some extent, supporting a rhetoric of sex as liberation, also provides a set of fundamental political tools to address the distorted, heterosexist accounts of women's sexual dissatisfaction in the comedies of the mid-1960s. These feminist views on women's lack of desire, then, give us a conceptual framework for demystifying the myth of the idle/unproductive woman, assigning a subversive potential to women's sexual agency as a way to subvert subjugation in the domestic sphere.

With all their limitations, deriving from their belonging to a 'male-centred frame of reference in which gender and sexuality are (re)produced by the discourse of male sexuality' (de Lauretis 1987, 17), the characters in the anthological comedies are anachronistically tied to a feminist operation of cultural and political rewriting, which aimed to resignify domesticity and sexuality as realms of political struggle. Putting these films in our feminist archive, then, is a way to see them beyond their overwhelming validation of male anxieties, as becoming part of a feminist-historical reappropriation of the cinematic text.

Notes

1. The term 'sexuo-economic relation', coined by the American writer Charlotte Perkins Gilman (1912), has been adopted by feminist theory with different goals and in different contexts to indicate the economic dimension of sexual relationships, from marriage to sex work. In this chapter I am using this expression loosely, as a working label to indicate the bond between sexuality, domesticity and capitalist values in the representational framework of these comedies.
2. In this chapter, I am using the term 'asexuality' as an anachronistic political move to counteract the adoption of a pathologising vocabulary. For this reason, in this context, the term doesn't refer to an identity or to a stable condition, but is rather closer to Ela Przybylo's use of the expressions 'strategic celibacy' and 'moments of asexuality' to indicate a transitory and ever-changing position in the asexual/sexual spectrum (2011).
3. Specifically, the anthological format allowed the serialisation of production and a rationalisation of the costs based on quick shootings and short, and therefore cheaper, contracts with expensive stars. These elements made these comedies closer to popular low-budget cinema than to *auteur* cinema in their modes of production, an aspect that increased the critics' limited enthusiasm.
4. Remarkably, most of the criticism (and the longest trials) targeted the actresses involved, Virna Lisi and Gina Lollobrigida, who had to respond in person for having accepted immoral parts.
5. During the 1950s, Pope Pious XII established an intense dialogue between the Church and medical professionals, including gynaecologists and sexologists. According to Isacco Turina, the Church began to address professionals and experts as a consequence of its increasing participation in the 'biopolitical challenge' posed by modernity (Turina 2013, 45–53). Not by chance, the first Italian 'marriage clinic' was founded in Milan in 1949 by a priest, Don Paolo Liggeri, who became 'one of the most active propagandists of the Catholic vision of marriage, using conferences, radio and television programmes, books, and magazines' (Wanrooij 2008, 114). Notably, Don Liggeri regularly penned an agony column for the women's magazine *Annabella*, and collaborated with *Grazia*.

6. *L'Espresso* is a weekly magazine, founded in 1955 by Arrigo Benedetti and Eugenio Scalfari and represents one of the most innovative tabloids of the time, thanks to its dry language, reporting on sexuality and American society and a renowned editorial staff composed of acclaimed journalists and left-wing intellectuals such Alberto Moravia and Nello Ajello.
7. The type and discourses on the 'single girl' are well summarised in the best sellers *Sex and the Single Girl* and *Sex in the Office* by Harley Gurley Brown, translated into Italian respectively in 1965 and 1967. In 1965 Brown became editor in chief of *Cosmopolitan*, and her long tenure at the magazine is associated with the introduction of self-help articles, including those about sexuality, and the first centrefold with a naked man in April 1972.

CHAPTER 7

Ines Pellegrini: Navigating (Post)colonial Representations in the 'Sexual Revolution'

In Igiaba Scego's novel *Adua* (2015), the main character, a Somali woman born and raised right after the end of the Italian colonial domination, clearly remembers the local cinema where she saw for the first time the alluring images of classic Hollywood. A few years later, in the 1970s, she moves to Rome to pursue a career in acting, but she ends up trapped in an abusive relationship with a director and producer of soft-core films. As an adult woman, Adua is now an icon of sexuality and the hypersexualisation of her body becomes a metaphor for the legacy of colonial domination.

The Italo-Eritrean actress Ines (Macia) Pellegrini worked in several Italian productions between 1973 and 1981. Like the protagonist in *Adua*, Pellegrini was requested mainly for roles tailored for her exotic beauty that emphasised her African origins: she starred in two films by Pier Paolo Pasolini (*Arabian Nights*, 1974; *Salò, and the 120 Days of Sodoma*, 1975), in several low-end comedies and sexploitation films, but also worked in 1978 as anchor-woman for the prime-time show 'Mille e una luce' for the national broadcaster RAI. The diversity of these productions suggests that the exotic and the colonial intervened at different levels of the cultural imagery of the time, to meet with the expectations and tastes of different types of audience. The 1970s, indeed, saw an increased diffusion of sexualised representations in the Italian media, which contributed to the configuration of a 'postcolonial predicament' (Ponzanesi 2005, 177–87) that went hand in hand with the diffusion of the cultural imagery of the so-called 'sexual revolution', with its conflicting rhetoric of 'liberation' and hypersexualisation of the female body. Throughout her career, Pellegrini was able to exceed the colonial archive and present herself to the public as a professional and career woman, but in most of her roles, her figure was flattened on the colonial stereotype of the 'black Venus' whose exotic beauty was both an attraction and threat to the white man (Giuliani Caponetto 2012). The interplay between the contemporary model of a professional young woman and the timeless, static, colonial imagery of the black

Venus can be seen as a synecdoche of the multiple socio-cultural transformations that invested Italy in the 1970s.

Drawing on the trajectory of Ines Pellegrini in the Italian media, this chapter analyses the role of racialised and colonial discourses in the media culture of the 'sexual revolution', and particularly in soft-core pornography. Specifically, I focus on three distinct aspects of Pellegrini's trajectory that intersected with a hypersexualised and racialised imagery: her collaboration with Pier Paolo Pasolini, her participation in low-end and soft-core films and her self-representation as a professional and career woman. To do so, I adopt an archival approach that combines the close reading of the high-end porn magazine *Playboy* with an analysis of low-end soft-core films and a survey of feminist sources and the general press. The heterogeneous array of sources researched for this chapter reflects the circulation of colonial and racialised tropes in multiple strands of the Italian media, and the complementary review of both activist materials and popular culture sheds light on the complex intersections between these two domains in the Italian public discourses of the time.

Race and the Sexual Revolution in Italy

The gendered technologies of domination described in Scego's book are at the heart of what Gaia Giuliani has called the 'Italian colonial archive', a set of images and shared beliefs centred on gender difference and race that shaped Italian identity in the twentieth century (2019).[1] Specifically, the colonial enterprises and later the fascist rhetoric of imperial domination established a definition of the racialised Other that went hand in hand with a process of 'whitening up' of the Italian collective identity, which continued well beyond the years of the dictatorship. During the 1950s and 1960s, by means of strategies of 'self-reflexive colour-blindness' (Portelli 2003), Italians built the impression of being racially unmarked, while a series of racialised discourses concurred with a process of class formation in which whiteness became synonymous with beauty, hygiene, modernity and social privilege, while blackness was associated with dirt, economic deprivation and sexual abjection (Lombardi-Diop 2012). These tensions were counterbalanced by the emergence of an internationalist and anti-colonial sensibility whose legacy resonated in the social movements of the 1960s and 1970s. Despite this, during the 1970s the 'colonial archive' re-emerged in a more explicit and sexually connotated iconography that found its most evident manifestation in pornographic and erotic media. Specifically, according to Gaia Giuliani, this iconography was based mainly on the hypersexualisation of black women, and worked primarily as a reassuring narrative in a context of crisis of Mediterranean masculinity that culminated with the emergence of second-wave feminism (Giuliani 2019).

At the same time, the sexualisation of the media and its racialisation is somehow connected with the ideologically porous context of the so-called 'sexual revolution', a socio-cultural transformation that impacted most Western capitalist countries between the end of the 1960s and the mid-1970s, by means of the converging processes of commercialisation, liberalisation and the politicisation of sex (Herzog 2005, 141). Jeffrey Weeks argues that despite there not being a single social imperative that controlled its emergence, the 'sexual revolution' saw 'the continuing, even accentuating, commercialization and commodification of sex; the shift in relations between men and women; changes in the mode of regulation of sexuality; and the emergence of ... social antagonisms and the appearance of new political movements' (Weeks 1985, 21). In this apparently contradictory framework, media contributed to increase the hypervisibility of sex in the public debate, ultimately revealing the coexistence of anxieties and hopes for a cosmopolitan, affluent and sexually liberated society (Schaefer 2015). The 'sexual revolution', in both its mainstream and counter-cultural versions, was about opening society to a liberated experience of sexuality, but the feminist and gay movement soon pointed at the pitfalls of these narratives. Questions like the commercialisation of sex (particularly of pornographic media), the pervasiveness of sexual and gender violence, and last but not least, a legislation that continued to certify double standards between man and women, made evident the need for a more radical agenda, namely for a project of 'sexual liberation' that rejected the patriarchal and heterosexist notions at the basis of the process. In Italy, feminist critiques of the 'sexual revolution' produced a conflict within the radical groups, especially between feminists and male left-wing militants who refused to question the persistent asymmetries of gender in their practices and agendas (Bellassai 2011, 126–37).[2] However, as R. W. Connell pointed out, by the mid-1970s hopes for a 'sexual revolution' had vanished almost completely and 'sex became a very fraught topic in feminism', although the relation between sexuality, power and oppression continued to be discussed (Connell 1997, 61).

A black actress like Pellegrini in the Italian media of the 1970s intercepted all the tensions and contradictions of the local media culture: she played hypersexualised characters centred on colonial stereotypes, but at the same time her figure of young professional embodied the values of capitalist cosmopolitanism; portrayed as a black Venus, she was desirable, but threatening at the same time; she worked in arthouse films, but also in low-end comedies and soft-core pornography, and on television. All these aspects signal the complex levels of negotiation that race and gender played in the Italian culture of the 1970s, and at the same time suggest difficult conversations about female sexuality in the media but also amongst the feminist circles. To introduce the figure of Pellegrini, I begin with her appearance in the Italian edition of *Playboy* magazine, whose overall use of racialised images provides a good example of the ruptures and continuities that porn and the sexual revolution brought into postcolonial Italy in this phase.

ARTHOUSE CINEMA AND GLOSSY PORNOGRAPHY: INES PELLEGRINI AND PIER PAOLO PASOLINI ON *PLAYBOY*

The cover of the first issue of the Italian *Playboy*, edited by the publisher Rizzoli in November 1972, portrays an African-American model, Darine Stern, who was the first black woman to appear on a cover of Hugh Hefner's magazine. Darine Stern had appeared in the US edition more than a year earlier, in October 1971, yet the choice of this cover evidently helped Rizzoli to differentiate his product from that of its domestic competitors, like *Playmen*, which already counted on a vast readership consolidated in over five years.[3] The image of Darine Stern was unprecedented for this type of publication, yet in its original destination was clearly a hint to Hefner's political leanings: he was renowned for his support of the civil rights movement.[4] In Italy, the same image evoked slightly different meanings, which the local readership associated mainly with American racial conflicts. Some readers would have interpreted Stern's natural hair as a reference to the look of civil rights movement activists, while others would have read her naked black body as a reflection of the American sexual revolution and multi-racial society, and therefore as an element of cultural difference.

Black women of African origin who worked in Italian films, like Pellegrini,[5] played a quite different role in the complex iconography of the magazine, which also included a specific interest in arthouse films. For instance, a series of articles published in the September 1973 issue of *Playboy* announced the release of *Il fiore delle mille e una notte* (Arabian nights, 1974) and included several pictures of Pellegrini. The ten-page article 'Le mie mille e una notte' (My Arabian nights) by Pier Paolo Pasolini (1974) consisted of a detailed and complex explanation of the film decorated by numerous pictures, with a particular focus on Pellegrini's nude scenes acting as the slave Zamurrud, and the thirteen-year-old Barbara Grandi, who starred a smaller part. Pellegrini was also on the cover of the same issue, which introduces her as Pasolini's 'black star'. Then, a five-page photo shoot titled 'Una stella dopo mille e una notte' (A star after the Arabian nights) completes the collection of articles about *Arabian Nights*, which includes pictures taken by the famous photographer of the divas, Angelo Frontoni (Frontoni 1974a). This extensive coverage of the film is somehow linked to Pasolini's regular collaboration with the magazine for the column 'Schermi', which consisted mainly of film reviews.[6] Like the work of other intellectuals such as Italo Calvino, Alberto Moravia and Alberto Arbasino, the writings of Pier Paolo Pasolini contributed to the 'Italianisation' of *Playboy*, whose first issues included mainly articles translated and adapted from the American edition, an aspect that didn't satisfy a readership hungry for original content.

However, the content dedicated to *Arabian Nights*, with its complex references to exotic, colonial and racial tropes, goes well beyond this primary level of cultural translation, hinting at multiple cultural meanings attributed to race in Italian culture. This is evident not only in the long text penned by the poet,[7] but also in the photographic article dedicated to Pellegrini, which reports some statements allegedly made by the actress herself. Here, she describes her arrival in Rome, her first meeting with Pasolini and her career aspirations: it was Pasolini who had changed her name from Macia to Ines, but the collaboration with him was also transformative for other reasons. The narrative of an estimated male director who shapes the identity of a young and naive actress resonates with the career stories of the American playmates published in Hefner's magazine; though, in this case, the change of name, as well as the orientalist iconography of the pictures and the origins of the actress, contribute to an Italianisation of this format, which is particularly striking in its racist connotations. The article explains Pellegrini's motivations to become an actress with her desire 'to make easy money' and her achieved popularity with her hypersexualisation: 'Initially Macia didn't want to be in the movies, because she was shy (you wouldn't say that while looking at these pictures!), but once convinced, she started to take her clothes off: a resounding success!' As such, the hypersexualisation of her body is framed in the capitalist terms of ambition and economic return, suggesting that Pellegrini's agreement to pose naked was a choice made for her own personal gratification. The article also hints at a future return to Africa, emphasising on the Otherness of the actress, who was actually born in Milan, the daughter of an Italian soldier: this narrative activates a particular discourse of the Italian postcolonial archive, and its tendency to estrange mixed-race Italians as uncomfortable reminders of interracial sexual intercourse (Petrovich Njegosh 2015).

Transnational Pornography and Colonial Difference in Low-budget Cinema

In the articles about *Arabian Nights*, the use of an orientalist and colonialist iconography successfully 'domesticated' formats and discourses perceived as 'culturally foreign'. At the same time, the representation of Pellegrini as a young woman looking for easy money and success, and ready to take off her clothes to achieve this goal, offers a narrative that is perfectly in line with the capitalist framework of 'sexual liberation'.

Colonial and exotic imageries have circulated in the transnational infrastructures of popular culture thanks to the commonality of figures and tropes at the basis of the European colonial archives, yet in these years, these tropes also became popular in countries without a colonial tradition but playing a delicate role in the context of the Cold War, like Finland (Saarenmaa 2017). The reason resides in the ductility of the postcolonial archive, and its adaptation to the discourses and images of modern capitalism. Typical examples are the films and pornographic articles centred on the sexual adventures of a white man travelling to exotic locations, or on a foreign woman on vacation, looking for local men. While the first is a reconfiguration of the colonial journey of conquest, which consists of fantasies about the predation of the land and the female body (McClintock 1995), the second variation puts women at the centre of the plot, introducing a degree of ambivalence that admits to the female character, as in the *Playboy* pictorials, a certain degree of agency, though only in the framework of her sexual availability. One example of this latter case is the famous Italian porn series *Emmanuelle*, starring Laura Gemser, a lone female photographer who travels around the world, and whose films would gradually turn hardcore. Similar stories have circulated in popular culture and cinema since the 1960s, like the 007 franchise and, going back to Italy, the travelogues and the *mondo films*, all genres that had a vast transnational circulation and strong connections with imperial and colonial narratives (Miller 2003; Giuliani 2019). This adaptation hints at the complex bond between mass-marketed pornography and pre-existent themes, genres and modes of circulation of popular culture, as well as to the flexibility of the exotic. Such hybridisation was particularly successful in low-budget and genre productions, which foresaw the formation of a specialised porn industry in a comparable, yet different, process in many national contexts.[8] Regarding Italy, Giovanna Maina and Federico Zecca (2012) have demonstrated that a good number of Italian soft-core and erotic productions were destined for foreign markets, and were subsequently adapted to comply with the stricter regulations of local censorship. These practices were well established in low-budget genre productions, which since the early 1960s have counted on transnational circulation (Baschiera and Di Chiara 2011). One of these markets has traditionally been Spain, where the transition to democracy and a relaxation of the censorship allowed the introduction of soft-core magazines and films, opening a new market to Italian producers, who were already exporting their products around the world. The soft-core low-budget comedy starring

Ines Pellegrini, *La bella governante di colore* (A beautiful black housekeeper, Luigi Rosso, 1976) was distributed to Spain in 1979, three years after its release in Italy. The original title was translated into Spanish as *Polvo negro*, a pun that alludes to gunpowder, to Pellegrini's skin and to dust, hinting at the profession of her character, Myriam, who was a maid. Myriam is a domestic worker for a family headed by a Christian Democrat and former soldier in the Fascist colonial campaigns. His son repeatedly tries to seduce Myriam and eventually orchestrates a group rape that gets her pregnant. Sexual violence, allusions to slavery, racist slurs and the hypersexualisation of the female body recur for the duration of the entire film, which is centred on the multiple attempts of the men to have sex with the black maid. Interestingly, these clear references to Italian racist and colonial tropes, and therefore to Fascism, found circulation in post-Francoist Spain suggesting, once again, the complex resignification of the colonial archive once immitted in transnational cinema circuits.

Overall, even when Pellegrini played smaller parts, the space for a black actress in the cinema of the 1970s struggled to exceed the limitations of well-engrained colonial and racial stereotypes, as in the parody film set in the era of the ancient Romans *Orazi e Curiazi 3-2* by Giorgio Mariuzzo (1977), where she appears in the role of a servant, immediately mocked with a reference to the fascist colonial song 'Faccetta nera' (Little black face). In Duccio Tessari's crime comedy *La Madama* (Sexycop, 1976) Pellegrini plays a very short part as a prostitute, a role that she also plays in the low-end sexy comedy *Il brigadiere Pasquale Zagaria ama la mamma e la polizia* (Luca Davan, 1973). A partial exception, that nonetheless doesn't contradict the typical use of the exotic in these films, is Umberto Lenzi's crime *Gatti rossi in un labirinto di vetro* (Eyeball, 1975), in which she is a tourist.

Objectified Women and Tentative Escapes: The Limitations of the Feminist Debate

As explained in Chapter 5, Italian feminists didn't engage in a systematic opposition to pornography as the Americans did, and produced no comprehensive theoretical debate that attempted to influence institutional aspects such as censorship and legislation. This can be partially explained by the relatively long hybridisation of porn with other formats and genres in Italian mass culture, which continued at least until the end of the 1970s. As such, the feminist movement understood pornography as the product of broader and systematic patterns of oppression and commodification of women's bodies and sexuality, a view that corresponded with their general approach to sexism in the media, in opposition to an enthusiastic rhetoric of 'sexual liberation'.

In other words, the diffusion of pornography was seen as a product of the patriarchy, while the triumph of eroticised and hypersexualised female figures in the media was read in relation to men's inability to represent women's 'inner reality' (Frabotta et al. 1979, 22). These reflections, which were derived mostly from the local debates in film criticism, didn't include race as a structural and analytical category. This doesn't mean that there was no anti-racist sensibility in the movement, but the analysis of women's oppression was focused primarily on gender difference, putting class, and especially race, in a secondary position. As Vincenza Perilli has pointed out, Italian second-wave feminism has consistently adopted the analogy between racism and sexism to explain its political intervention during the 1970s, and this analogy as well as the prevailing of essentalist views of the feminism of the difference in the 1980s have hindered the development of an intersectional perspective that can rearticulate race and gender in a more nuanced political analysis (2007). This question had also influenced feminist debates about women's role in the cinema, also exemplified by a special issue of the feminist magazine *Noi Donne* (1977) that was emblematically titled 'Il cinema e la donna: qualcosa é cambiato, ma l'attrice é sempre negra' (Cinema and women, something has changed, but the actress is always black). In this title, the juxtaposition of women and black people generically hints at comparable conditions of exploitation and subjugation. But despite this, none of the articles in the special issue discussed race at all as they focused only on the problems of white actresses who had a more established career. In other words, Italian second-wave feminism was confronted with the theoretical and pragmatic difficulty of contesting pornography in a period when it wasn't perceived entirely as an autonomous industry and market; at the same time, its reflections about gender and race didn't admit the specificity of black women's experience of patriarchal oppression, including in the very visible mechanisms reproduced and nurtured by the media.

These limitations are evident in a handful of feminist and independent studies addressing topics such as the absence of women in the cultural industries (Buonanno 1978; Bellumori 1972), and the representation of women in films and television shows (Cif 1977; Garaguso and Renzetti 1978; Frabotta 1979). In these examples of feminist cultural critique, notions such as 'objectification' and 'objectified woman' (donna-oggetto) are employed frequently, becoming part of the feminist vocabulary of discussing pornography. Interestingly, such notions were adopted by both explicitly Catholic organisations, like the Centro Italiano Femminile (CIF), and the most radical areas of the movement. In 1975, at a presentation of the study on the representation of women in the cinema commissioned by the Catholic organisation, the president Alda Miceli affirmed that 'the model of femininity that cinema offers is still that of the objectified woman', and launches an appeal to the young actresses starring in erotic cinema, asking them to boycott misogynistic films and their humiliating characters (L.T. 1975). Interviewed by a journalist in regards to this proposition, a group of soft-core cinema actresses (Edwige Fenech, Gloria Guida, Stella Carnacina, Maria Pia Giancaro and Jenny Tamburi) responded that they disagreed for two reasons: first, they refused the label of 'objectified women', as they were well aware of their decision to pose naked, as a stepping stone to a better career; second, they saw in nudity something natural and innocuous that didn't need to be judged (Ronza 1975).

Similar questions had been raised at the talk show *Proibito* aired by the Italian public broadcaster RAI in 1977, where a feminist activist described as 'victims' the actresses Eleonora Giorgi and Ines Pellegrini and the porn star Ilona Staller, who had been invited to the programme. The debate was moderated by the journalist Enzo Biagi; present also in the studio was a group of men with an 'informed opinion', including the priest Leandro Rossi, a therapist and the porn producer Riccardo Schicchi. Despite Giorgi and Pellegrini saying they were proud of their bodies and their careers, the activist seemed indifferent to their perspective. Pellegrini, for example, explicitly affirmed that she was aware of the compromises she had made for her career, and explained that soft-core films were the only option to start a career in Italian cinema. By saying this, she was reclaiming a form of agency that the activist refused to acknowledge or address, which also made a point about the lack of opportunities for women in the cinema, a question that many other actresses and feminist film critics have stressed repeatedly in their public interventions. This episode is one of the few public appearances in which Pellegrini discussed her profession in a context that was not shaped on her Eritrean origins or a colonial imagery. However, in the context of the sexist and moralising debate of the talk show she still occupied a contested and stigmatised position, this time for agreeing to act in sexually explicit roles.

This debate eventually deadlocked in a sterile confrontation between women, in which the pragmatism of the young actress Pellegrini illustrated the ideological rigidity of the activist. In other words, the category of the objectified woman immediately revealed its limitations when confronted with the realities of the women who worked in the film industry, as it offered no answer to the very material issue of the shortage of job opportunities, while erasing the possibility of agency to a woman who was sharing her views and experiences. At the same time, the idea that agency corresponded with making career choices and 'compromises' reveals that an incipient 'post-feminist sensibility' (Gill 2007) was already circulating in the Italian media culture of the time, as a powerful counter-discourse to second-wave feminism.[9]

BETWEEN HIGH AND LOW THEORIES OF SEXUALITY

As we have seen throughout the chapter, in the Italian media and public discourse of the 1970s race was hyper-visible and neglected at the same time, working as a flexible signifier for Italian identity and as a critical category that perturbed the narratives of sexual liberation, while negotiating the contradictions of a postcolonial society. At the same time, race made evident the limitations of gender difference as a political and interpretative framework that couldn't acknowledge the specificity of Pellegrini's experience, marked by colonial and racist stereotypes, but also by the promise of one day achieving a better position in the cinema.

In her seminal analysis of the pornographic magazine *Hustler*, Laura Kipnis suggests reading both 'pornography' and feminist protests as theories of sexuality, that can be associated with 'low' or 'high' cultures (Kipnis 1992). In high-end, soft-core magazines like *Playboy*, women, rather than being mysterious or threatening sexual creatures, were key to accessing a world of pleasure and commodities. In this framework, colonial tropes and orientalist stereotypes concurred to produce a reassuring narrative in which the agency of a sexually liberated woman like Pellegrini was contained by her position of economic and racial subalternity. The 'lower-theories of sexuality' typical of low-end and sexploitation films revealed a similar tension, in which Pellegrini's opportunities of exceeding stereotypical and hypersexualised characters seemed even narrower. At the same time, the feminist responses to these narratives were based on the abstract notion of the 'objectified woman' to challenge the logics of commodification and exploitation of female sexuality prompted by the sexual revolution. However, by talking about the women who agreed to pose naked as 'objectified', they also erased their perspective, which could have actually helped to understand how the lack of working opportunities for young actresses affected women. *Noi Donne*'s choice of focusing especially on those professionals who had acted in non-sexy films, and the CIF's request to actresses to reject roles in erotic films failed to consider the systemic limitations that confronted many young actresses in the film industry.

One can say that it is not mandatory to be an actress, and these young women could always do other jobs that didn't force them to 'sell their bodies'. This argument is very slippery, as it somehow implies that it is acceptable for women not to even try to work in cinema, basically leaving things as they are while waiting for 'dignified' and feminist roles to be (sooner or later) available, or hoping that a 'respectable' director would choose them. As we see in the following chapters, none of these options actually worked, as what happened at the level of representation and stardom was just the product and reflection of a more complex entanglement between sexism and the film industry.

Notes

1. My use of the expression 'colonial archive' is borrowed from Gaia Giuliani's working definition, which understands it as a site of knowledge production and shared beliefs articulated through the dissemination and circulation of 'figures of race'. The figures of race are a set of 'images that sediment transnationally over time and crystallise some of the meanings assigned to bodies – which are gendered and racialised in colonial and postcolonial contexts' (Giuliani 2019: 20).
2. A detailed feminist reconstruction of the fractures and tensions between Italian feminism and other leftist groups and movements from 1968 to the late 1970s is in Bettini 1978: 158–209.
3. *Playmen* was the monthly edition of *Men*, the first soft-porn magazine legally sold in Italy, an erotic weekly launched at the end of 1966 by two publishers based in Rome: Adelina Tattilo and Saro Balsamo. Before then, porn and sexually explicit pictures circulated clandestinely, or were confined to down-market publications. After a few requisitions and trials for obscenity, *Men* and its monthly edition *Playboy* eventually succeeded in the legitimisation of a niche market for erotica, which would grow dramatically in subsequent years (Maina 2018).
4. This choice was interpreted as a clear reflection of Hugh Hefner's renowned support for the civil rights movement and progressive politics in this phase. Elizabeth Fraterrigo identifies 1967 with the beginning of a liberal turn in the American edition of *Playboy*, which also endorsed the liberalisation of marijuana and opposed the Vietnam War (Fraterrigo 2009, 159–66).
5. Other than Pellegrini, in these years another Eritrean actress debuted, Zeudi Araya, who would later marry the producer Franco Castaldi. Araya's first film, *La ragazza dalla pelle di luna* (Luigi Scattini, 1972), launched Araya's image as a sexy, exotic beauty. See Giuliani 2019.
6. The special collaboration between Pasolini and *Playboy* is confirmed by the coverage that *Arabian Nights* received in the competitor magazine *Playmen*, which published an article with pictures taken by Angelo Frontoni, accompanied only by a couple of quotations from the film (Frontoni 1974b).
7. A discussion of Pasolini's use of the exotic and of the colonial archive goes beyond the scope of this chapter. For a preliminary assessment of these questions see Giovanna Trento, 2012, 'Pier Paolo Pasolini in Eritrea', in Cristina Lombardi-Diop and, Caterina Romeo, eds, *Postcolonial Italy* (New York: Palgrave Macmillan); Luca Caminati, 2017, 'Pasolini's Southward Quest(ion)', *Estetica. Studi e Ricerche*, no. 2 (July–December): 273–92.
8. To date, the most extensive studies on this topic concentrate on the American case (Schaefer, ed., 2015; Gorfinkel 2017).
9. For a further exploration of the intersections between post-feminism, pornography, popular culture and second-feminism in Italy, see also Missero 2019.

CHAPTER 8

The Beginning of the End? Depoliticised Feminism in Fellini's City of Women

> Woman [are] a series of projections invented by man. In history, she became our dream image.
>
> Federico Fellini[1]

As Áine O'Healy has noted, feminist interventions about Federico Fellini's cinema have generally been split between attempts at recuperation and the sharply critical (1992, 325). Teresa de Lauretis' discussion of *Giulietta degli spiriti* (Juliet of the spirits, 1964) represents the latter group: the author focuses on the 'cinematic contract' that the director establishes with the female spectator, which in her view consists of 'a heterosexual contract designed to bind or "entertain" . . . within the male-designed social technology of gender that is cinema' (1987, 105). In other words, de Lauretis reminds us that cinema reflects 'the social reality and political consequences of gender asymmetry' (105) by means of its production mechanisms and structures of representation, and elevates Fellini as one of its most emblematic examples.

Almost thirty years later, while the polarisation between recuperative and critical scholarship is not completely over, de Lauretis' invitation to analyse Fellini's work for its material and political consequences remains compelling. Drawing on this suggestion, this chapter focuses on a late film and a less-discussed aspect of Fellini's relationship with women, *La città delle donne* (City of women, 1980), a project that pushed him to collaborate with a group of feminist intellectuals, artists and activists. In particular, this chapter focuses on the multifaceted strategies of depoliticisation that Fellini successfully pursued during the production of this film by means of specific creative, ideological and production strategies.[2] It is not my intention to map the feminist reception of the film, draw conclusions about Fellini's sexism, or reconstruct how the activists discussed his cinema. Rather, I am interested in the material aspects and political consequences of the representational agenda pursued by the film and its symptomatic relation to the political and critical tensions that Italian feminism was experiencing in the late 1970s.

La Città Delle Donne: A Political Film?

Besides involving feminist activists, *City of Women* openly 'addresses head-on Fellini's own self-professed fear and bewilderment of women, which, this time, he foregrounds in light of Italy's recent feminist movement' (Reich 2004, 92). In *City of Women*, indeed, feminism has a significant presence and occupies a central position in the fears of 'every Italian man at a certain point of his life (middle age) at a certain point in history' (Reich 2004, 95).

The plot is based on a dream-like structure that echoes *8½* (1963), and begins on a train, where Marcello/Snàporaz (Marcello Mastroianni) meets and tries to seduce a mysterious stranger (Bernice Stegers). Suddenly, their train stops, and the woman gets off the coach to walk towards the woods. Marcello follows her as far as the Miramare Hotel where a feminist congress is taking place. Women of all ages and from different parts of the world are gathered to debate, perform, sing and watch films, but they are too busy to pay attention to Marcello. Once the group notices his presence, he is forced to escape until Donatella (Donatella Damiani), the only woman who speaks to him, saves him from a lynching. When Snàporaz eventually manages to escape from the hotel, he is chased and harassed by other women (a peasant and a group of loud girls who are driving a car, listening to loud music and smoking) until he finds shelter at the villa of Dr Katzone (Ettore Manni). As his name suggests – it means 'dickhead' or literally 'big dick' – Katzone is obsessed with his sexual prowess, so much so that his entire house is decorated with penises and photos of his lovers, exhibited as trophies. That night he is celebrating his ten thousandth conquest by holding a party, where Snàporaz unexpectedly bumps into his ex-wife. All of a sudden, Donatella reappears and rescues him from his ex, but then a couple of gay men escort him in front of a court composed of a pool of feminists who are going to judge him 'for being born male' and for his masculinity. Once dismissed, Snàporaz boards a hot air balloon in the shape of Donatella, but the young woman, who initially helped him, is now shooting at him with an automatic rifle. At this point, Marcello wakes up, finding himself back on the train, and the film ends.

Overall, *City of Women*'s dream-like structure has been interpreted as a regressive journey to the maternal womb, where the fears and anxieties of a middle-aged man about women and sexuality gravitate around feminism, marriage and masculinity.[3] The scenes in which references to feminism are most visible are the convention and the trial. In the first, the movement is portrayed as a series of extravagant performances, in which feminist politics is reduced to a festive, chaotic assembly of women behind closed doors. The scene of the trial, however, is characterised by a darker atmosphere, in which anxiety prevails about the bewilderment and curiosity of the first part. This duality also represents Fellini's ambivalent relationship with feminism. Indeed, although he argued that all his films were concerned with the liberation of men and women and therefore could be considered as feminist films (Scalfari 1979), at the time he began to work on *City of Women*, he knew very little about the activities, ideas and practices of the movement. In line with his working practice, eminently based on a creative combination of research, inspiration and intuition (Minuz 2012), the director repeatedly tried to attend the meetings of Roman collectives in via Del Governo Vecchio to get inspired and gather ideas, but every time he was kicked out by activists (Tornabuoni 1980). Despite these initial efforts to conduct 'research' and his alleged liaison with Germaine Greer,[4] Fellini never hid his scarce enthusiasm for the movement, that he contested not so much for its 'ideals', but for its 'political nature'.[5] In an interview released to the Italian *Playboy* magazine in 1973, the director confessed to being

> irritated by today's tendency to make political something that is psychological or artistic... If feminism is a pseudo revolution in which women who are incapable of being women wish to validate their own ineptitude... well, I don't think this is an appreciable form of feminism. (Fellini in *Playboy* 1973, 43)

These words resonate with the comments he exchanged with the co-author of the *City of Women* script Bernardino Zapponi on the set of the film:

> Look at these girls, tight in the pants, with heavy heels, who smoke nervously and without respect for anybody... And their feminist meetings, the rallies where they articulate their incomprehensible slogans, with their faces drawn by anger... I don't understand, what has happened between us, between women and me... We were getting along so well! (Zapponi 1979, 75)

The trope of the angry, unpleasant feminist returns in the words of the character Snàporaz as well, when he says: 'I understand feminism and all, but why be so angry!' Both Fellini's opinions about the movement and his reduction of women's activism to an irrational state of anger tend to minimise the political character of feminism. These views can be read in the framework of his discussed tendency to depoliticise his work. According to Francesca Cantore and Giulia Muggeo, Fellini 'sought repeatedly – but in vain – to diminish the political aspects of [City of Women]' in different versions of the screenplay, and subsequently by denying his intention and ability to make a film about feminism, an aspect apparently confirmed by his search for 'feminist consultants' (2021). However, as noted by Andrea Minuz, such attempts often hid the ideological aspects of Fellini's cinema, which the director often failed to control (2012). In Minuz's reconstruction, Fellini's 'politics' appears like a product of the socio-cultural context surrounding the director, rather than a result of his political leanings. But looking at the case of *City of Women*, what are the consequences of diminishing the political content of a film that deals explicitly with a social movement like feminism? And why, as Cantore and Muggeo suggest, has the director failed to contain the ideological aspects of his film?

IN-BETWEEN CONTRADICTIONS: PRODUCTION STORIES AND FEMINIST COLLABORATIONS

The 'depoliticisation' of second-wave feminism has frequently been associated with the contamination of feminism by the neo-liberal agendas of the 1980s and 1990s.[6] The depoliticisation of feminism in *City of Women* is somehow symptomatic of this process, as it makes visible the complex role of the media in the fragmentation of the movement. As anticipated, Italian feminists were also very critical of Fellini's work. On the release of *Amarcord*, Adele Cambria elected Fellini as the 'anti-feminist of the month' (Cambria 1973, 10–11), while Patrizia Carrano criticised the female characters of his films for being mere products of his imagination (Carrano 1977).

Despite this, after the initial difficulties in establishing contact with the movement, Fellini changed his strategy and decided to get in touch individually with a group of intellectuals and artists who were involved with or were close to the collectives, and it seems that one of his first contacts was Adele Cambria. Indeed, Cambria's name appears on the printed edition of the screenplay of the film, along 'with all the other feminists who collaborated with tips and suggestions to the construction of that part of the tale about the sequence of the feminist convention' (Fellini 1980, 5).[7] Despite this, in the feminist magazine *Quotidiano Donna*, Cambria tried to minimise her involvement, though Ippolita Avalli, a feminist writer and artist who similarly agreed to collaborate with Fellini, invited her 'to tell things as they were' (Avalli 1979, 7). Indeed, it appears that Cambria helped more than she was keen to admit, as she not only contributed to the script, but also facilitated the contacts with other feminist artists and intellectuals, like the collective Le Nemesiache, who agreed to meet with Fellini at Cinecittà and show their films (Mangiacapre 1979). According to Lina Mangiacapre, the director wanted Le Nemesiache in *City of Women*, but the contacts ceased when he refused to give them full control of their role. It seems that this was standard practice: having established a contact and obtained some information, Fellini offered the activists a little part in the film, promising economic compensation, and reassuring them that he wasn't going to make 'a documentary about feminism but a . . . a projection of the main character, a man in his fifties, a provincial professor of literature' (Cambria 1979b).

This was also the experience of Méri Lao, a feminist musicologist and writer who authored the song 'Una donna senza uomo é' (A woman without man is), which was included in one of the last sequences of the feminist convention. In a public lecture she gave in 2010, Lao lamented not having being credited for the song.[8] She was also particularly embittered by the lack of acknowledgement for the dance sequence present in the film that was based on her laboratory of yoga and voice, *Musica Strega*.[9] Méri Lao's experience reflects the affective response of many other feminist 'consultants' for the project of *City of Women*, especially those who have worked as extras. *Quotidiano Donna* published a brief article discussing the bad working environment on set and denouncing the pay discrimination perpetrated by the production (Anon. 1979). The topic of money, indeed, recurs in almost all the justifications that the feminists gave for getting involved in the project, but other activists rejected this excuse as a clumsy attempt to conceal a desire for fame and success (Tamburrini 1979). Looking at this debate, it seems that Fellini's request for help, which Lina Mangiacapre describes as a proper 'ransack', not only positioned the activists against each other, but also won over every possible ideological objection. The director, indeed, was touching a sensitive nerve in the second-wave movement, which was dealing with the progressive exhaustion of its radical agenda as it confronted the political and social turmoil of the end of the decade.

It is also interesting to look at these debates in relation to the very different treatment reserved to Donatella Damiani, the actress who played the part of the salvific Donatella in the film. Christie Milliken has suggested an interpretation of Donatella's character as the mythological figure of Medusa in the context of a Freudian–Bakhtinian reading. Milliken's hypothesis is that this character encapsulates a 'female power' that supports a 'potentially progressive feminist reading of the film' (1990, 28). However, if we extend our analysis beyond a strict interpretation of the text, this possibility appears much more elusive than in theory. Like many other young actresses who worked with prominent Italian arthouse directors in these years, Damiani posed naked for the local edition of *Playboy*, which presented her as Fellini's last discovery and as the next Anita Ekberg (*Playboy* 1980).[10] In line with the formula of the girl-next-door that was typical of *Playboy* centrefolds, Donatella Damiani presents herself as a young woman who is lucky to have been chosen, and who is happy to pose naked while waiting for better professional opportunities.

The article begins with a comment about her breasts: 'Since Fellini liked them, I am almost proud of them too!' (Damiani in *Playboy* 1980) and then continues: 'Feminist critics? This is not my business: in the film I was who Fellini wanted me to be. I am happy that I accepted that role' (Damiani in *Playboy* 1980). In this framework, Damiani's disinterest in feminism consolidates a model of femininity that is sexually emancipated and available to the male gaze, but also subjected to an asymmetric relationship of power (the one with the director) that is eminently a working and economic relation. In the fantasised narrative of the *Playboy* article, then, Damiani's disinterest in politics pairs with an alternative model of femininity, one that, unlike the feminists, is not angry, but smiles and is happy to be what the director asks her to be. This image certainly reflects *Playboy*'s editorial line more than Fellini's intentions; however, most of these promotional materials had been shot on set, also portraying Mastroianni and the director with a semi-naked Damiani in an iconography that seems to confirm that the essential difference between Donatella and the other women in the film resides in a more condescending relationship with men.

The Film and the Political Materiality of Feminist and Queer Spectatorship

According to Frank Burke, *City of Women* is characterised by the 'collapse of referent into sign and signified into signifier' (2002, 36). For this reason, in *La città delle donne*, women are 'merely one term within a chain of significations', and none of them can be 'real' (Burke 2002, 36–7).[11] However, if we move outside a strict textual interpretation of the film, I would argue that for some spectators, and I am thinking about feminist and queer spectators, the 'signs' in Fellini's chain of significations were easily recognisable references to their own reality. Indeed, as seen in the previous section, Fellini's strategies for extraction and resignification of the 'real' had political, gendered and ideological consequences. This is especially true of those parts in which the film explicitly represents feminism, which put feminist and queer spectators in a difficult position, suspended between the erasure of their political experience and the opportunity to repoliticise the text by means of an eminently individual act of resignification. All these questions highlight the complex textual and extra-textual gendered aspects of *City of Women* as well as the consequences of 'depoliticising' feminism in a context of imminent changes within the movement.

The scenes of the feminist convention are based on information and practices obtained from women who had spent years involved in activism and creative research: the *musicastrega* laboratory, feminist political chants, feminist cinema, feminist social theatre – with the little sketch *La giornata gloriosa di una casalinga* (The great day of a housewife). Just to mention this latter example, while references to feminist theatre easily go unnoticed by the general public, they remain perfectly recognisable for a feminist spectator who might have attended a play like that. The emphasis of *City of Women* on the artistic and creative aspects of feminism reflects Fellini's idea that the problems posed by feminism pertained to the sphere of the artistic and the psychological.

Similar considerations can be made about the trial scene that preludes the final part of the film. Here we see a group of androgynous characters training for a boxing match while the pool of feminist judges is ready to condemn Marcello, who is escorted by two gay men. The alliance between emancipated feminist judges and queers is not just a projection of the emasculation fears of the heterosexual male character, Snàporaz, but it is also an accidental hint at the contemporary politicisation of gay and lesbians, which is historically tied to feminism. This political allusion evidently exceeds the representational agenda of the film, as an example of 'queer asynchrony' (Freeman 2010), in which the political history of queerness forces the constraints of Fellini's cinematic contract. Glimpses of queer asynchronies are suggested also by a scene of the on-set documentary *Notes on City of Women*, where we see Fellini controlling the performance of an actor impersonating the gay man at the trial. The director shows him how to walk swaying the hips and chuckling, while exhorting him to do it in the same way: 'C'mon! This is what sissies do!' (é questo che é da frocio!). Despite this, the actor continues to fail to perform as illustrated, so Fellini scolds him and yells: 'Come on, smile! SMILE!!!'. This brief exchange well encapsulates Fellini's fixation with his own significations, as he attempts to repeat a representation of queerness that is very close to those seen twenty years earlier in *La dolce vita*.[12] The actor's failure to do so, and the exhortation to smile in the face of his embarrassment, are a consequence of Fellini's anachronistic understanding of queerness, so much so that he believes he can perform a better 'sissy' than the man he has hired to do it.

Conclusion

The collaboration between Fellini and the feminist intellectuals and artists on the scene of the congress is emblematic of a delicate moment for both Italian arthouse cinema and feminism. *City of Women* didn't meet with the praise of the critics or the public, and seen today, it seems a product of bitterness, if not of the dark anxiety, of the director. At the same time, the divisions that Fellini managed to bring out among the Roman feminists reveal the internal and individualising tensions that were beginning to run in the movement, precisely among those activists who had come closer to professionalising their activism as writers, performers and public figures. From this point of view, the destabilisation and depoliticisation of second-wave feminism seemed to be close to an end point. A similar tension is also reproduced at the level of representation, in which the scenes with feminists and queers are marked by a high degree of ambivalence.

All these contradictions result from an analysis of the interplay between textual and the extra-textual aspects, namely the study of the historical and material context of production and signification of the film. Besides enriching our understanding of the socio-cultural impact of cinema, this approach to *City of Women* helps to recuperate neglected positionalities and perspectives (those of the activists, of Donatella Damiani and the feminist and queer spectators) that exceed the 'vision and intentions' of the author, to reveal the mechanisms of power and resistance activated within and outside the film.

Notes

1. Gideon Bachmann and Federico Fellini, 1980–81, 'Federico Fellini: "The Cinema Seen as a Woman . . .": An Interview on the Day "City of Women" Premiered in Rome', *Film Quarterly* 34, no. 2 (Winter): 8.
2. Like most of Fellini's films, a vast array of material discussing the making of *City of Women* is available, including Sonia Schoonejans' production diary (1980), Raffaele Monti's photographic book *Bottega Fellini* (1981), the printed edition of the screenplay published by Garzanti (1980), and behind-the-scenes documentary titled *Notes on City of Women* (Ferruccio Castronuovo, 1980). Although these sources emphasise the craftsmanship behind Fellini's cinematic creations and his artistic genius, they also provide helpful contextual elements to aid understanding of this collaboration, giving also an idea of Fellini's intentions and perspective. These materials also offer a framework for contextualising the debate about the making of the film that appeared in the feminist weekly *Quotidiano donna*, in which several activists discussed their experience with the director.
3. For a detailed analysis of the film in regards to masculinity, see Reich 2004, 92–104.
4. Fellini first contacted Greer when he was working on *Casanova* (1976). He also repeatedly claimed to have read her book *The Female Eunuch* (1970). In 2010 Greer revealed the details of a night she spent with the director in 1976. See Helen Pidd, 2010, 'Germaine Greer breaks cover on tryst with Federico Fellini', *The Guardian*, 11 April, available at https://www.theguardian.com/world/2010/apr/11/germaine-greer-affair-federico-fellini, accessed 5 May 2021.
5. Interestingly, both Minuz (2012) and Peter Bondanella (1992) make a point about Fellini's complex – or contradictory and therefore not politically categorisable – views on feminism by mentioning the appreciation of his work by two prominent feminist intellectuals, Germaine Greer and – in the case of Bondanella –

Camille Paglia. It is noteworthy that both these figures are widely and notoriously considered controversial, as they have shaped their academic and public presence around provocative and aggressive statements about contemporary queer, antiracist and transfeminist movements. Specifically, their views on transgender folk have problematically tied them to the most conservative factions of academic feminism. By saying this I am not implying a direct correlation between the ideas of these intellectuals and Fellini's cinema, but rather suggesting a careful consideration of the different positions that coexist within 'feminism'. Greer and Paglia's 'pro-fellinist' interventions, from the late 1980s, belong to two intellectuals who have detached from feminism as a social movement to embrace a specific strategy of philosophical and intellectual activism that is not necessarily representative of 1970s feminism or of contemporary movements. About the controversies around these two authors, see Tara John, 2016, 'Germaine Greer Defends her Controversial Views on Transgender Women', *Time*, 12 April, available at https://time.com/4290409/germaine-greer-transgender-women/, accessed 5 May 2021; Joseph McAndrew, 2019, 'Camille Paglia's transphobia made students feel alienated. Here's how we responded', *Queerty*, 5 May, available at https://www.queerty.com/camille-paglia-made-school-unsafe-trans-students-heres-responded-20190505, accessed 5 May 2021.

6. This particular phase has also been discussed in the conceptual framework of the 'backlash' since the publication of Susan Faludi's *Backlash: The Undeclared War against American Women* (New York: Crown Publishers, 1991). I am not adopting this term, as it suggests too clear a distinction between a 'before' and an 'after'. Two readings that specifically discuss the depoliticisation of feminism and its entanglement with neoliberalism are Nancy Fraser, 2009, *Fortunes of Feminism: From State-Managed Capitalism to Neoliberal Crisis* (London: Verso) and Angela McRobbie, 2009, *The Aftermath of Feminism: Gender, Culture and Social Change* (London: Sage).

7. According to Cambria, Fellini asked her about some bizarre American self-help groups that he thought were composing a mysterious 'music of the vagina' (Cambria 1979a; Cambria 2010, 35). Cambria, who had never heard anything about this group, decided to send him a story about an ageing Latin lover who was attempting to stay young.

8. The video 'Meri Lao racconta il suo Fellini e canta Una donna senza uomo è' is available at https://www.youtube.com/watch?v=yW6BbjTXgPM, accessed 5 May 2021.

9. A description of the sequence is present in the second edition of Meri Lao's book *Musica Strega* (1980).

10. The promotion of the film in a glossy soft porn magazine is particularly interesting in relation to the production history of the film, which was initially produced by Bob Guccione, the founder of the American porn magazine *Penthouse* (Kezich 1988, 480). Guccione wanted to invest in a high-budget pornographic narrative film, and the initial negotiations with Fellini went very well, so much so that the director described him as 'a congenial companion' (Chandler 1995,

211–12). However, the production soon went over budget, and the two disagreed on fundamental creative aspects, such as casting and the ways sex should be portrayed. On this, Fellini commented: 'He [Guccione] thought I was prude. I was, by his definition. He wanted to show much more sex than I like to show, and in close-up' (Chandler 1995, 212). Eventually, the American decided to work with another Italian director, Tinto Brass, for the controversial *Caligula* (1979), a film that was notoriously marked by similar disagreements about the level of explicitness of the sex scenes, and was released more or less at the same time as *City of Women* in the spring of 1980.

11. In this respect, Jacqueline Reich (2004), using a psychoanalytic framework, proposes a reading of the entire film as a sequence of jokes.
12. In his discussion of *La dolce vita*, Richard Dyer remembers that in the wake of his activism in the 1970s he rejected the representations of gay people in the film, but he also acknowledges that when he saw it at the time of its release, he welcomed the presence of so many queer characters (2018, 4–9). Dyer words perfectly illustrate the asynchronies typical of the acts of queer (and feminist) spectatorship, and the ambivalent interplay of feelings of validation and political sentiments of refusal.

Part III

Cultures of Production: Maps, Labour and Archives

The marginalisation of women in the cinema industry is a process that has characterised most national cinemas and which have been influenced by technological, industrial and cultural matters. This has inevitably contributed to consolidating women's exclusion from a canon of national cinema based on the exceptionality and genius of a handful of directors (Higson 1989), yet the histories of technical professionals, popular genres and low-budget filmmaking have similarly continued to exclude women by reproducing the same categories of artistic merit and value. This section aims to situate women's filmmaking in these intertwined, complementary historiographies, considering the evolution of the overall institutional framework, the gendered production cultures consolidated in the film industry, of both below-the-line and above-the-line professionals. The following chapters provide a genealogical perspective on women's role in filmmaking, to emphasise its problematic relationship with notions of authorship and national cinema. To do so, this part of the book adopts a materialistic approach, which draws from women's practices, experiences and networks to reconstruct their position and contribution in the material and ideological frameworks of film production. This approach also enables me to emphasise the collective and processual nature of cinema history rather than a notion of historiography that prioritises singularity and excellence.

The section splits into two main parts, each consisting of two chapters, one providing a more general reconstruction and one focusing on a case study. Chapter 9 discusses the professional trajectory of the production manager Mara Blasetti, to focus on the informal practices of recruitment and training in the Italian film industry and discuss the topic of sexism in her work environment. The research is based on Mara Blasetti's personal archive, which is held at the Cineteca di Bologna and represents a rare example of a complete collection of documents that belonged to a female film professional. Her career covered a time span from approximatively the mid-1950s to the early 1980s, and offers an insider perspective on the main difficulties faced by female professionals working in below-the-line and managerial positions. Chapter 10 analyses the career paths of a group of female graduates at the Centro Sperimentale di Cinematografia (CSC), the first public film school in Italy. Drawing on the official list of alumni, the chapter reconstructs a genealogy of female practitioners in order to understand the complex interplay of structural and individual aspects determining women's trajectories in the film industry.

The last two chapters focus on feminist film directors and collectives during the 1970s in both cinema and television. Chapter 11 analyses labour and collective filmmaking in the Collettivo Femminista Cinema and the Arcobaleno Cooperative, as well as films by Dacia Maraini and a mainstream project, *Io sono mia* (Sofia Scandurra, 1978). The last chapter focuses on the case of Adriana Monti, a feminist filmmaker and author of the film *Scuola senza fine*, drawing on a study of her archive, which is preserved at the Fondazione Micheletti in Brescia.

CHAPTER 9

Sexism and Women's Work: Mara Blasetti, Production Manager

This chapter focuses on the structural and material consequences of sexism in the film industry, drawing on the case of the production manager Mara Blasetti, daughter of the director Alessandro Blasetti. To this extent, I have studied her personal archive, preserved at the Cineteca di Bologna, to which Mara also donated her father's archive.[1] As a unique example of a comprehensive collection belonging to a female below-the-line professional currently available in the Italia archives,[2] this fund gives access to film history from a gendered, material and affective perspective, which is scarcely present in Italian production studies. Before focusing on this case study, I offer an overview of the historical sources and studies on the Italian film industry of the past, while interrogating their scarce interest in gender.

FOR A GENDERED AND ARCHIVAL PERSPECTIVE ON THE ITALIAN FILM INDUSTRY

In his investigation of the American film industry, John Thornton Caldwell demonstrated that film practitioners attribute intangible cultural values to their profession that inevitably influence working practices and relationships (Caldwell 2008). Caldwell talks of these 'production cultures' as processual and relational formations that result from the negotiation of individual and collective experiences by means of particular forms of 'industrial reflexivity'. In the growing literature in the field of production and 'feminist production studies' (Banks 2018), investigations into the Italian case are still sporadic and limited to a few case studies. A possible reason is the persistent influence of established lines of inquiry, which have been proven to be particularly resistant to gender. One is the anecdotal approach, which has been pursued mainly by film critics since the early 1980s, when Franca Faldini and Goffredo Fofi published their classic two-volume collection *L'avventurosa storia del cinema italiano* (The adventurous history of Italian cinema, 1981). These volumes gather anecdotes and testimonies from film practitioners – mostly directors, screenwriters and actors – about the making of famous films and the working practices of a few renowned directors.[3] Although this book provides important contextual information, its emphasis on industrial narratives based on the values of camaraderie and technical and creative genius,[4] has inevitably prevented a systematic study of gender inequality. Female practitioners have generally worked in less recognised clerical professions, therefore their know-how has rarely been considered essential to understanding the creative process of filmmaking, which is conventionally attributed to the director and a handful of his collaborators (screenwriters, cinematographers and music composers). This confirms that the historical link between creativity and masculinity has contributed to establish gender inequality and sexism in the creative industries, with consequences for today's working practices too (Nixon 2003; Conor et al. 2015). Another group of influential studies has been inaugurated by the classic research of Lorenzo Quaglietti, *Storia economico-politica del cinema italiano* (An economic-political history of Italian cinema, 1980), which proposes an economy-centred perspective that privileges aspects such as institutional policy, financing, production and legislation. Quaglietti's seminal book has been joined more recently by systematic investigations based on archival research, like Barbara Corsi's *Con qualche dollaro in meno* (With a few dollars less, 2001), and Marina Nicoli's *The Rise and Fall of the Italian Film Industry* (2017).[5] However, this line of research has no specific focus on gender, although it provides essential contextual analysis to frame an historical assessment of women's role in the industry. The last group of scholarly research that I should mention in this brief overview consists of studies mainly focused on technological aspects and technique, which also gives no specific attention to gender.[6]

These three tendencies have dominated the scholarly debate so far, despite the issue of gender discrimination in the film and communication industries has been raised by Italian feminist criticism since the 1970s.[7] For the specific case of cinema, there are at least two examples: the special issue of the film journal *Bianco e Nero*, titled *Le donne del cinema, contro questo cinema* (Women of cinema, against this cinema, 1972) by Cinzia Bellumori and Patrizia Carrano's *Malafemmina* (1977), a book that addresses feminist debates, such as the marginalisation of women's creativity and the objectification of female sexuality in films. It is not a coincidence that these publications appeared in a period that coincided with the peak of the Italian feminist movement and the significant weight of the unions and the workers' movement. Covering two decades, from 1951 to 1969, Bellumori's study engages explicitly with a feminist perspective, linking the gender discrimination characterising the film industry with patterns of inequality affecting female workers in other sectors. This study represents the only systematic attempt, to date, to investigate the working conditions of female film professionals, combining different methodologies, such as surveys and interviews with practitioners, and including the workers of a film stock developing plant, as well as continuity supervisors, editors and actresses. Carrano's book, albeit using a journalistic approach, collects testimonies from female film practitioners and surveys the public debates about women and cinema, with quotations and comments from newspapers and popular magazines. Despite their different approach, these studies share the merit of framing gender segregation in the film industry as part of diffused unequal working conditions. Moreover, both these publications have a definite conception of the role that women should play in the media, one that rejects the romanticisation of creativity to focus on material and pragmatic aspects, such as labour and discrimination.

Despite this, these publications had no follow-up until recent years, when a series of comparative studies analysed the patterns of gender inequality in the industry and produced data sets and reports about the film sector in Europe.[8] In 2019 the Italian research group DEA – Donne e Audiovisivo (Women and the audio-visual) – has published a report about gender in film professions such as film direction, production and screenwriting, focusing also on copyright and funding policies but leaving aside the technical professionals (DEA 2019). In all these areas, researchers have met difficulties in gathering systematic data, pointing to the absence of concerted action by institutions and professional organisations. This situation pairs with the difficult reception of these questions in public debate, as testified by the Italian reactions to #metoo and #wetogether campaigns. Among a series of embarrassing episodes, in which members of the Italian film industry were involved with or publicly defended the US producer Harvey Weinstein,[9] the Italian #metoo was characterised by multiple attacks on the few women who denounced and named their abusers, such as Asia Argento and Miriana Trevisan.[10] The trope of the *il divano del produttore* (literally the sofa of the producer, the Italian epigone of Hollywood's casting couch) has been evoked multiple times to indicate that, to use the words of the film critic Natalia Aspesi, 'the producers . . . have always acted like this. And the girls, on the famous sofa, would sit knowingly' (Aspesi 2017).[11] The idea that the casting couch has always existed and women have happily taken advantage of it somehow normalises sexual harassment as a form of recruitment in the entertainment and film industry. As film historians, it is our task to revise this idea that sexual harassment and gender discrimination are a 'timeless' aspect of the film industry, to reframe the topic in a broader conversation about women's labour, its precarisation and devaluation, inside and outside the film industries. Indeed, the #metoo campaign, including the related Italian hashtag #quellavoltache, involved an unprecedented number of young women who publicly discussed episodes of sexual harassment at the workplace.[12] This mobilisation could have been an opportunity to refocus on central issues like the gender pay gap, welfare and the low rates of employment outside the house. Instead, a fixation with the status and credibility of VIP denouncers has overshadowed the participation of thousands who relied on forms of digital and hashtag feminism, joining a global trend in feminist and queer activism.[13] The idea that 'certain things' happen only to 'certain women' in the entertainment industry or that their privileged status makes them unrepresentative of those who endure pervasive harassment and discrimination in the workplace is particularly slippery. On the one hand it seems to imply that sexual harassment is more tolerable in some working environments than in others; on the other hand, it suggests that what happens at the level of representation and the media has no reference to the society we live in. For this reason, it is important to undertake research that retraces the historical and material consequences of sexism in the film industry, a task that can't be achieved without understanding the role of historical narratives in naturalising women's segregation and marginality and in reproducing patriarchal power relations at the workplace.

Mara Blasetti's archive can help in this task, as it gives insights into the practical aspects of her profession, production management, which requires constant mediation between creative and economic needs. These characteristics also allow the focus to shift from the 'glamourous' experience of celebrities and actresses, and reframe the centrality of a 'production culture' dominated by elusive values such as camaraderie, creativity and genius to concentrate on the materiality of women's labour.

Mara Blasetti, Production Manager

The documents in Mara Blasetti's archive can be divided into three main categories: correspondence, a large number of dossiers related to the management of each individual film with the relevant working papers (final balance sheets, production plans, estimates, location surveys), and technical materials, such as brochures, catalogues, maps and price lists for the rental of studios. The information in these documents provides a comprehensive picture of Blasetti as a professional, illustrating her network of relationships and professional capital (in the correspondence); how she understood her profession in her working practices (in the dossiers), and the technical knowledge necessary to her profession. Moreover, the fact that she worked for both Italian and foreign companies makes it possible to attempt a comparative view, albeit fragmentary, between different production contexts.

Born in Rome in 1924, Mara Blasetti started to work with her father in 1951 as assistant continuity supervisor for the film *Altri tempi* (Infidelity, 1952).

In a recent interview, she recalls that that position was particularly badly paid, 'even less than a key grip', and that her father hindered her determination to get a job.[14] Her determination to work came from her desire to be economically independent after separating from her husband and her wish to raise her son on her own. The film industry represented the most natural place to look at, as she was raised in that environment. It was thanks to the insistence of her father's assistant directors, Luigi Filippo D'Amico and Isa Bartalini, that Mara was eventually hired, to begin a collaboration that continued for almost ten years.[15] Soon after that first experience, she was promoted to the position of continuity supervisor, although her duties were those of an assistant director, a position the she officially took in 1954 when D'Amico left to direct his first feature film *Bravissimo* (Very good, 1955).[16] Despite this promotion, being the daughter of a prominent director like Blasetti was a complicated position: the technicians and other crew members considered her need to work 'pointless' and other film directors didn't want to collaborate with her, as they suspected that she would tell her father the details of their projects.[17] Mara recalls that 'As Blasetti's daughter, it was really hard to be hired by others: they say that because of my dad's money, I didn't need to work (although I am divorced and I have a kid)' (Bellumori 1972, 45). The turning point in her career came with *Europa di notte* (European nights, Alessandro Blasetti, 1959): she was the only member of the crew who spoke English, therefore the producer Antonio Altoviti proposed her as production coordinator as they had to film in different locations all around Europe. After few experiences as production inspector for Italian films, in 1962 the producer Jerry Bresler from Columbia Pictures hired her as production manager for *Gidget Goes to Rome* (Paul Wendkos, 1963), marking the beginning of a twenty-year career in this position, working in dozens of films such as *Darling* (John Schlesinger, 1965), *Modesty Blaise: The Beautiful One Kills* (Joseph Losey, 1966), *What?* (Roman Polanski, 1972), *Flesh For Frankenstein* (Paul Morrissey, Antonio Margheriti, 1973), *Blood For Dracula* (Paul Morrissey, 1974), *Lion of the Desert* (Moustapha Akka, 1980) and *For Your Eyes Only* (John Glen, 1981). The move to the production department also allowed her to pursue her career independently of her father, an aspect that increased the weight of her gender in many aspects of her profession, beginning with her professional relationships with her male colleagues. The importance of her network clearly emerges in the correspondence kept in her archive, a question that is particularly important for two closely related reasons: the first is the informal nature, based mainly on word of mouth, in which recruitment took place and collaborations were usually established; the second, is the need to prove her professional credentials through a network of references. Much of her correspondence, in fact, is dedicated to maintaining, over time, professional relationships that would guarantee a certain continuity of work with foreign producers, but also a solid base of collaborators in Italy, including directors and actors with whom she exchanged thank you cards and appreciation letters. The consistency of this correspondence further testifies the importance of such practices to progress in an industry that relied extensively on recommendations and informal training. Indeed, as we discuss in the next chapter, the Centro Sperimentale di Cinematografia (CSC) offered a curriculum in film production, but the graduates didn't necessarily continue to work in that department, and most professionals, including top-level ones, accessed the industry by means of family and friends. Such aspects reflected a diffused industrial attitude towards improvisation and contingency that Valentino Brosio lamented in the introduction of his manual for film producers, hoping that his contribution would support the standardisation of working practices (1956, vii–viii).

But how does informal recruitment and training intersect with gender, and to what extent has it contributed to reproducing patterns of gender discrimination? To answer this delicate question, let's take a step back to look at the professions and gendered dynamics typical of the production department. At the top of the hierarchy, there is the production manager, who in major film productions can be also referred as general organiser (organizzatore generale),[18] who is responsible for the economic efficiency of the production. Brosio describes this professional as a 'businessman, with good intuition and a lively business acumen' (1956, 56). He is generally assisted by the production coordinator (*ispettore di produzione*) and the production secretary (*segretaria di produzione*). This latter profession has been historically associated with women, as it mainly consists of clerical and secretarial tasks, such as minute taking, scheduling meetings and travel accommodation, organising supplies and relaying messages. Women in this position rarely progressed to roles with more responsibilities and possible reasons for this could be explained in the words of production secretary Vivien Boden, who in the 1970s released an interview to Patrizia Carrano:

> [If you are a woman] They only want you if you work like crazy, shut up and obey. But once you try to move up in rank, there's the wall, the ostracism... They're always ready to make any kind of comment about your appearance... If you're not a ghoul, they're well-disposed, but then they also become paternalistic, full of advice... And maybe I don't need their advice, [...] but in order to not to go up against everyone, I have to pretend to accept it. (Carrano 1977, 41)

At the time of the interview, Boden was twenty-eight and had three years of experience in the industry: in that relatively short time, she rapidly became used to gender discrimination, and accepted mansplaining and paternalism as part of the job. At the same time, she was well aware that her gender represented an obstacle to any ambition of career progression, even if she was unmarried and had no children. On top of this, there was also a question, so to speak, of respectability:

> I would have no trouble to impose myself as a 'person'. But as a woman I always had to pay a price. Not to mention the gossip: they always find a reason to explain why you have work, and generally they say that is because you are a mistress [of a member of the crew]. I have worked a lot with a good production manager, Bruno Altissimi [. . .]. Well, in the end we had problems because everyone said I was his mistress. (Carrano 1977, 41)

Allegations about sexual relationships represented a limitation for many women who wished to work in filmmaking. Carrano reports that the cameraman Pino Pinori admitted that whenever he attempted to hire a female assistant, he changed his mind because it would have compromised him: 'All productions claimed that if I had a woman as an assistant it was because I slept with her. Which wasn't true at all. Nobody cared if she was doing her job well' (Carrano 1977, 49). In such context, it is important to bear in mind that Mara Blasetti moved to the production department mainly because she could provide an essential skill to complete a film (she spoke English), namely her promotion was prompted by the contingency of the moment. Moreover, her father was 'enough to explain' her career progression without implying an affair with other professionals. All these questions are unsurprising as the professional networks in the area of production management were traditionally dominated by men who referenced mostly each other.[19] According to the sources available, between the 1950s and the 1970s, there were only three women officially working in this role out of a total of one hundred professionals: Blasetti, Jone Tuzi and Bianca Lattuada.[20] Interestingly, they all moved from the role of assistant director to the production department, meaning that after a consistent training in film direction, they became top-level below-the-line professionals, taking managerial/organisational roles that are still subordinate to the director and stay behind the scenes.

As such, it is particularly revealing that Blasetti worked mostly with a niche of clients, the foreign producers who came to shoot in Italy. According to Blasetti, foreigners were more willing to work with women, as 'Italians were not used to seeing women in decisional positions' (Tola 2002). Despite this, homosociality prevailed in the international film industry too, affecting her professional experience and leaving material traces in her archive. As a woman in a sexist working environment, she had to accept sexism as a sign of comradeship, an aspect that was evidently considered part of a good professional relationship. In a letter dated 11 December 1968, the production manager Frederick Muller, who was in Colombia for the movie *The Adventurers*, wrote her a letter that expressed a mix of sexism and Western superiority:

> Colombia is not the easiest country in the world, but one cannot expect them to fully understand film problems as they hardly know the existence of film making... So you know, Bogotá is one of the most horrible cities in the world, while the other places have somewhat of charm; incidentally, girls are kept practically in seclusion, worse than in Sicily, but in other parts one can find many nice girls.[21]

In other instances, a similar mix of patriarchal ideas and stereotypes gave foreign producers the opportunity to question her professional integrity. In 1963, Blasetti was hired by Frank Ross for the film *Mister Moses* (Ronald Neame, 1965), which had to be shot in Africa. Ross contacted Mara thanks to the recommendation of a former employee, Jerry Bresler, and she was enthusiastic about the project, so she accepted the job and immediately started to work full time on the film. By the end of the year, Ross ceased his contact and refused to pay her for the work done, and Blasetti decided to sue him. In a letter to Roger Good, the production representative of Columbia Films in Rome, Mara explained the real reasons for Ross disappearing:

> At our meeting he said that as a woman I was unsuitable to manage a location in Africa. You can imagine my surprise... I have been a woman from the day I was born and certainly all the time Mr Ross was in contact with me.[22]

The same folder contains many letters of appreciation from former – male – employees (like Antonio Altoviti and Dino De Laurentiis), aiming to confirm her ability to work in Africa and support her legal action, somehow reproducing the patriarchal bias that women need a man to guarantee for them. However, despite all her efforts, Ross never paid Mara. These episodes demonstrate how sexism was pervasive in Blasetti's professional life and how the formal tone of most of her working papers could only partially conceal the emotional and affective consequences of gender discrimination in her career. It is probably because of experiences like this that Blasetti became involved in the Italian production management guild, the Associazione Organizzatori e Direttori di Cineteleproduzioni (Association of Organisers and Directors of Cinema and TV Productions, AODC), which aimed to achieve institutional recognition for her profession by the Italian Ministry of Tourism and Show Business and the governmental agency Ente per la Gestione Cinema (Cinema Management Board) (Bellumori 1972, 65).

These episodes somehow illustrate how sexism and sexual harassment were structural and functioned to maintain and reproduce men's exclusive privilege to express their creativity and management of decisional and economic power. Without these limitations, how many films could have been made and managed by female assistant directors and production secretaries? And what kind of environment would the film industry have been if patriarchy and sexual allegations had not have conditioned every working relationship on set? Of course, it is impossible to answer these questions. As we see in the next chapters, feminist film collectives and directors made films without hiring men in an explicit attempt to develop non-hierarchical, ethical working practices. However, these attempts had no impact on the film industry, and revealed a series of practical and political limitations. Perhaps there is no way of fixing the practices that sexism and misogyny have established so far, yet as a film historian I think it is possible to look at the experiences of the past to reflect on alternative pathways in the present, and Mara Blasetti's archive gives us this opportunity.

Closing Notes about Sexism and Mara Blasetti's Archival Singularity

Blasetti's being 'the daughter of a more distinguished one' has contributed to the preservation of her working documents, confirming that the importance of a 'male connection [that] was deemed historically important' crucially impacts on the fate of women's papers (Dever et al. 2009). Both the institutional acquisition of the archive and the beginnings of Mara's career have to do with her affective and emotional relationship with her father. In this respect, 'affect' represents a productive notion, which prompts political and materialistic consequences in 'doing' (Labanyi 2010), orienting people towards certain objects and actions. As archivist and gatekeeper, Mara Blasetti performed a particular kind of emotional work by disseminating the historical legacy of her father, who died in 1987 after a long battle with illness. This also means that for thirty years, from 1987 until the donation of the papers to the Cineteca in 2007, Mara became the custodian of her father's archive. In *Archive Fever*, Jacques Derrida describes the archive's institutional life, its exclusiveness and relationship with power, in terms of 'domiciliation' (Derrida 1995). The whole domiciliation process resounds in opposition to the word 'domesticity', which is generally the main characteristic of the pre-institutional life of archives like this: the private papers of a practitioner are kept in some space in the house, to obtain an institutional life only subsequently. In its 'domestic phase', the preservation of Alessandro Blasetti's documents was entirely owed to his daughter's 'labour of love', which left material traces on the archive. The Cineteca has kept some traits of the original organisation, which was conceived by Mara, intact in her own collection, which comprises very heterogeneous materials. Many papers are also annotated and dated with an erasable pencil, providing additional details or clarifying some unreadable parts. These notes avoid any personal comment and apparently confirm the general impression of emotional detachment typical of working papers. Nevertheless, in the history and materiality of this archive, the notions of the private and the public collapse: these papers pertain to a public aspect of Mara Blasetti's life, her job, but also reflect, at multiple levels, a practice of 'self-care'. Looking at this archive, it is possible to notice how the same 'labour of love' performed for the sake of her father's memory, has become a self-reflexive practice of care and self-aknowledgment. A similar mechanism is at play when Mara is invited to speak in public or is interviewed: she receives an opportunity to talk about her experience in the industry, while providing a direct testimony about the work of her father. In other words, the history and singularity of Mara Blasetti's archive gives us an opportunity to think about the importance for us to share and valorise our experiences, and establish new protocols of knowledge, in which the experience of sexism also emerges in its practical and material consequences. It is only by recognising the importance of what we do every day that we can continue to care, transmit and pursue an anti-patriarchal, feminist agenda. In other words, it is on us to take care and assemble feminist archives as dynamic, multifaceted historical objects with a crucial role in the present and our futures.

Notes

1. The description and inventory of the fund are available at www.cinetecadibologna.it/biblioteca/patrimonioarchivistico/mara_blasetti, accessed 5 May 2021.
2. In film production, 'below the line' is a term derived from the layout of the top sheet of a film budget. The 'line' separates the costs of the creative, mainly on-set crew (director, cinematographers, actors) from those of the technical, mostly off-set practitioners (editors, location managers).
3. See Faldini and Fofi, 1981. In the same category the only volume that includes a contribution on the history of unions in film industry is *La città del cinema* (1979) which, other than its opening essays, is entirely composed of interviews with film directors, actors and film critics. Assessorato alla cultura et al., 1979, *La città del cinema. Produzione e lavoro nel cinema italiano 1931/1971* (Rome: Napoleone).
4. For a detailed analysis of these narratives, see Francesco Di Chiara and Paolo Noto, 2016, 'Appunti per una storia un po' meno avventurosa: produzione e cinema italiano 1945–1965', in Luca Barra, Tiziano Bonini and Sergio Splendore, eds,

2016, *Backstage. Studi sulla produzione dei media in Italia* (Milan: Unicopli), 113–25.
5. A recent development in this field is the AHRC-funded project 'Producers and Production Practices in the History of Italian Cinema, 1949–1975', led by the University of Warwick. See https://warwick.ac.uk/fac/arts/film/research/current/italian_producers_project/, accessed 5 May 2021.
6. See for instance Giacomo Manzoli and Guglielmo Pescatore, 2015, *L'arte del risparmio. Il cinema a basso costo in Italia negli anni Sessanta* (Rome: Carocci); Federico Pierotti, Paola Valentini, and Federico Vitella, eds, 2017, 'Cinema italiano: tecniche e pratiche', *Quaderni del CSCI. Rivista annuale di cinema italiano*, no. 13.
7. On women's difficulties in the journalism professions, see for instance Milly Buonanno, 1978, *La donna nella stampa. Giornaliste, lettrici e modelli di femminilità* (Rome: Editori riuniti).
8. The European Women's Audiovisual Network (EWA) published 'The Gender Equality Report on Female Directors 2006–2013', which brings together data about seven European countries: Austria, Croatia, France, Germany, Italy, Sweden and the UK. A series of other reports with the same focus have been conducted nationally in countries such as Slovenia, Spain, the United States, Finland, France and Germany.
9. Luciano Lombardo was allegedly employed by Weinstein at Miramax Italy 'in part to help satisfy [his] voracious appetite'. Cf. Jason Horowitz, 'Harvey Weinstein's Italian Friend is now in the Eye of a Media Storm', *New York Times*, 24 October 2017, available at https://www.nytimes.com/2017/10/24/world/europe/fabrizio-lombardo-harvey-weinstein-italy.html, accessed 5 May 2021. Another example with international resonance took place at the 2018 Venice Film Festival, when director Luciano Silighini wore a T-shirt reading 'Weinstein is Innocent' on the red carpet. For a detailed reconstruction of the Italian media coverage of the Winstein scandal see also Claudia Torrisi, 'Harvey Weinstein: Italian Media Coverage of the Scandal Has Been Predictably Outrageous', *Open Democracy*, 20 October 2017, available at https://www.opendemocracy.net/en/5050/italian-media-harvey-weinstein-asia-argento/, accessed 5 May 2021.
10. A detailed reconstruction of the backlash against the Italian #metoo is available at https://www.nytimes.com/2018/08/21/world/europe/asia-argento-italy.html, accessed 5 May 2021. Following heated reactions to Argento's denunciation, more than 100 women employed in Italian entertainment signed a letter against the systemic patterns of sexual abuse in the film and media industry. However, to mark their distance from the #metoo movement, the campaigners did not give the names of any molester or explicitly endorse Argento. It is also relevant that the letter does not account for any specific experience of harassment, but rather uses abstract and even psychoanalytical notions to approach the question. It was published originally in *La Repubblica* in 2018.
11. In 1973, the journalist and film critic Aspesi published a book on women's condition (*La donna immobile*), which found a certain resonance in the feminist

movement. At the time, the book helped to consolidate her reputation as a feminist journalist sympathetic to the cause of women's equality.
12. One week from its launch, on 12 October 2017, the hashtag #quellavoltache ('that time that') obtained more than 20,000 references on Twitter. Source: Redazione, '#quellavoltache, le molestie raccolte in un libro', *Wired*, 10 March 2018, available at https://www.wired.it/play/libri/2018/03/10/quella-volta-che-molestie-libro/, accessed 5 May 2021; some of them were collected in a book, '#quellavoltache. Storia di Molestie', released on 8 March 2018. See also Angiola Codacci-Pisanelli, 'La galleria degli orrori di 'quella volta che': tra rabbia e disgusto le denunce delle donne', *L'espresso*, 7 March 2018, available at http://espresso.repubblica.it/visioni/cultura/2018/03/06/news/quante-molestie-quellavoltache-1.319237, accessed 5 May 2021.
13. On the increasing weight of this form of activism, and its contradictions please see: Hester Baer, 2016, 'Redoing Feminism: Digital Activism, Body Politics, and Neoliberalism', *Feminist Media Studies* 16, no. 1: 17–34.
14. Interview with Mara Blasetti for the radio programme 'Hollywood Party', Radio 3, 14 August 2014.
15. Interestingly, in 1944 Bartalini assisted Blasetti as secretary for *Fabiola* (1949). This role consisted mostly of typing the filmscript, and led to her promotion as assistant director (Blasetti in Gobbato 2015, 177).
16. Interview with Mara Blasetti, 'Hollywood Party'.
17. Interview with Mara Blasetti, 'Hollywood Party'.
18. I couldn't identify an equivalent in English professional titles to the Italian 'organizzatore generale'.
19. This aspect has consistently affected Blasetti's job opportunities: 'I have always worked prevalently with foreigner producers . . . But also very often, Italians suggested my name only to them, when their male colleagues were busy' (Bellumori 1972, 45).
20. I have cross-referenced this information, reported by Patrizia Carrano in 1972 and based on the data sets of the professional organisation Associazione Organizzatori e Direttori di Cineteleproduzioni (AODC), directed by Mara Blasetti, with the data published in Patrizia Carrano's book (1977, 39). Such information has been further verified in the following professional guides: Alessandro Ferraù, ed., 1971, *Annuario del Cinema Italiano* (Rome: Cinedizioni); AA.VV., 1971, *Set. Guida Categorica professionale per lo spettacolo* (Rome: Set); Informaset 1979.
21. Letter dated 11 December 1968, folder 'Film Mara girati 1', Archive Mara Blasetti (AMB), Cineteca of Bologna.
22. Letter to Roger Good, dated 19 December 1963, folder 'Frank Ross (Mister Moses)', AMB, Cineteca di Bologna.

CHAPTER 10

A Map of Open Questions: A Feminist Genealogy of Women Directors (1935–70)

This chapter analyses the trans-historical, systemic barriers that generations of female film professionals have encountered in the Italian film industry, from training to later stages in their career paths. My goal is addressing some compelling questions in the histories of women's participation in the film industry by providing a transgenerational and materialistic perspective. The chapter thus focuses on a specific case study, namely a reconstruction of the trajectories of a group of women who studied film direction at the CSC (Centro Sperimentale di Cinematografia), the oldest and most prestigious Italian film school based in Rome. Feminist scholarship has been interested in film schools for multiple reasons.[1] The histories of these institutions are helpful in understanding the impact of top-down policies, as well as the production cultures and professional values present in the industry, and their archives can open up interesting considerations about gender. In the specific case of the CSC, most of the documentation is inaccessible, or it is irretrievable.[2] Moreover, despite the existence of studies on its history, no systematic research on the gender composition of the student population and the teaching body has been undertaken so far.[3] However, being one of the best training programmes in filmmaking and offering a more defined pathway for access filming professions, the school could overcome the barriers typical of informal training, facilitate the admission of women and international students, and in some instances allow forms of experimentalism, otherwise invisibilised in mainstream production. As such, the analysis of this case study is mostly an opportunity to access neglected stories and narratives in film history, and pose a series of methodological and theoretical questions about the role of gender, labour and creativity in Italian cinema. To do this, the present chapter is presented in five sections: the first two introduce the case study and the methodology and sources adopted; the following three have thematic and narrative focuses centred on the gendering of labour, the interplay between politics, activism and filmmaking, the experiences of international students, and marginalisation from mainstream productions.

The Position of the CSC

To better understand the role of the CSC in Italian cinema history, it is also important to have in mind the major shifts occurred in the positioning of women in the local film industry. The first steps of women in Italian cinema, as in several other national contexts,[4] trace back to the pioneers who took part, since the early days, in every aspect of filmmaking, in both creative and technical roles, as well as working in related industries such as film development and processing.[5] The fragmentation of the centres of production and the local preference for certain genres favoured the development of small-scale and family-run companies, a model that encouraged women's participation, as in the case of Elvira Notari in Naples.[6] The crisis brought on by World War I and the advent of the fascist regime led to a centralisation of film production in the capital, Rome, which in the 1930s also saw strong involvement by the state in legislation and policy making. The increasing industrial and technical complexity of film production required a wider range of specialised professional figures, transforming the working dynamics and the organisation of labour, while the circulation and reception of avant-garde and aesthetic principles led to an acculturation of the film professions. All these aspects impacted on women's participation in the film industry, yet female workers continued to prevail in fields like film development, editing and costume design, and later, with the definition of clerical roles, in positions like the continuity supervisor and the production assistant, who removed from the director and the producer (who were usually men) the need to comply with secretarial and repetitive tasks.

The institution of the CSC in 1935 somehow reflected all these trends, as well as the film policies of the fascist regime, which aimed to renovate Italian cinema in the name of 'youth and virilism' (Chiarini in Andreazza 2019, 68). At the CSC, students learned technical skills, but crucially received a solid theoretical and cultural foundation from the most prominent film professionals of the time. Originally, enrolment required the membership of the Fascist Party and a high school diploma, an aspect that reveals the existence of significant barriers in terms of class, and confirms the scope of the school to train an elite of film professionals. In the academic year 1939/40, the CSC ran programmes in acting, cinematography, sound production, set design (scenotecnica) and film direction, but women were officially admitted only in acting and scenotecnica, a programme that consisted of makeup, costume, and set design (Baldi 2010, 33). After 1943, with the Nazi occupation of Rome and the institution of the Republic of Salò, the CSC suspended its activities to resume in 1947–8, and subsequently transition to a phase that reflected the new political climate of the Cold War, with a renovation of the management.

A Feminist Genealogy 123

Since the 1950s, the school has assigned scholarships to foreign students, who enrolled especially in the direction programme, reflecting the international prestige achieved by Italian cinema in the post-war years. In the early 1960s, the diffusion and popularity of television made inevitable the establishment of closer collaboration with the national broadcaster, RAI, and the training of professionals who could work for both cinema and television, while the school continued to develop its international partnerships with other film institutions abroad (Laura 1976).

METHODOLOGIES: FROM THE LIST TO THE MAP

In order to recuperate the career paths of different generations of students I had to turn to a list that was uploaded on to the CSC website, with the names, year of attendance and chosen curriculum of each student since the inauguration in 1935.[7] Between 1935 and 2017 the CSC admitted 619 students in film direction, but only sixty-six of them were women. I attempted to retrace additional information about those twenty-two who attended the school before the 1970s, and I was successful for only twelve: Gemma de Aloysio (1936), Marisa Romano (1937), Franca Maranto (1951) Ornella Vasio (1951), Olga Bianchi (1952), Gabriella Rossetto (1951), Lily Venman-Rademakers (1957), Benilde Vittori (1958), Laura di Nola (1960),[8] Liliana Cavani (1961), Helena Lumbreras Giménez (1962), Rosalia Polizzi (1964).[9] My interest in the film direction programme aims to address a persistent issue in feminist cinema history, namely the supposed 'absence' of women directors, which has led feminist scholars to challenge canonical notions of authorship and consider other professional figures. This chapter contributes to this scholarship by focusing on a group of women who were trained as directors, yet in most cases ended up working in other roles, or had to wait years before making their own feature film.

However, basing our study on a document such as a list raises a series of methodological and theoretical issues that I have been only partially able to fix throughout the chapter. Indeed, a list is an operation of extraction that privileges some trajectories instead of others, and can easily turn into a canon; then, a name alone, without contextual information, calls for further investigation and complementary sources that are not always available; finally, working with a list of names means dealing with a limiting notion of gender identity, one that relies on institutions identifying a person's name exclusively with a specific gender. In other words, lists, and especially institutional lists like that of the CSC, can help a feminist historiography like this one, only on condition that these epistemological limitations are made evident and addressed. In my specific case, a vast array of complementary sources has worked as a corrective to the fragmentary and partial knowledge offered by the list, considering also the impossibility of accessing the original archive.[10] I have also renounced a strictly chronological and biographical order in favour of a thematic structure, focusing on four questions that have impacted most of the students here considered, albeit in different ways: politics, transnationality, the gendering of labour and its marginalisation from mainstream production. This approach means giving up on linearity to privilege aspects such as repetition, identification and commonality. With these correctives, the CSC list enables a transgenerational approach that is particularly beneficial for this research, allowing me to overcome the risks of reducing women's cinema history into a collection of individual stories, whose relevance resides in their uniqueness and to attempt a cartography of broader theoretical and methodological questions; at the same time, it gives me the opportunity to link specific national trends within wider transnational issues, intersecting topics in feminist cinema history, activism and theory beyond the Italian case.

GENDERING OF LABOUR: ASSISTANT DIRECTORS AND SCRIPT-GIRLS

The endemic invisibilisation and marginalisation of women's work in the industry has been reproduced and institutionalised by the CSC since its very beginnings; despite this, the resurfacing of these histories from the archives allows us to complicate our understandings of the interplay between invisibility and visibility.

The example of Gemma de Aloysio, a painter, designer and artist who was involved in the Futurist avant-garde and enrolled in the school in 1935, is particularly interesting in this respect. Despite her young age – she was born in 1906 – in 1932, she had already published an article, 'Sensibilità e personalità nell'ambiente moderno' (Sensitivity and personality in the modern environment), in the Roman journal *Futurismo*, a theoretical piece about aesthetics and furnishing styles (de Aloysio 1932), whose considerations can be seen under the light of her Futurist interior design projects published in the same magazine in the following issues. Two years later, in 1934, the painter Giacomo Balla portrayed de Aloysio with his two daughters, Elica and Luce, in the painting *Andiamo che é tardi* (Let's go, it's late) (Altea 2019, 360). As Giuliana Altea has pointed out, Elica and Luce 'are two of the many Italian artists of the first half of the twentieth century who have been excluded or relegated to the margins of the modernist canon' (Altea 2019, 360); however their kinship with an important male artist enabled some attention to be given to their work, a piece of good fortune that de Aloysio, who took part in the same cultural and artistic milieu, didn't have. At the time of her application for the CSC's programme of film direction, de Aloysio was only twenty-six and she had already attended the Scuola Nazionale di Cinematografia at the Royal Academy of Santa Cecilia,[11] and participated in a couple of national painting exhibitions.[12] However in 1936 she was excluded from the school after failing an exam, proving to the commission that she 'did not possess, to the desired extent, those qualities of taste, sensitivity and ability that are indispensable for pursuing a career as a *segretaria di produzione* [production assistant] with a minimum chance of success'.[13] According to a letter sent to her mother, Gemma contested the results, lamenting the way in which the director Luigi Chiarini informed her about the failed exams, described as 'sybilline'. It is obviously impossible to know if de Aloysio really lacked the qualities needed to become a production assistant. However, considering her previous experience at the Santa Cecilia film school, her publications and exhibitions, as well as her technical high school diploma, it is quite dubious that she scored so badly in an exam for a secretarial, organisational role such as that of production assistant. At the same time, it is also true that at this early stage, the programmes of the school were still not finalised, and women were actually excluded from the film direction curriculum. In this respect, it is interesting to note that in 1935 among 'the 49 students admitted to the curriculum in film direction, thirteen were *segretarie di produzione*' (Laura 1976, 15).[14] This suggests that although they applied to the programme of direction, women were subsequently diverted towards the clerical and feminised profession of the production assistant, revealing that there was little room for women's directorial aspirations at the school, and that the gendering of film professions was already institutionally embedded in the slogan 'virilism and youth'.

The experience of Luisa Alessandri, a student who enrolled in the curriculum of film production in 1936, confirms how informal practices and the gendering of film professions impacted women's career opportunities. Her first recorded experience on set was as continuity supervisor in Camillo Mastrocinque's *Voglio vivere con Letizia* (1938), but most of her career developed during the post-war years, when she worked, almost exclusively, as assistant director for Vittorio De Sica, in films like *Bicycle Thieves*, *Miracle in Milan*, *Umberto D.*, *Two Women*, and *The Garden of the Finzi-Contini*. She stayed in this position from 1938 to 1976, working in thirty-five features. In an interview released to Patrizia Carrano in the mid-1970s, Alessandri explains why she never became a director:

> when I started, for women it was difficult, terrible to make cinema... For 11 years they didn't pay the contributions for my pension, and nobody listened to me because I was a woman. Then, there was the question of De Sica: if I were the assistant of a little director... but also if I were a man it would

have been different, I would have focused much more on work. But instead, there was the family . . .' (Carrano 1977, 45)

Such difficulties were evidently common to other women during the 1950s, as Alessandri's career trajectory –graduation at the CSC, first job as continuity supervisor and promotion to assistant director – is shared by most CSC female graduates of my list. The students of the 1950s, Franca Maranto (1951), Gabriella Rossetto (1951) Ornella Vasio (1951) and Benilde Vittori (1958), all worked as continuity supervisors, but never directed a full-length film. Rossetto and Vasio, who took both the specialisations in continuity supervision and film direction, never progressed from that role, like Benilde Vittori who graduated in film direction few years later. The continuity supervisor is a professional who works closely with the director and his assistants, and assures the continuity between different scenes and scenarios. It is an entry-level position that became common in film production between the 1920s and the 1930s, when the director and his assistants abandoned this particular duty that required clerical and secretarial tasks such as note taking, minutes and stenography. As Ellis Hill has reconstructed, the continuity supervisor rapidly became a feminised profession, so much so that in the American and British productions the person working in this role was commonly referred to as 'script-girl' or 'continuity girl' (Hill 2016, 177–88). In Italy this profession has been similarly associated with the feminine term *segretaria di edizione* ('script girl'), reflecting a broader tendency to feminise the names of lower-grade professions usually occupied by women, like *le passafilm*, the film checkers working in the editing department who supervised the 'continuity' and 'invisibility' of the editing work (Missero 2018). In the description of the film crew in Valentino Brosio's manual for production managers edited by the CSC in 1956, the continuity supervisor is the only profession explicitly linked to a gender – 'the continuity supervisor [is] a role normally filled by a woman' (Brosio 1956, 28) – while the other professionals are indicated with masculine terms, which in the Italian language generally indicate the 'neutral'. As noted by Melanie Williams, continuity hinges on invisibility: the goal of this professional is concealing the aspects of filmmaking that should not to be seen, and its work becomes visible only when it is not properly done, like housekeeping (2013, 608). On set, this means combining authority and modesty: 'The continuity girl must never direct but she must stand up for her decisions and instructions, often in the face of intimidating disagreements from crew or cast' (Williams 2013, 609). As such, it is evident that a training in film direction and production would make a great continuity supervisor, yet it was the particular 'in-betweenness' and its invisible contribution to the quality of the film that made this position so 'suitable' for women.

Politics: Trespassers and Films Never Made

The involvement of female CSC students in politics could actually help them to trespass beyond the gendered norms of the school and of the industry, as testified by the example of Marisa Romano (Maria Luisa Scala). Romano enrolled in 1937 in the film direction programme, and directed a handful of documentaries such as the collective *Il seme* (The seed) and *Sinfonia in bianco* (Symphony in white) for the Luce Institute, and a couple of fiction shorts when she was still studying at the CSC, *Dopoguerra* (Post-war) and *Il passo* (The step) (both 1937).[15] She also contributed to two full-length features, the colonial film *Sotto la corce del sud* (Under the Southern Cross, Guido Brignone, 1938) specifically for the script, in collaboration with her husband Jacopo Comin,[16] and the historical drama *Pietro Micca* (Aldo Vergnano, 1938). She is the only accredited female director working in this period, a status that can be explained by her proximity to the regime, which is confirmed not only by her work and private life, but also by her involvement in the Fascist intelligence, since the mid-1920s, when she was still an aspiring actress.[17] Her production is entirely devoted to fascist propaganda, beginning with the collective documentary *Il seme* (The seed), presented at the Venice Biennale in 1937, whose title allude to the 'seed sown by Fascism, which, by growing, produces the lush ramifications ... of the empire' (Cinema Illustrazione 1937, 81). Romano's case reflects the gender and cinematic politics of the regime, in which modernising and traditionalist discourses were complementary to each other and intersected with specific notions of national identity (De Grazia 1992). As Ruth Ben-Ghiat has pointed out, Romano is a good example of 'fascist modernity' (Ben-Ghiat 2001, 91), a woman whose achievements were functional to an image of Fascism as a modernising and transformative force. A brief article published in the popular film magazine *Cinema Illustrazione*, which discusses the films of Dorothy Azner, mentioned Marisa Romano as the only example of an Italian female director. While wondering about the lack of women in this profession, the short piece ends with a humorous comment: 'women should succeed in directing ... First of all, women have a lot of sensitivity. And then, come on, they really like to be in charge!' (*Cinema Illustrazione* 1937). The disproportionate comparison between Azner and the freshly graduated Romano evidently aimed to support an idea of Italian cinema as modern and competitive, at every level, against Hollywood.

However, Romano's untimely death in 1940, at the age of thirty-six, complicates the picture. At the time of her passing, the journal *Cinema* published a short memorial praising her skills, mentioning also the existence of preparatory materials for a new film, presumably her first full-length feature (Cinema 1940). This mysterious bequest sheds a different light on Romano, as we have no idea of the nature of this or her next unmade films. Would have she continued to make films after the fall of the regime, like many of her male colleagues, including her husband? And what is the legacy of a female director and screen-writer who was so involved with fascism? In her study about Mexican women filmmakers, Elissa J. Rashkin (2001) calls those isolated female directors, who worked before the 1960s in an industrial context characterised by high degrees of gender segregation, 'trespassers'. According to Rashkin, although these exceptional figures have certainly 'trespassed' beyond the patriarchal constraints of Mexican society and its film industry, their work and experiences can't lead to a coherent notion of 'women's cinema', as they negotiated and somehow reproduced patriarchal notions of national cinema and its gendered structures (2001: 31–4). These contradictions explode with figures like Romano who have been directly involved not only with a dictatorship's propaganda, but also in its repressive structures, working as a spy. A more visible example of this paradox is Leni Riefenstahl, whose critical and scholarly reception was split between 'two tendencies, either defending the transcendent virtues of aesthetics/gender ('the greatest woman film-maker ever'), or attacking the all-too-political vice of propaganda ('Hitler's favourite director')' (Soussloff and Nichols 1996, 23). Considering the trajectory of Riefenstahl, Ruby B. Rich affirms that 'the mere existence of a woman within a patriarchy's power structure does not belie its pervasive sexism. On the contrary, the complicity of the token woman ... advances the patriarchy's consolidation of power' (1998, 47). In other words, Rich suggests going beyond the reification of women who achieve visibility, and coming to terms with their ambivalent contribution to consolidating women's oppression. Coming to terms, then, means taking Judith Mayne's suggestion to approach the work of women filmmakers 'against a background, shaped and defined by the ways in which women have been associated with the cinema' (1981, 29). Therefore, going back to Romano, her becoming the 'female token' of fascist cinema confirms the troubling relationship between women's visibility and patriarchal power structures, a question that persists today when we look at individual career achievements and advancements without considering their consequences in the bigger picture of women's condition.

The full integration of Romano in fascist cinematic and political structures was tied to the role that the cinema had for the regime. With the advent of democracy and the consequent evolution of the institution, the ways in which women combined filmmaking with politics have also changed. The CSC, with its programme of international scholarships and its lively intellectual and creative environment have become a site of possibilities. The school was a stepping stone for Helena Lumbreras, a Spanish student, who was admitted to CSC in 1961 with a bursary and who completed the programme in 1964, with an essay titled *Spagna*.[18] Relatively little is known about her years at the school, but there is trace of an exchange between Lumbreras and Pier Paolo Pasolini at one of his lectures at the school held in 1964, which was partially published in the journal *Bianco e nero*. On that occasion, Lumbreras told the poet:

> It seems to me that you do not love your characters, but rather contemplate them with the detachment of the intellectual; [...] and I do not understand this well, but it seems a little dishonest on your part, it is a literary attitude not to seek salvation for these people who suffer. (Lumbreras in Pasolini 1964)

As Annalisa Mirizio (2017) pointed out, this comment embodies the idea of cinema as an instrument of political and social intervention that would characterise Lumbreras' subsequent work. In 1968 Lumbreras made her first film produced by the Unitelefilm *Spagna '68 – El hoy es malo, pero el mañana es mio*, a medium-length documentary that was shot clandestinely between Madrid and Barcelona, to bring to Italy images of students' and workers' demonstrations against the regime of Francisco Franco.[19] In *Spain '68*, as in all her films, Lumbreras gives women a say in social and political issues, while the internationalist spirit of her work finds its best expression in its circulation in Italy. In the spring of 1970, Lumbreras returned to Barcelona to work on a second film, *El cuarto poder*, which analysed the control of the press by Franco's regime. After filming the material clandestinely, Lumbreras left for Rome to edit and develop it, to return to Spain with the positive copies and organise some clandestine screenings.[20] The exceptional circumstances in which she made her films, as well as her commitment to a transnational project of political transformation, reveal a form of transnational film activism that is at odds with static notions of national cinema, as well as with any understanding of film authorship based on extensive and coherent filmographies.[21] As Barbara Zecchi notes, Lumbreras is the only female director emerging from the culturally and artistically vibrant context of the post-1968 Spanish left, and despite this, her work has been recuperated only recently using the same categories that determined her erasure (Zecchi 2019; Cami-Vela 2009). At the same time, in Italy, she is largely unknown among scholars and film critics, as her political films don't fit with Italian notions of artistic value and politically engaged cinema, for multiple reasons: she made low-budget, non-theatrical documentaries that were thought to be aimed at a transnational public and were also in line with her internationalist views.

To sum up, despite their opposing political views, the experiences of Romano and Lumbreras reveal the weight of gender in the relationship between political commitment and filmmaking, as well as the different roles of the CSC in the context of the Italian film industry. Romano's unique position in the years of Fascism was functional to the gendered politics of the regime, and was institutionally embedded; Lumbreras' militant cinema, despite her 'classical' training, refused to compromise with the cinematic institutions and decided to stay at the margins, in line with her internationalist political commitment, which couldn't fit with a static notion of national *auteur* cinema.

Transnational Paths

Lumbreras' experience illuminates a transnational trajectory in anti-fascist and radical filmmaking that has ensured her a long historical oblivion, an aspect that finds an interesting analogy with Olga Bianchi, a Latin American student who enrolled at the CSC in 1952. As we have already mentioned, since the 1950s the CSC has offered several bursaries to foreign students who were also attracted by the opportunity to study in the country of neorealism. Among them there was a group of South American students such as Fernando Birri and Gabriel García Márquez, who arrived at the school to study with Cesare Zavattini.[22] Like her male peers, Olga Bianchi, after her experience at the CSC, returned to her country of origin, Chile, where she participated in the development of the New Chilean Cinema. As a member of the board and teacher of the Cine Club de Viña del Mar, an association that promoted film criticism and cinema as an art form, Bianchi was involved in teaching and the production of films, and later in the International Film Festival de Viña del Mar, which would become an international hub for the promotion of Latin American cinema. In a bulletin of the Cine Club de Viña del Mar dated 1965, Bianchi is mentioned as the producer of a 16mm documentary (Cine Foro 1965), an aspect that suggest the multifaceted activities of the organisation. After Augusto Pinochet's coup, Bianchi actively supported the formation of anti-regime groups, using the film club to host clandestine screenings with films against the dictatorship. She subsequently fled the country as a refugee to move to Costa Rica, where, in 1974, she became the director of the local National Cinematheque (Cinemateca Nacional), working with María de los Ángeles 'Kitico' Moreno, a crucial figure in the development of the local industry (Cortés 2002).[23] During her exile, until her death in 2015, Bianchi continued her political activism, as a member of the Women's International League for Peace and Freedom. Bianchi's contribution to the cinematic cultures of Latin America has scarcely been investigated so far, and one of the reasons is certainly her transnational mobility, which makes her a crucial figure in the cinematography of two national contexts, which are nonetheless difficult to tie together. Her story, characterised by the experience of exile and her passion for cinema, bonds the two sides of the Atlantic, and suggests the existence of a more complex relationship between feminism and the formation of transnational cinematic cultures, representing also an historical antecedent to the contemporary mobility experiences of many female filmmakers and producers from the Global South.

A mirror example of transnational mobility is Lili Rademakers, whose trajectory is inextricably tied to the formation of European *auteur* cinema. Born in Utrecht in 1930, she moved to Rome in the mid-1950s to study at the CSC. In that period, she met her future husband, Fons Rademakers, who was in Rome on a scholarship. Lily began to work with him in 1958, becoming his assistant director for decades, and before moving back to the Netherlands, she worked as second assistant director for Federico Fellini in *La Dolce Vita*. Her first feature film, *Menuet*, was produced by Fons in 1982, and was awarded the Jury Prize at the Festival of Cannes. Her short biography, published on the website of the EYE institute of Amsterdam, says: 'Lili Rademakers made greater contributions to Fons Rademakers' films than the credits lead one to believe: she helped with choosing locations, determining camera angles and making storyboards' (EYE 2020).[24] Despite her tie to author and national cinema, a full recuperation of Lily's story requires us to look beyond authorship, to evaluate the intense affective and emotional implications of filmmaking.

The trajectories of Bianchi and Rademakers mirrored two trends that reflected the internationalisation of the student body of the CSC – the influence of New Latin American Cinema and the formation of European *auteur* cinema. Unlike to their male peers, their experience of mobility and their eccentric positioning in film direction have translated into a late recuperation of their historical legacy. In both cases, their work has been crucial to the cinematic cultures in which they were involved, yet the organisational and invisible nature of their contribution continues to pose challenges in terms of the gendering and recognition of behind-the-scenes labour.

THE MARGINALITY FROM THE MAINSTREAM

Given the many institutional and cultural obstacles that prevented women from accessing film direction, it is unsurprising that non-theatrical and documentary films soon became a staple for those attempting this career. One example is Franca Maranto, who after graduating in 1951 and working as a script supervisor, directed a handful of newsreels and educational films, such as *Le donne del Risorgimento* (The women of the Risorgimento, 1960), an historical documentary, co-written with Paola Angelilli, about the women who contributed to the unification of Italy.[25]

The turn to marginal, non-theatrical and low-budget productions is more evident in the trajectories of those students who debuted in the industry in the 1960s, when opportunities to work as directors widened thanks to television.

Liliana Cavani, who graduated in 1961, is certainly one of the most famous Italian female directors worldwide, and the exceptionality of her case deserves a separate analysis that exceeds the aims of this chapter. Here, I mention just her early experiences with the national broadcaster RAI, a career step that she shares with other two graduates of the 1960s, Rosalia Polizzi and Helena Lumbreras, who both graduated few years later than she did. At RAI, they all worked as directors and authors for documentaries and news programmes. While Cavani turned to feature films, Polizzi and Lumbreras continued to work at RAI and engage with militant filmmaking and documentaries. In the late 1960s, both began to work for the Unitelefilm, the production company of the Italian Communist Party (Partito Comunista Italiano), and continued to make political films. After graduating in 1964, and until 1970, Lumbreras worked as director and scriptwriter for *Cordialmente*, a programme broadcast on the second RAI channel. For this work, Lumbreras filmed short investigative reports in Turin, Naples, Potenza and Bari, where she documented the living conditions of the working class and peasants. This experience had a significant impact on her sensibility, giving her the opportunity to consolidate her abilities in storytelling and the investigation of social issues through rapid production methods and light technologies. The contracts that Helena Lumbreras signed with the RAI between 1966 and 1969 for the programmes *Cordialmente* and *Panorama Economico* reveal that this phase of her career was characterised by precarity and extreme mobility.[26] Indeed, although she was a regular collaborator, Lumbreras was paid by the episode, and given a lump sum to cover the costs of the preliminary inspections and the shooting, the purchase of film supplies, editing and other post-production costs. The broadcaster had all the rights of reproduction and exploitation of the finished product, and these were the conditions that television usually gave to authors and directors. This meant that the creative possibilities offered by this type of collaboration were very constrained.

For all the differences between them, the experience of Rosalia Polizzi, who was born in Buenos Aires of an Italo-Spanish family and graduated in 1964, resonates with that of Lumbreras. Since the very beginning of her career, Polizzi worked in several productions and roles. In 1965 she began to work at RAI for programmes like *Enciclopedia della natura* (Natural encyclopaedia) and *Habitat*, while she also worked at two short films with Giorgio Pellari, *La giovane Arabia* (The young Arabia) and *Il mito* (The myth), released in 1966, and collaborated with Bruno Corbucci as continuity supervisor/*segretaria di edizione* (*James Tont, Operazione U.N.O.*, 1965) and Nanni Loy (*Le nostre mogli*, 1966). In the early 1970s, her collaboration with the Unitelefilm, begun few years earlier, intensified. She directed a series of documentaries about the condition of women and the feminist movement, none of which exceeded a medium-length duration, and with the usual characteristics of low-budget production, made with a small crew of no more than four or five people, generally all women.[27] From 1974 to 1978 she ran her own production company, the Paranà film, whose documentation is preserved at the library of the CSC. This archive contains an impressive number of screenplays and scripts for cinema and television, about women and/or Argentina and specifically about its culture and migratory exchanges with Italy. Most of these projects have never been made into films, while others were produced by the broadcaster RAI. Among them, there is *I mille volti di Eva* (The thousand faces of Eve), created and directed by Polizzi with Tilde Capomazza, Mariuccia Ciotta and Ada Acquaviva and transmitted by the second channel in August 1978.[28]

Overall, Polizzi's experience in the audio-visual field has been vast and varied (writing, production, documentary, television, fiction film), and for this reason, her trajectory, like that of Lumbreras, is at odds with cinema history, but at the same time is emblematic of the precariousness of labour in this field. Many of the films she conceived and wrote have never been shot, or have never found a circulation outside militant circles, and even the TV programmes she authored and have been broadcast were destined to an ephemeral consumption. Only in 1997 did she achieve the direction of a full-length feature film, the Italo-Argentinean co-production *Anni ribelli* (Laura: the rebel years, 1997); and she made her second and last full-length film, *Riconciliati* (Reconciled, 2001), just three years later.

A Map of Open Questions

The different experiences of this group of students map and pose a series of questions that are consistent with the evolution of women's position in cinema, showing also the complex role of an institution like the CSC, which reproduced patterns of discrimination but also opened up new opportunities. The case of Marisa Romano illuminates the contradictions inherent in women's visibility and career achievements within patriarchal systems of power; Olga Bianchi and Lili Rademakers are representative of the transnational exchanges that characterised post-war cinema and the late recognition of women's contribution in these networks; Luisa Alessandri's trajectory and the graduates who ended up working as continuity supervisors show a phase in which the invisibilisation of women's labour and feminisation of certain professions were embedded in the organisation of work; finally, the careers of the graduates of the 1960s, such as Lumbreras and Polizzi, but also Liliana Cavani – who, it is important to remember, worked in RAI for seven years before making her first feature film, *Galileo* – are emblematic of the precarious working conditions characterising the Italian audio-visual industry, as well as the importance of television and non-theatrical filmmaking for women directors. All these questions persist in the contemporary film industry, and are stimulating new strands of feminist scholarship internationally, confirming that most of these issues were shared in many different national contexts. In other words, these histories challenge our idea of Italian cinema at multiple levels, with histories of women who trespassed, adapted and transformed its boundaries, both physically and metaphorically.

This genealogy clearly indicates what type of work is ahead of us, a research that uses the recuperation of individual histories, by considering multiple archival sources and testimonies, to build a cartography of questions that supports our understanding of recurring narratives and problems across time and space, including across borders.

Notes

1. There are several studies, with a historical and industrial approach, about the role of film schools in supporting feminist cinema and fostering gender equality. Two examples of these two areas of investigation are: Julia Knight, 1992, 'Institutional initiatives', in *Women and the New German Cinema* (London: Verso), 102–21; Miranda J. Banks, 2019, 'Film Schools as Pre-Industry: Fostering Creative Collaboration and Equity in Media Production Programs', *Media Industries* 6, no. 1, available at https://doi.org/10.3998/mij.15031809.0006.105, accessed 5 May 2021. Film schools have been also crucial in fostering feminist film and women's film production in Latin American countries (Rashkin 2001; Nair and Gutiérrez-Albilla 2019).
2. When I was conducting my preliminary research for this chapter in 2018, I contacted the archivists of the CSC, who were very sympathetic with my research. Unfortunately, as the documentation is still not accessible to researchers, the results have been very fragmentary, if not inconsistent. In 2010, Giulio Bursi published an article with some preliminary findings based on the school's archive, which at the time had just been inventoried and digitalised (Bursi 2010). To date, these scans are not publicly available.
3. See for instance, Alfredo Baldi, 2018, *La scuola italiana del cinema. Il Centro sperimentale di cinematografia dalla storia alla cronaca (1939–2017)* (Soveria-Mannelli: Rubbettino); and also the special issue of the journal *Bianco e Nero* 71, no. 566 (January–April 2010).
4. The website of the Women's Film Pioneer Project (https://wfpp.columbia.edu/, accessed 5 May 2021) adopts the structure of the hypertext to emphasise the transnational connections between the experiences of silent pioneers working in different national contexts around the globe. However, this project is the coronation of years of feminist research about the participation of women in early cinema beyond acting. Cf. Jennifer Bean and Diane Negra, eds, 2002, *A Feminist Reader in Early Cinema* (Durham, NC: Duke University Press); Sofia

Bull and Astrid Söderbergh Widding, eds, 2010, *Not So Silent. Women in Cinema before Sound* (Stockholm: Acta Universitatis Stockholmiensis).
5. For the Italian case see: Monica Dall'Asta, ed., 2007, *Non solo dive: pioniere del cinema Italiano* (Bologna: Cineteca di Bologna).
6. See Kim Tomadjoglou, 2013, 'Elvira Notari', in Jane Gaines, Radha Vatsal, and Monica Dall'Asta, eds, *Women Film Pioneers Project* (New York, NY: Columbia University Libraries), available at https://doi.org/10.7916/d8-zdmp-rs37, accessed 5 May 2021. Other than Tomadjoglou's essay, the most comprehensive study on Notari is still Giuliana Bruno's *Streetwalking on a Ruined Map: Cultural Theory and the City Films of Elvira Notari* (Princeton, NJ: Princeton University Press, 1993).
7. The list is divided into the main programmes, follows alphabetical order and reports the year of enrolment or graduation. It is available at https://www.fondazionecsc.it/wp-content/uploads/2019/11/ELENCO_DEFINITIVO_EX-ALLIEVI_aggiornato_al_19.12.18.pdf, accessed 11 December 2020. Another list that reports only the graduate students appears in the special issue of *Bianco & Nero* 5–6, 1976: 31–41.
8. Given the very short career of di Nola, I was unable to incorporate her story in this chapter. However, I believe it is worth outlining her profile. She graduated with an essay titled 'Giovanna dei Macelli' – an adaptation of Bertolt Brecht's play, starring the future show girl Raffaella Carrà – and is credited as assistant director in the adventure film and Italo-French co-production *Il Naufrago del Pacifico* (Jeff Musso and Amasi Damiani, 1962). Her name re-emerges only in the 1970s in a very different context, as editor of two collections of feminist poetry, *Da donna a donna. Poesie d'amore e d'amicizia* (1977) and *Poesia femminista italiana* (1978). During the 1970s, Di Nola took part in the Roman feminist movement, and participated in the group La Maddalena, specifically in the homonymous collective of experimental theatre. She also joined the gay and lesbian activist group FUORI, and hosted a show broadcast on Radio Radicale about lesbian sexuality and consciousness raising. She was allegedly involved in the kidnapping of the Italian Prime Minister Aldo Moro, who was held hostage and assassinated by the terrorist group Brigate Rosse in May 1978. Di Nola died in 1979 of a heart attack, and her role in this crime hasn't yet been clarified.
9. I have concentrated on the years before 1970, because after that date a group of filmmakers graduated from the CSC who were actively involved in the feminist movement, a phase that will be covered in the last two chapters of the book.
10. The most difficult aspect has been the reconstruction of the filmographies, for which I have relied on three on-line databases, IMDB, Archivio del Cinema Italiano ANICA, and the Database of Italian Cinema. The latter has been particularly helpful, as the entries are crowdsourced from the opening and closing credits of different versions of the same films. Complementary research has been conducted on the database of the project Italia Taglia, which gathers the mandatory censorship clearance that films need to obtain to be publicly screened.

This source has been particularly helpful, as it includes also documentations about short and educational films.

11. This school was founded in 1932 and was directed by Alessandro Blasetti until 1934, when it was closed to make way for the CSC.
12. Gemma De Aloysio, f. 'Gemma de Aloysio', Allievi Regia, 1935, CSC (Application).
13. Anon., Letter to Marzia de Aloysio, 30 April 1936 f. 'Gemma de Aloysio', Allievi Regia, 1935, CSC.
14. It is possible that these thirteen students were added to the 'Production' section of the list, which at this early stage wasn't a separate curriculum.
15. These films are now irretrievable.
16. Comin was a prominent film critic, teacher of cinema history at the CSC, and official of the regime, who had a primary role in the development of Fascist cinema. In 1938, the negative reception of *Under the Southern Cross* at the Venice Biennale was motivated mostly by its melodramatic plot, gravitating around a mixed-race woman, Mailù. As Ruth Ben-Ghiat points out, although Romano was presented as the 'first female screenwriter in Italy' who brought 'a female perspective' to a colonial film, the film was a 'low point in the history of women within empire film' (2001, 208).
17. Marisa Romano, whose real name was Maria Luisa Scala, had her first contact with the Fascist political police (OVRA) in 1925. At the time she helped to foil an initial plan to assassinate Mussolini, hatched by former socialist deputy Tito Zambonini. She would become a regular informant of OVRA, especially about the anti-fascist activities of Italians exiled in France. Her husband Comin helped her to recompile information at the French embassy (Franzinelli 2000, 19–20). In confidential police documents, Romano is described as a 'very young and excessively made-up woman, with big poses and discreet jewels' (Franzinelli 2000, 19). See also Mauro Canali, 2004, *Le spie del regime* (Bologna: Il Mulino), 725.
18. Between 1959 and 1961, Lumbreras studied film direction at the Instituto de Investigaciones y Experiencias Cinematográficas in Madrid. This film school was founded by the dictator Francisco Franco and was active between 1947 and 1975. Despite it admitted several women, most of them didn't achieve a career in the local film industry. A programme of their films was screened in 2019 at the Mostra Internacional de Films de Dones in Barcelona.
19. A digital version of the film is available at the website of the Audiovisual Archive of the Democratic and Labour Movement (AAMOD), which preserves the audiovisual archives of the Italian Communist Party and its affiliated organisations, such as Unitelefilm. The archive also contains a folder holding Lumbrera's working documents. Available at http://patrimonio.aamod.it/aamod-web/film/detail/IL8300001743/22/spagna-68.html, accessed 5 May 2021. It was shot with very limited means: in a letter the director tries to obtain more economic support from Unitelefilm, to pay a higher fee to some local operators and technicians who, due to their political views, struggled to work in other productions. See

letter dated 20 May 1968, available at http://patrimonio.aamod.it/aamod-web/film/detail/IL8300001743/22/spagna-68.html, accessed 5 May 2021.

20. On the link between Lumbreras' experimental filmmaking and her anti-Franco activism, several contributions have recently been published, highlighting her transnational influences, particularly on New Latin American Cinema (Ledesma 2014) and Italian political cinema (Mirizio 2017). Not least, she has also attracted the attention of feminist scholars interested in addressing her pioneering figure (Cami-Vela 2009; Martin-Márquez 2012; Zecchi 2019).

21. Having decided to leave Italy for good, Lumbreras started working as a teacher in high school, continuing to make films and support the local anti-Francoist movement. It was in this context that she met Mariano Lisa, her future husband, and co-founder of the Colectivo Cine de Clase. The Colectivo would make a series of militant films that were characterised by a collective approach to direction and centred on the participation of the filmed subjects. Amongst these are *El campo para el hombre* (1975), dedicated to the conditions of exploitation of the workers in rural Spain, *O todos o ninguno* (1976) and *A la vuelta del grito* (1977–8) centred on the struggles of the Catalan workers' movement. She also imported into Spain forbidden films held by Unitelefilm, such as *The Spanish Earth* by Joris Ivens.

22. There is a quite vast literature on the 'global impact' of neorealism, including its impact on the New Latin American Cinema. Feminist scholars have challenged the 'canon' of the New Latin American Cinema but no analysis of the intertwined marginalisation of women in both neorealist and NLAC cinematic cultures has been undertaken so far. See B. Ruby Rich, 'An/other history of Latin American Cinema', first printed in *Iris* 13, 1991, reprinted in Michael T. Martin (ed.), 1997, *New Latin American Cinema*, Vol. 1 (Detroit: Wayne State University Press): 281; Deborah Martin and Deborah Shaw, 2017, *Latin American Women Filmmakers* (London/New York: I. B. Tauris).

23. As reported by Costa Rican film historian María Lurdes Cortés, during her tenure at the Cinemateca, Bianchi organised several film festivals dedicated to European cinema, programs of film training, and several film exhibitions of Costa Rican cinema, including of Super 8 films. Despite Bianchi's remarkable results, achieved despite the few resources available, in 1979 she was replaced by Gabriel Gonzáles Vega, who suspended all the initiatives put in place by Bianchi, as he considered them 'poorly made and lacking of rigour'. Under Gonzàles Vega, the Cinemateca practically ceased its activities. (Cortés 2002: 182–4).

24. Her personal archive is also deposited at the EYE institute.

25. Maranto's filmography has been reconstructed thanks to the 'Italia taglia' database, which lists the titles *Italiani nel mondo* (1952), *Arte e realtà di Bruno Munari* (1955), *Di giorno e di notte* (1955), *I portoghesi* (1960), *Donne del Risorgimento* (1961).

26. Digital copies of this material (11 contracts) have been given to me by Mariano Lisa via our correspondence, begun on 24 April 2020. I wish to thank him for his precious collaboration and generosity.

27. These documentaries combined stock footage materials with the testimonies that Polizzi and her collaborators took in several locations, such as family counselling

centres, demonstrations and occupied factories. This structure characterises the two films dedicated to motherhood and abortion, *Madre, ma come?* (Mother, but how?, 1977) and *Madri e figli* (Mothers and children, 1977), as well as documentaries about women's political participation: *Non ci regalano niente* (They don't gift us anything, 1977), shot for the Unione Donne Italiane (UDI, Italian Women's Union), and *Insieme per cambiare* (United for change, 1979). In *Mother, but how?*, the camera captures a group of women in a counselling room discussing work, sexuality, intimacy and motherhood: topics that are sometimes addressed with ambivalence, if not dismissively. These conversations are fragments of a wider feminist debate about motherhood that Polizzi connects to specific political policies, including reforms in family legislation and welfare, mostly reflecting the programme of the Communist Party.

28. The show consisted of four episodes, broadcast weekly, analysing stereotypes of women and femininity in cinema history, and following chronological order. It is, in essence, a collective exercise of film analysis, similar to those practised in the feminist festivals that we analysed in Chapter 3; however, reception by the feminist press was quite lukewarm. Specifically, *Effe* published a negative review of the programme, accusing it of being a mild critique of overwhelming cinematic stereotypes that failed to address 'the specific experience of the cinema and the work of the spectator' (Pasqua in Pasqua and Tagliaferri 1978). The review is divided into two parts, the first authored by Maricla Tagliaferri and the second by Mariella Pasqua.

CHAPTER 11

A Materialist Trajectory in Feminist Filmmaking: Rethinking Labour and Consciousness-raising

In the 1970s, women's access to film direction remained hampered, and the impact of feminism on existing production cultures differed across Europe, with more success where cultural and film institutions were willing to support experimental and independent filmmaking, such as in the UK and in Germany (Maule 2009, 197–202). In Italy, this kind of support was practically absent, and given also the anti-institutional character of the local movement, feminist filmmaking remained confined to niche and activist productions, with the partial exception of collaborations with the national broadcaster, RAI. Despite this, as we have seen in the previous sections, Italian feminist critics and film collectives were very active in the organisation of film festivals and the support of alternative circuits that could disseminate feminist films, a production consisting prevalently of experimental and low-budget documentaries often made through forms of collaborative work. All these aspects resonate with a transnational trend in feminist filmmaking, that led, from Europe to the Americas, to innovative forms of theoretical and political production.[1]

With this in mind, this chapter explores the political and material links between collaborative filmmaking and the activist practices developed in Italy, drawing on an archival and materialist perspective. As Bono and Kemp put it, 'what is characteristically Italian ... is the uneasy, conflictual but nevertheless sustained relationship between theoretical separatist speculation, the effort to analyse and create an autonomous subject-woman, and practical political activities' (1991, 20). For this reason, this chapter focuses on the reconstruction of the theoretical reflections, creative choices and economic constraints that have characterised this period of intense feminist film production. As such, the chapter doesn't aim to cover the totality of feminist films made, or make considerations of aesthetic value; rather, it concentrates on aspects of production and their interplay with theoretical and political practice, in contexts such as film cooperatives, collaborations with RAI and the 'mainstream' film industry.[2] I also reflect on the political and pragmatic consequences of the decision of many filmmakers to use 'poor' technologies such as the Super 8 and the videotape, to concentrate on the historical and practical outcomes of these choices without falling into the trap of technological determinism.[3] This approach allows me to reconstruct, and at the same time understand, the strengths and pitfalls of the Italian feminist cinematic agenda by taking into consideration the coexistence of systemic and structural barriers, and their consequences for individual trajectories. My goal is to provide a complex and lively portrayal of the debates and strategies that feminist filmmakers have adopted to pursue their artistic and political objectives, but also to reflect on their limits. Addressing the limitations of a creative and political project doesn't mean denying its importance: it's actually a way to make sense of the present through the past, and think more productively about the political strategies that we can adopt today. Indeed, as we have seen in Chapter 10, women filmmakers and film practitioners are still experiencing gender discrimination and huge difficulties in accessing both public and private funding. Looking back at the 1970s helps us to put these issues into an historical framework as well as offering points of reflection.

WORKING TOGETHER: GRASS-ROOTS AND MAINSTREAM ATTEMPTS OF COLLECTIVE FILMMAKING

My analysis begins with two experiences that apparently lie at opposite ends of the corpus of Italian feminist cinema: the collective and experimental films of the grass-roots Collettivo Femminista di Cinema (FCC) and Sofia Scandurra's *Io sono mia* (I belong to me, 1978), a mainstream production made by a crew composed entirely of women. Despite their huge differences, these two examples share a utopian view on women's collective labour, and a difficult approach to professionalism.

As discussed in Chapter 3, the FCC was founded in 1971 and promoted by the two filmmakers Annabella Miscuglio and Rony Daopoulo, who were actively involved in the Filmstudio cine club.[4] Daopoulo graduated in 1971 at the Centro Sperimentale di Cinematografia (CSC) with the essay *L'aggettivo donna* (The adjective woman, 1971), which was also the first film of the FCC.[5] The CSC produced the graduation essays of its students and lent them some of the equipment they needed, a practice that encouraged forms of experimentation with low-budget formats and technologies, like the 16mm. In the same year, the FCC published its manifesto, *For a Clito-Vaginal Cinema*, which explains the group's approach to filmmaking: '[this is why] we are interested in the audiovisual means: to talk to other women, and to express a new way of being a woman' (Collettivo Feminista di Cinema 1971 in *Almanacco* 1978, 135).

This idea was an extension of the theories and practices developed by the movement, in particular those linked to *autocoscienza* (or consciousness-raising groups), which consisted in separatist meetings where women shared their experiences to analyse mechanisms of patriarchal oppression and produce new collective interpretative categories. To use Lea Melandri's words, with the practice of *autocoscienza*, Italian feminism 'counterposed the big philosophical interpretative systems (Marxism, psychoanalysis, Hegelianism) . . .[the] attention to individual experience, rethought by means of collective listening' (Melandri 2000, 43). This also meant that the practice of *autocoscienza* supported a form of activism in which there was 'a split neither between theory and experience, thinking and action, ends and means, nor between the enunciated and the subject of enunciation, the transformation of reality and the self' (Dominijanni 2005, 26).

The transposition of *autocoscienza* into filmmaking meant adopting separatism and a self-reflexive style based on experimentalism, which found in documentary its natural aesthetical translation. Indeed, the *Lessico Politico delle donne* defines *autocoscienza* as 'the main tool that the Italian Feminist Movement has given itself to analyse and make an intervention in the real' (Bettini 1978: 125). The small groups of *autocoscienza* reflected mostly on two topics: the method and practice of 'staying among women', namely the meanings and affects of separatism; and the importance of reaching out to and meeting with different women and destabilising male institutions (Bettini 1978: 127). All these aspects are reflected in *La lotta non é finita* (The struggle is not ended, 1972–3), the second and last film of the FCC, which was 'born from the Feminist Cinema Collective with and for the Feminist Movement' [opening titles]. The closing credits take up the metaphor of birth and motherhood by saying that the 'film was conceived, handled, bred, socialised, by a troupe entirely composed by women'. As such, *La lotta non é finita* is an activist film made for the movement using the movement's theoretical and political tools, and for this reason, it expresses a subjectivity that is collective and individual at the same time. However, despite these intentions, Daopoulo was soon confronted with the dilemma of working with a medium, the cinema, that was too masculine to interpret women properly. In the transcription of an assembly held on February 1972 at via Pompeo Magno, Daopoulo shared her concerns about the cinema as

> a means of expression that is clearly masculine . . . I thought it was possible to do it from a women's perspective, but the method remains male. However, [if I don't make films] I would remain completely silent, so I don't know . . . This is my problem, which I realised with the film.[6]

These reflections resonate with the brief text 'Autobiografia di una esperienza' (Autobiography of an experience, 1978) written by Daopoulo to explain the firm intention of the collective to make *La lotta non é finita* with a crew composed entirely of women. The main issue, though, was that they didn't have enough technical skills:

> the movie, on the technical side, is a big mess, but this is not important, because things can be learned. The real problem was that mechanisms of competition, power, etc. have been unleashed. And for this reason, we began to see very clearly how the things we used to say in the movement, such as 'there should be no leader', 'no ideology', 'no competition', were just slogans that did not correspond to our achievements as individuals. (Daopoulo in *Almanacco* 1978, 133)

In other words, this experience confirmed Daopoulo's concerns about the masculine nature of the cinema, an aspect that also made evident the political contradictions of the activists.

It is interesting to read Daopoulo's views in relation to the experience of the professionals who worked at Sofia Scandurra's *Io sono mia*, the only Italian mainstream film made entirely by a crew of women. The film is an adaptation of Dacia Maraini's novel *Women at War* (1975); it starred a cast of renowned actors, such as Stefania Sandrelli, Michele Placido and Maria Schneider, and involved a group of practitioners who had previously worked on other feminist productions, like Nurith Aviv (cinematography), Vanna Paoli and Nieves Zenteno (sound department). Notably, despite their intention to hire a team of women, Scandurra and the executive producer Lù Leone could find no electricians or grips, and the production team refused to get them from abroad. The lack of these figures confirms the strong gendering of film professions in the Italian industry, and also the unprecedented nature of Scandurra's project. The film, indeed, sought to intercept a wide, non-activist audience, testing for the first time the feminist experiments of collective and separatist filmmaking into a mainstream and commercial production. The promotional materials of the film emphasised these feminist credentials, creating a certain level of expectation among both activists and the general public. However, despite the intentions, the film didn't hit the box office and had a lukewarm critical reception, including in feminist circles: almost unanimously, both the specialist press and feminist critics considered the film excessively pedantic and didactic, and did not appreciate its dramatic style (Cavallaro 2007). However, this project is the culmination of a line of experimentation in collaborative filmmaking which, as in the case of the FCC, soon made its limitations evident. Although Scandurra and Leone attempted to introduce the practice of *autocoscienza* within the crew, the rhythms imposed by the production team made it impossible to take regular moments of collective self-reflection. This is also reported in the promotional booklet *Io sono mia*, which includes a collection of stage photos and texts written by the members of the crew, focusing on their feelings and opinions about the experience of working together with other women (AA.VV. 1977). These testimonies, edited in a format that echoes the dialogues and exchanges of a group of *autocoscienza*, mention several times issues such as competition and a lack of collaboration. According to the assistant director Mimmola Girosi, a regular practice of *autocoscienza* would have made the experience more positive. For her part, Scandurra regrets how things went, noticing that the whole process was much more difficult than expected because the other women questioned every aspect of the film. Despite this, there are also other testimonies that are more positive, especially when comparing this film with experiences in predominantly male crews. These conflicting opinions reveal the problematic relationship between the separatist practices of feminist filmmaking and the organisation of labour typical of mainstream productions, a political and theoretical impasse that Italian filmmakers didn't solve. It is also interesting to note that the practice of *autocoscienza* was intended as a possible solution to eminently organisational problems, as if more attention to women's relationships could fix issues brought on in a professional context. Like the FCC, which similarly relied on separatism and *autocoscienza*, Scandurra's project capitulated before cinema's technical needs and labour organisation, which were practically incompatible with her initial intentions. However, feminist filmmakers and practitioners were well aware of these structural limitations, and for this reason attempted to think of other critical practices to challenge precisely these material and practical constraints.

QUESTIONING LABOUR: FILM COLLECTIVES AND COOPERATIVES

After the experience with the FCC, Daopoulo and Miscuglio joined the film cooperative Maestranze Tecnici e Cinema (MTC) and began to collaborate with RAI, contributing two of the most famous Italian feminist films, *Processo per stupro* (Trial for rape, 1978) and *AAA Offresi* (1981).[7] Thanks to the mediation of a group of professionals employed at RAI and close to the movement, like Loredana Rotondo and Marina Tartara, the broadcaster opened a series of opportunities for feminist filmmakers. The importance of these initiatives must be read in the context of a company characterised by a heavily gendered workforce. As reconstructed by Daniela Brancati, in 1977 only 25 per cent of the employees at RAI were women, employed mainly in secretarial and administrative positions; among the creatives and technicians, there were only eighteen women (working as editors), against the 440 men employed in all the other departments. The situation was decisively better in the direction department, where 40 per cent were women, working mainly as assistants and production secretaries (Brancati 2011, 78–81).[8] Miscuglio remembers that many feminist filmmakers struggled with the obstruction and sexism of RAI's technicians, a problem that pushed many of them to work freelance, and constitute their own companies and cooperatives. This strategy allowed them to hire and chose practitioners from outside, and therefore have more control of the film (Miscuglio in Bruno and Nadotti 1988, 159). The film cooperative, indeed, offered a mode of production that could meet institutional constraints and gender discrimination, while making a critical and anti-capitalist stance in line with a tradition of Italian film cooperatives initiated by the Cooperativa spettatori produttori cinematografici, which was founded in 1950.[9] At the same time, the Italian film cooperatives of the 1970s were also the result of a diffused desire for alternative culture and participation that animated the social movements of the time, including the forms of experimental and militant cinema inspired by initiatives like the the Film-makers' Cooperative in New York and the London Film-Maker Co-op.

The Arcobaleno Cooperative (1976) is an interesting encounter between the cooperative model and original feminist reflections about labour, based on a political project centred on the question of work and founded by a group of film professionals: Anna Brasi, Fausta Gabrielli, Nieves Zenteno, Caroline Laure, Marilú Parolini, Eva Piccoli, Rosetta Froncillo, Paola Muzzi and Silvana Abbrescia.[10] At least three of them, Zenteno,[11] Gabrielli and Brasi,[12] graduated in film direction at the Centro Sperimentale, while Froncillo was a professional production secretary,[13] Muzzi had experience as assistant editor and Piccoli as a camera operator. Their intention was subverting, through feminist practice and theory, established modes of cinematic production, which they considered 'a field where women traditionally work and express themselves subordinately to men' (Cooperativa Arcobaleno in *Almanacco* 1978, 140). Their first film, *8 Marzo, giornata di festa e di lotta* (8 March, day of celebration and struggle), which was produced and aired by the second RAI channel on Women's Day in 1977, also focused on labour, specifically on the history of the women who participated in the strikes and revolts of the 1910s. The documentary opens with images of contemporary feminist demonstrations, and a reconstruction of the events from the beginning of the century through the memories recorded in three testimonies, in combination with archival materials. The use of stock images and interviews suits an analytical and materialist approach to history, which the filmmakers adapted to the investigative style of RAI productions.[14] To some extent, *8 marzo* shares many features of Gabrielli and Anna Brasi's graduation essay for the Centro Sperimentale, *Marghera come Marienbad* (Marghera like Marienbad, 1974), which is set at the petrochemical plant at the Venice lagoon and alternates images of the landscape and the factory, with few excerpts from Marx's *Capital*, an interview with the workerist theorist Mario Tronti and images of the strikes of the Hot Autumn of 1969/70. This structure combines political analysis with a visual and historical display of class conflict, anticipating the style of *8 marzo*.[15] However, the ideas on women's autonomy, history and work at the basis of the Cooperativa depart from the strictly Marxist and workerist approach of *Marghera*. Although Fausta Gabrielli explicitly reclaims her affinity with workerism,[16] *8 marzo* developed 'a line of research that recuperates the moments of the past in which women had developed their completely autonomous struggles' (Cooperativa Arcobaleno in *Almanacco* 1978, 140). In an article published in *Effe*, five members of the Cooperativa (Anna, Paola, Silvana, Rosetta and Gabriella) explain that working only with women is a way to be autonomous that 'overcomes the myth of professionalism as a form of surveillance-expression, proposing an approach to teamwork that aims to the collective reappropriation of the design, the image, and the technical means' (Cooperativa Arcobaleno 1977, 29). A feminist rejection of professionalism, indeed, overthrows the gendered division of work, letting the entire group participate in every stage of production to 'counteract the efficiency of the set with an organisation of work that is actually a way of staying together' (ibid.).[17] In other words, for the Cooperativa, making films was a practice that transformed the individual by 'developing social relations, collective work, and cooperation' (Gabrielli 1976, 28). This approach expands the notions of authorship and film direction to promote a radical critique of the 'author/authority [as a form of] command on work and money' (Brasi and Gabrielli 1979, 43). Drawing on a feminist analysis of power, the Cooperativa sees in the notion of the author/director an epitome of the gendered mechanisms that make the cinema an art of capital, which values women's work only in terms of sexualisation and femininisation (Brasi and Gabrielli 1979, 42–3). As such, in the work of the Cooperativa, separatism is a strategy that aims to disrupt the patriarchal mechanisms of film production, drawing on a materialist perspective that mirrors in its practice the (critical) proximity of the Italian feminist movement with the ideas of workerism and the contemporary struggles of the workers' movement.

Dacia Maraini's Films with the Iskra Cooperative

The experience of the Arcobaleno Cooperative was distinctive in its Marxist approach to labour and its rejection of authorship, yet the production mode of the cooperative was flexible enough to allow a variety of political and creative experiments. Indeed, in 1975, the writer, intellectual and feminist activist Dacia Maraini joined the cooperative Iskra cinematografica, which produced her first documentary, *Aborto, parlano le donne* (Abortion, women talk), a 16mm film consisting of a collection of testimonies of working-class women who had experienced illegal abortion.[18] *Aborto* represented Maraini's return to film direction after *L'amore coniugale* (Conjugal love, 1970), a negative experience that, using Maraini's words, 'prevented [her] from falling into the trap of mainstream cinema' (Maraini in Frabotta 1979, 62).[19] After *Aborto*, she made other two documentaries: *Ritratti di donne africane* (Portraits of African women, 1976–7), for RAI, and *Le ragazze di Capo Verde* (The girls from Cape Verde, 1976), produced by Iskra. *Ritratti* consisted of three parts, dedicated respectively to the women of the Lobi, Abidji and Fanti West African tribes, and benefited from the collaboration of the camera operator Nurith Aviv.[20] According to Maraini, the project encountered several difficulties before being approved by RAI, perhaps because of its explicit feminist aim: the documentary, indeed, explored how gender impacted the organisation of these communities, an aspect that interested Maraini because it would prove the existence of 'a feminine consciousness and strong sentiment of independence along with [. . .] a separation between the feminine and masculine worlds, which is lived in a conscious way; not without conflict, but with clarity' (Maraini in La Stampa 1977). *Ritratti* is ideally linked to *Le ragazze di Capo Verde*, an investigative documentary that focuses on a group of Cape Verdean domestic workers in Rome. The idea for the film came to Maraini from a Cape Verdean woman whom she met at the Casa Internazionale delle donne in Rome:

> We became friends and she introduced me to other Cape Verdean women, and then I wanted to make a documentary to tell their stories and show their difficulties as migrants, almost always forced, even if they graduated, to do humble and badly paid jobs. (Correspondence of the author with Dacia Maraini, email, 12 November 2020)[21]

The film reveals the exploitative conditions faced by African women in Italy, constantly threatened with being 'sent back to their countries' (Perona 1976, 6), to 'denounce the consequences of colonialism and the contradictions of society' (La Stampa 1976), in the context of the inertia of unions, parties and cultural associations. The political relevance of this film remains particularly high: it is the only feminist Italian film of the 1970s focusing on migrant women and post-coloniality, anticipating later feminist reflections on the 'global care-chains' and reproductive labour.

Le ragazze was distributed by the Turin-based cooperative Art Kino, which also supported the feminist film festival Kinomata, where this film was also programmed;[22] however, like *Aborto*, the copies of this film are currently lost, and Maraini didn't own them, as they belonged to the producer (Maraini 2020).[23] As such, a copy of *Ritratti*, produced by RAI, is accessible at the archive of the broadcaster, while the experimental Super 8 films that Maraini shot later were deposited and digitalised at the film archive of Stanford University. As such, the accessibility of these films is evidently linked with their different modes of production and circulation, confirming also that after the completion of their works the filmmakers had a very limited control over the finished product, an aspect further confirmed by the fact that the Arcobaleno Cooperative couldn't circulate *8 Marzo* as they pleased, because the film was RAI's property.

THE PROBLEM OF THE SUPER 8

As we have mentioned, Maraini eventually transitioned from the 16mm to the Super 8, a choice motivated by the author's need 'to look, touch, understand, poking around with the eye' and control every stage of the film, from filming to editing (Maraini in Frabotta 1979, 59).[24] This shift towards a personal and self-reflexive style resonates, once again, with the idea of *autocoscienza*, or rather, with its declination closer to psychoanalysis, the *practice of the unconscious* (pratica dell'inconscio).[25] Maraini, indeed, is one of the many women filmmakers who approached the Super 8 to make experimental films with an artistic and aesthetic vocation. However, the quantity and the often amatorial quality of this production raised some criticism in feminist circles. In 1978 Moira Miele published a polemical article in *Effe* expressing her discontent for the improvisational and poor technical quality of many Super 8s screened at the Italian feminist film festivals (Miele 1978, 34). The topic was also posed in *Quotidiano Donna* by Daniela Rotunno, who hoped that the fourth edition of 'Rassegne del cinema di Sorrento' (1978) would address questions such as:

> how much the laws of the market condition the freedom of expression? What compromises in terms of content should be paid in order to be disseminated? [. . .] Is it possible to continue to produce films that are made with smaller means and are increasingly marginalised from any circuit?

However, from our perspective, it is interesting to look at the Super 8 as a response to the pitfalls of the film cooperative model: although the Super 8 format favoured individual practice and experimentation at the expense of collective work and accessibility, it also gave the author full control of every aspect of her work, including its circulation and preservation. In this respect, the Super 8 films, which resulted from a practice that was liminal to the visual arts,[26] reintroduced the question of self-expression that was left aside by the cooperatives, and reproduced the duality between the individual and the collective that haunted feminist cinema and its experiments in separatist filmmaking.

AAA Offresi: The End of Collaborations with RAI and the Impossible Revolution of the Videotape

Despite the polemics about the Super 8 were based on its lack of professionalism and the difficulty of distributing work in this format, the movement was also critical of the feminist films produced by RAI (Miscuglio in Bruno and Nadotti 1988, 158). A review of Anna Carini and Annabella Miscuglio's documentary *Il rischio di vivere* (1977), published in the catalogue of the Rassegne del Cinema di Sorrento (1978, 58), expresses strong reservations about a format that sacrifices the radicalism of the message in order to meet the expectations of the general public. In response, Miscuglio explains:

> Having chosen the media to disseminate the analysis and contents of the women's movement, we feel the need to reach a wider audience than the alternative circuits. [. . .] We are interested in bringing our information to women who are still locked in their homes. [. . .] The making of a film, or even video tapes, involves costs that make the production impossible [. . .] without the support of an economic structure that also guarantees the remuneration of work. (Rassegne 1978, 59)

This brief exchange illustrates another contraposition within the movement that was split between attitudes of rejection and compromise with the institutions, while highlighting the persistent lack of infrastructure and funding.

The sudden suppression of the programme *Si dice donna*[27] in 1981 and the case of *AAA Offresi* definitively ended a phase of intense collaboration with RAI that began in the mid-1970s, somehow marking the end of the project of media transformation brought on by the second-wave movement.[28] Here, I focus on the case of *AAA Offresi* as it better encapsulates the complexity of this political phase, and its material and practical consequences for filmmaking. The documentary was made by the MTC cooperative and compiles footage of the meetings of a French sex worker, Veronique, with her clients, obtained with a hidden video camera. The filmmakers wanted to analyse the behaviour of the clients, showing how they approached Veronique, what kind of requests they made and how they treated her, from the first contact over the phone until they left her apartment in Rome. According to *Effe*,

> *AAA Offresi* is a mature product of feminist creativity, neither vindictive nor victimising: by means of ruthless images it puts male sexual misery in front of everyone's eyes [. . .]. The roles are innovative in the imagery: the prostitute

is neither the exploited nor the cheerful hooker nor the 'whore' by tendency; HIM, the client, through this process of disenchantment, is ridiculed; he is literally left there in his underwear! (E.M. 1981, 6)

In both the feminist magazines, *Effe* and *Quotidiano Donna*, the documentary stimulated an interesting debate about sex work, which also emphasised the film's ability to show Veronique's personality and self-awareness. In a short interview published in *Quotidiano Donna*, Veronique explicitly rejects the feminist movement, as she believes that women, as individuals, can emancipate without the support of others, posing herself as an example: 'look at me. I do what I want [...] and I am completely free in my relationship with men' (*Quotidiano Donna* 1981a, 11). The filmmakers explained that initially Veronique was worried about their 'feminist judgment', but when they explained that they were interested in her 'as a woman and not as a prostitute', the relationship improved (*Quotidiano Donna* 1981b: 10). Though the clients' voices and faces had been anonymised and no personal details about Veronique had been revealed, transmission was suspended after the first part was aired, responding to a formal request made by members of the parliament.[29] This fact raised a harsh debate about censorship and the political control of the public broadcaster, while the filmmakers were accused in a long criminal trial of aiding and abetting prostitution and violating privacy (Belmonti et al. 1981, 125–7). As a result of the investigation, the film and all the materials related to this project were seized by the police and are still irretrievable today.

According to the reviews of the time, what made this film unique was the ingenious use of the videotape, a technology that had raised the enthusiasm of Italian militant filmmakers since the early 1970s for its low cost and ease of use.[30] The videotape could fulfil the desire to bring the cinema within reach everyone everywhere: inside houses, in assemblies, on the streets, in the factories. Several feminist organisations promoted workshops to teach women how to use videotape, and the technology was also adopted by film cooperatives collaborating with RAI. However, Miscuglio was particularly cautious about the 'revolutionary' potential of this technology, as she had started to use it because of the persistent economic constraints suffered by her productions. Indeed, she believed that it was more important to think about the use of technologies rather than drawing abstract and enthusiastic conclusions about their accessibility (Miscuglio 1979). Miscuglio's words are particularly important as they deromanticise the use of the videotape to redirect our attention to the problem of the scarcity of resources and infrastructures.

In 1982, in the middle of the *AAA Offresi* case, Daopoulo and Miscuglio organised one of their videotape workshops at the Roman bar Zanzibar, which since its foundation in 1978 had been a reference point for the local lesbian community (Biagini 2018, 147–52). However, it seems that the women who attended the Zanzibar were more interested in dance nights and entertainment than in cultural and political activities, such as the videotape class (Conte 1982, 15). Only five years earlier, a similar workshop, stemming from the Kinomata festival and known as 'Laboratorio a', raised significant interest and attracted several applications (*Almanacco* 1978: 140): the declining interest in these initiatives was symptomatic of a broader transformation of the political practices of the movement at the beginning of the 1980s. At the same time, hopes for an Italian 'women's cinema' were rapidly being absorbed by a new trend of *auteur* cinema, embodied in the experience of (few) female authors not directly linked to the movement, like Francesca Archibugi and Cristina and Francesca Comencini, while the feminist filmmakers of the 1970s, such as Miscuglio, continued to make their films for the underground.

Beyond the Glass Ceiling

These very different experiences illustrate that Italian feminist filmmaking faced three main questions: first, the duality between the individual and the collective, which created political, creative and relational tensions; second, the problem of technique, which was also linked to the organisation of labour; finally, limited access to funding and infrastructure. The directors tried to address these issues using the political and material tools available, like *autocoscienza* and the adoption of low-budget, cheap technologies; however, none of these correctives had a long-term impact or offered a solution to issues that were structural and intrinsic to the cinema itself. Moreover, the evolution of the political context closed the few spaces that had opened up for feminist film production, worsening an already difficult situation. All these questions reveal the political and material limitations of a feminist cinema project that was split between the urgency of making films and disseminating feminist ideas and the necessity of transforming the cinema as a whole. At the same time, we can't deny the vitality of the political and creative laboratory of feminist filmmaking and its original combination of theory and practice.

However, despite the weaknesses of this project, it is also important to put them in an historical perspective. According to the report published by EWA (European Women's Audiovisual Network) in 2014, only 25 per cent of directors and screenwriters registered in Italy were women, while in the 2006–13 period the number of female-directed films supported by the national film fund was 11 per cent of the total, and among the films funded by RAI, only 21 per cent were directed by women (EWA 2016). These numbers speak volumes of the persistent gender inequality in film direction and funding today, with impressive consistency with the past. In this respect, the ideological and political approach of the 1970s evidently failed to tackle the structural nature of these issues, and can't represent a model for today's policy makers, practitioners and activists; at the same time, those experiences also signal the urgency of focusing on the organisation of labour in terms of economic and gendered relations, stimulating a reflection on the relationship between the individual, the cinema and the community. In other words, that project of feminist filmmaking can help us imagine a model of women's participation in the cinema that goes beyond the breaking of the glass ceiling towards a more radical, transformative agenda.

Notes

1. See for instance Diane Waldman and Janet Walker (eds), 1999, *Feminism and Documentary* (Minneapolis: Minnesota University Press); Alexandra Juhasz, 2003, 'No Woman is an Object: Realizing the Feminist Collaborative Video', *Camera Obscura* 54, vol. 18, no. 3: 71–96; Deborah Martin, 2015, 'Slipping discursive frameworks: Gender (and) politics in Colombian women's documentary', in Parvati Nair and Julián Daniel Gutiérrez-Albilla, eds, *Hispanic and Lusophone Women Filmmakers: Theory, Practice and Difference* (Manchester: Manchester University Press).
2. In this context I am using the terms 'mainstream' and 'commercial' loosely to indicate in the first case those productions that aspired to reach a non-activist audience, and in the second, those films made within the structures of the Italian film industry that were meant to circulate in the national theatrical distribution.
3. Optimistic and often utopian views about the role of technology in promoting social change have constellated the history of social movements, especially since the 1990s, with the massification of the internet. An analysis of this question exceeds the objectives of this chapter, yet the question is relevant, as the accessibility of formats like the Super 8 and other cheap technologies certainly impacted the debates and practices of feminist filmmaking in the 1970s.
4. Since its constitution in 1967, the Filmstudio has been a hub for underground Italian cinema, hosting retrospectives, events and presentations, including the first screenings and festivals of the women's cinema festival Kinomata (see Chapter 3).
5. The members of the crew were Paola Baroncini, Clelia Boesi, Rony Daopoulo, Umberto di Socio, Anna Giulia Fani, Roberto Farina, Lara Foletti, Margie Friesner, Annabella Miscuglio, Silvia Poggioli, Marco Rossi and Angelo Vicari.
6. 'Registrazione dell'assemblea tenutasi 16/2/1972', Fondo Pompeo Magno, Fascicolo 1, Centro Documentazione Alma Sabbadini, Archivia, Rome.
7. Other than Daopoulo and Miscuglio, other members of the MTC were Maria Grazia Belmonti, Anna Carini, Paola De Martiis and Loredana Rotondo, who

also made programmes such as *La donna e la salute* (Woman and health) and *Riprendiamoci la vita* (Let's take back the life). For a reconstruction of these collaborations focused on the figure of Rotondo see Sara Filippelli, 2011, 'Le ragazze con il videotape. La tv secondo Loredana Rotondo', *Bianco & Nero*, no. 3: 97–107.

8. It is interesting to note the similarity between these numbers and those for the film industry, an aspect that suggests a commonality between different creative industries that deserves further investigation.
9. The cooperative was founded in Genoa and produced two films directed by Carlo Lizzani: *Achtung! Banditi* and *Cronache di poveri amanti*.
10. Silvana Abbrescia attended the German Film & Television Academy from 1982 to 1986 and has worked since then as a freelance filmmaker.
11. With Vanna Paoli, Zenteno directed the film *Una razione mensile di atrocità*, discussed in Chapter 5.
12. Brasi and Gabrielli discuss their experience at the CSC in their essay 'Espressione' (Frabotta 1979, 57–9) and in Arcobaleno Cooperative in *Almanacco* 1978, 141.
13. Froncillo was a central figure in the politicisation of Italian lesbian feminists and published two books about lesbianism: the first – with Matilde Finocchi and Alice Valentini – *E la madre, tra l'altro, è una pittrice ... Dialoghi fra lesbiche* (Rome: Felina, 1980); the second, in German, is described in the blurb as the story of 'a period of her life, interrupted again and again by reflections, dreams, memories – questions that are staged like film flashbacks, shots, camera angles': 1983, *Confusa Desio. Eine Reise in Abschweifungen.* (Confusa Desio: a journey into digressions) (Munich: Frauenoffensive).
14. On the relationship between woman, found footage and historical materiality see Alessandra Chiarini and Monica Dall'Asta, 2016, 'Editors, Introduction: Found Footage: Women Without a Movie Camera', *Feminist Media Histories* 2, no. 3 (1 July): 1–10; and Missero 2016.
15. The short also benefits from the cinematography of the champion of Italian underground cinema, Antonio Grifi, and includes music by Philip Glass, which gives the impressionistic petrochemical images a vibrant experimental touch that is lost in the Cooperativa's film.
16. Gabrielli indeed explains: 'it was my healthy background in workerist thought that preserved me from the fascinations ... of the cinephile. [...] Analytical thinking allows you to understand that the cinema doesn't exist if not in terms of the social relations of production' (Gabrielli in Cooperativa Arcobaleno 1977, 30).
17. A similar approach to collective work was promoted by the Roman film collective Alice Guy, born in 1976 from a group of women who responded to a call posted in *Effe* for a feminist film collective to be founded. The collective shot one Super 8 film, *Affettuosamente ciak* (1979) (*Almanacco* 1978, 140–1).
18. In 1975 the Iskra produced its first and last full-length feature, *Il caso Raoul* (The Raoul case, Maurizio Ponzi, 1975), and was about to start a series of

medium-length 16mm documentaries on the peripheries of Rome. Maraini's *Aborto* was the first of the series.
19. Dacia Maraini, 'Tema' in Frabotta 1979: 58–64.
20. Maraini remembers that she insisted on working with a camerawoman, and the production team assigned her Nurith. Including the two women, the troupe was composed of four people; the others were sound technician Roberto Faidutti and a production director. Cf. Correspondence of the author with Dacia Maraini, email, 12 November 2020.
21. Correspondence of the author with Dacia Maraini, email, 12 November 2020.
22. It was also screened in Turin in July 1976 at one of the open-air arenas set up by the city council during the summer (La Stampa 1976). This mode of exhibition well exemplifies the non-commercial and at the same time ephemeral character of alternative circuits of distribution in Italy at the time.
23. I have attempted to reach the former members of the Iskra cooperative without success, while an ex-member of the Art Kino has confirmed that they have no copies of these films.
24. Maraini made three Super 8 films: *Mio padre amore mio* (1976–9), *La bella addormentata* (1978) and *Giochi di latte* (1979). All focus on her relationship with the father and investigate the topic of motherhood. For an analysis of this production see Picchietti 2002 and O'Healy 2000.
25. For an introduction to the practice of unconscious see Teresa de Lauretis, 1990, 'The Practice of Sexual Difference and Feminist Thought in Italy. An Introductory Essay' in *Milan Women's Bookstore Collective, Sexual Difference: A Theory of Social-Symbolic Practice* (Bloomington: Indiana University Press).
26. It is impossible to summarise here the contribution of feminist activists, artists and theorists to the Italian arts of the 1970s, and to date there is no systematic study on women's experimental filmmaking in Italy. For an introduction see, Giulia Simi, 2018, 'Soggetti imprevisti. Le avanguardie dagli anni Sessanta a oggi', in Laura Buffoni, ed., *We want cinema: sguardi di donne nel cinema italiano* (Venice: Marsilio), 82–109. For theatre see, Daniela Cavallaro, 2017, *Educational Theatre for Women in Post-World War II Italy A Stage of Their Own* (London: Palgrave); on the visual arts and specifically on Carla Lonzi see Francesco Ventrella and Giovanna Zapperi, eds, 2021, *Feminism and art in postwar Italy: The legacy of Carla Lonzi* (London: Bloomsbury).
27. Started in 1977 and aired on the second channel, it was conceived and hosted by a group of women and dealt with issues and news with a feminist agenda. Other than Tilde Capomazza, the editor-in-chief of the programme, *Si dice donna* was developed by a team of feminist journalists and filmmakers like Daniela Colombo, Sofia Scandurra, Annamaria Guadagni and Alessandra Bocchetti.
28. Although some projects had been approved and the women who worked in RAI acquired greater autonomy and respect within the company, also thanks to their increasing unionisation, the overall situation continued to be difficult owing to internal bureaucracy and the persistence of a male top management not sensitive

to the agenda of the feminist filmmakers. Cf. Marina Magaldi, 1981, 'Una voce di uomo doppiava i nostri servizi', *Quotidiano Donna* 4, no. 6 (20 March): 10.
29. The stages of the debate in parliament are reconstructed in Belmonti et al. 1981, 101–8.
30. See for instance the manual by Roberto Faenza, 1973, *Senza chiedere permesso. Come rivoluzionare l'informazione* (Milan: Feltrinelli).

CHAPTER 12

Feminist Spaces and Knowledge Exchange: Adriana Monti's Archive

Before leaving for Toronto in the mid-1990s, the filmmaker, activist and educator Adriana Monti donated a collection of her films and working papers to the Luigi Micheletti Foundation, a research institute for contemporary history based in Brescia. Nobody studied this archive until 2007, when the director Alina Marazzi recuperated and digitalised some of Monti's experimental Super 8 reels for *Vogliamo anche le rose* (We want roses too, 2007).[1] In collaboration with the editor Ilaria Fraioli, Marazzi worked with Monti and re-edited some unfinished footage present in the archive, giving new life and a new audience to the material (Dall'Asta et al. 2016, 122–6). Though resulting from an idea of Marazzi, this collaboration is symptomatic of Monti's inclination to collaborative work, an aspect of her filmmaking that intersects with her political trajectory. Indeed, between the 1970s and the 1980s, Monti took part in several experiences of grass-roots feminist activism in Milan which reflected, at different levels, the evolution of the feminist movement more broadly. In the early 1970s, she joined the Milanese group of Lotta Femminista (Feminist Struggle, LF), and then took part in the separatist Gruppo dell'Inconscio (Group of the Unconscious), and in the 1980s, while continuing her career as filmmaker, she founded the experimental film school Albedo.

This chapter provides an archive-based reconstruction of the different phases of Monti's political engagement and cinematic work, focusing on her political practice and her films. The archive reflects both these aspects by means of a heterogeneous array of sources, including audio-visual materials (16mm, 8mm, U-Matic, VHS), pamphlets, personal correspondence, film festival catalogues, production plans, technical brochures, teaching notes, press cuttings, film reviews. This documentation hasn't been catalogued or reorganised since the filmmaker moved to Canada, and the materials are still preserved following the inventory that the filmmaker left at the Foundation. Like Mara Blasetti, Adriana Monti decided autonomously to make them accessible to the public, so my goal is to interrogate this powerful act of self-historicisation by offering a narrative that puts together Monti's individual trajectory with the collective history of feminist politics and filmmaking. This reconstruction has also benefited from the dialogue, via Skype and email, with the filmmaker, who has responded to my questions with generosity.

Given its comprehensive and heterogeneous nature, this archive gives access to an experience of feminist filmmaking that is not documented in feminist magazines like *Effe* and *Quotidiano Donna*, or in other collective publications of the late 1970s like the *Almanacco* and *Lessico Politico delle donne*.[2] As such, Monti's experience enables the recuperation of a creative and political trajectory developed in a city, Milan, where the presence of the audio-visual industry was significantly different from how it was in Rome, and where the cinema had a different position in the reflections of local feminist collectives. Monti's production, indeed, was initially developed individually, then in collaboration with activists with similar interests, and subsequently relied on her direct involvement in Milanese film institutions.

Monti's films and political history reveal the existence of a path of feminist filmmaking that differs significantly from those explored in the previous chapter, while the biographical approach of this section provides access to an insider and situated perspective. For all these reasons, the chapter follows a chronological order, splitting in two main sections: the first concentrates on the 1970s, and specifically on Monti's militancy in LF, and the Gruppo dell'Inconscio (Group of the Unconscious), including her participation in the 150-hours educational programme; the second part focuses on the years she worked at the experimental film school Albedo, the conference 'Italian and American Directions: Women's film Theory and Practice' (New York, 1984), and her experience as film critic for *Ragazza In* (1985–6). These examples reflect well the political transition of the Milanese groups from the second-wave movement to the 'femminismo diffuso' (diffused feminism) phase of the 1980s (Calabró and Grasso 2004).

Lotta Femminista and the 150 Hours: Filming Women's Work and Community

Monti's beginnings with cinema date back to 1971, when she enrolled at the Civica scuola di cinema Luchino Visconti (Municipal School of Cinema) to obtain a diploma in film editing.[3] She soon took her first job as assistant editor with Carla Simoncelli, and worked in few productions with the Italian Swiss broadcaster, Televisione Svizzera Italiana, while she continued to work as a fashion designer at a Milanese factory to ensure herself a stable income.

In the same period, Monti joined the feminist collective LF, which was part of the network of the Wages for Housework campaign. LF used to meet at the Palazzina Liberty, a space managed by Dario Fo and Franca Rame, where the group discussed politics and shared creative ideas for the promotion of their initiatives. In this context, Monti, Chiara Gamba, Franca Geri and Grazia Zerman put together an audio-visual show in support of the campaign against the referendum for the repeal of divorce in 1974. The filmmaker remembers that this show consisted of a series of 'common images, images of politicians ... a sort of found footage film with public images' accompanied by a political text, which was a big success: 'the women's movement used it a lot, because it talked about the depression in the households and within the family, illustrating the devaluation of women's work'.[4] The portability and flexibility of the show suited well the practical needs of the activists, who could set up projections in factories, schools and other public spaces, without using expensive equipment,[5] an aspect that resonates with the rest of LF's creative practice, consisting of political songs and short plays that could be performed publicly and collectively at the demonstrations.[6]

This early phase evidently influenced Monti's approach to cinema, which ultimately went beyond her work as professional editor, with her first Super 8 films. A good example of this phase is *Le casalinghe di via Plinio* (The housewives of via Plinio, 1976), which shows, with scrupulous attention, the gestures of two women hanging up the laundry on their balconies, emphasising the repetition and the everydayness of this work. This analytical approach is also evident in the Super 8 *Il piacere del testo* (The pleasure of the text, 1978), a 'visual supplement' of the journal *A Zig Zag*,[7] in which Monti films an assembly, with a group of women sitting in a circle looking at each other, taking notes, smoking and debating, and the camera observing in great detail their expressions and gestures. At the same time, the audio track, which consisted of background noises, including those of the editing machine, emphasises Monti's analytical approach to the images. The audio-visual show and the Super 8 films, then, highlighted different aspects of women's work, from the isolated dimension of housekeeping to the collective experience of consciousness raising. This change in her subjects reflected Monti's engagement with the Group of the Unconscious and her progressive abandonment of LF. Particularly emblematic of this phase is the film *Scuola senza fine* (School without end, 1979–83), a project born within the group of women who participated in the '150 hours' educational programme designed by the Gruppo dell'Inconscio activists.[8] This curriculum was especially aimed at female workers and housewives, and introduced moments of *autocoscienza*, as well as a writing class, body awareness laboratories, photography and film analysis (Bruno and Nadotti 1988, 101–7).[9] Monti, who was also a teacher, started to bring a Super 8 at the school, attracting the interest of the students and her colleagues.[10] The casual introduction of the camera led eventually, in 1979, to the project of the collective film *Scuola senza fine*, whose structure reflects its difficult production process. The film indeed is split into two sections, one filmed collectively with the students and teachers that illustrates the 150 hours initiative, and a second, more experimental, focusing on visual reconstructions of the writings of participants in the 'Women and writing' class.[11] This latter part was directed almost entirely by Adriana Monti, who was eventually left alone with the unfinished project to edit.[12] She eventually completed the film on her own in 1983, borrowing equipment from the film cooperative Albedo Cinematografica, that she had joined in 1981 in order to start the project of an experimental film school designed with another '150 hours' teacher, Giulia (Bundi) Alberti.

After learning about the difficulties of *Scuola senza fine*, I asked Monti if she had in mind a specific audience for this film, and she replied: 'No. I didn't think of any particular destination, the thing that pushes me to make films is that nobody tells these stories, and I think someone has to tell them, so . . .'[13] She also remembers, with a note of disappointment, that the lack of support from the other women concurred with the scarce resonance of *School Without End*, a question that she also links with the difficulties experienced later, when attempting to get funding for a feature film.[14] In her view, the problem was not only the absence of producers willing to support films made by women, but also that women didn't go to see women's films. Monti explains this as women's struggle to abandon male culture, a problem that she has analysed in feminist groups for many years in her work on the unconscious and the symbolic.[15]

FEMINIST AGGREGATIONS: THE ALBEDO FILM SCHOOL, A CONFERENCE IN NEW YORK AND *RAGAZZA IN*

The evolution of *Scuola senza fine* from a collective project to an individual endeavour is symptomatic of the changes that were taking place within the feminist movement at the end of the 1980s. In this phase, as pointed out by Anna Rita Calabró and Laura Grasso, feminist groups began to pursue curtailed objectives and goals that responded to a more immediate and pragmatic agenda, by means of 'feminist aggregations' typical of the 'femminismo diffuso' (diffused feminism) (2004, 63). Calabró and Grasso use this expression to describe the transition from the collective dimension of the movement to smaller projects often carried out by individuals or associations, within specific fields such as academia, education and cultural promotion. The experiences reconstructed in this section give a sense of the impact of these changes in the activities of Adriana Monti, whose creative work has been much entangled with feminism and the feminist networks.

As already mentioned, in 1981 Monti joined the cooperative Albedo,[16] which approved her proposal to constitute an experimental film school funded by the European Union and the Lombardy region, to assign bursaries to the young unemployed. The school offered practical and theoretical training based on the foundations of cinema history and encouraged an analytical approach to the film text. In that context, Monti, as well as coordinating the school, led, with the help of Giulia (Bundi) Alberti, a class on feminist film analysis, insisting that the school adopt an equal admissions policy:

> In the first selection, among twenty-five selected students there was only one woman... this was not our project. Bundi and I wanted to enhance the Italian female vision, not just the dominant male one, which was raging. So, I put my foot down by quoting the Berlin film school, where by political choice, 50% of the students were women. I was the source of funding, so the selection changed radically.[17]

This fact illustrates well Monti and Alberti's intention to bring change within the structure of film training and recruitment by applying their feminist experience to a context outside of the movement.

Another example of the circumscribed nature of the feminist spaces of the 1980s is the conference organised by Giuliana Bruno and Maria Nadotti, 'Italian and American Directions: Women's film Theory and Practice', which took place in New York from 6 to 9 December 1984. This event inspired the publication of *Off Screen: Women and Film in Italy* (1988), which includes several essays by Italian feminist filmmakers, activists and critics. We have already discussed the importance of this publication, so here I would rather focus on the impact and relevance of the conference, in which Monti not only presented her films, but also took part as 'secretary and coordinator' in its preparatory stages.[18] The event consisted of a series of panel discussions with both Anglo-American and Italian feminist theorists and filmmakers, such as Yvonne Raider, Laura Mulvey, Mary Ann Doane, Judith Mayne, Annabella Miscuglio, Gabriella Rosaleva, Adriana Monti, Giovanna Grignaffini, Giulia (Bundi) Alberti, Paola Melchiori, Lucilla Albano and Lea Melandri. The conference also included a composite programme of film screenings – held at the Kitchen art centre, with experimental films and videotapes as well as full-length features like Giovanna Gagliardo's *Maternale* (1978). Other than *Scuola senza fine*, Monti screened *Frammenti per sé* (Fragments for the self, 1984),[19] a video originated from the training class *Donne e cinema* (Women and Cinema, 1980–3) organised for 150 hours teachers and ideated by Monti with Bundi Alberti.[20] However, after the conference, which was conceived, not by chance, by two Italian feminists who worked between Italy and the US, the transatlantic dialogue somehow stopped. Albeit the legacy of the derived publication is indisputable, it hasn't been translated into Italian, and therefore its dissemination in the peninsula was limited mostly to specialist and academic circles. This fact in itself doesn't erase the importance of the conference and the innovative project at its base, yet it highlights the absence of structures in Italy to repeat that experience, as well as the fragmentation of the feminist networks of the 1980s.

In the same year as the conference, Monti was working as assistant director for Luigi Comencini's mini tv-series *Cuore*, but at the end of that experience she was unemployed. As such, her friend Lea Melandri, who at the time was penning the agony column *Inquietudini* (Relentless)[21] in the girl's magazine *Ragazza In*,[22] put Monti in contact with editors who needed someone to write about films. Monti's archive holds several drafts of film reviews, and a couple of articles about relationships and reports about teenagers, which she wrote using a pseudonym, Gloria Maffei. She reviewed blockbusters like *The Goonies* and *Rambo*, but also Italian comedies like Carlo Verdone's *Troppo forte* (Great! 1986), classics like Federico Fellini's *Ginger e Fred* (Ginger and Fred, 1986) and films directed by women like Agnes Varda's *Sans Toit ni Loi* (Vagabond, 1985) and Susan Seidelman's *Desperately Seeking Susan*, whom she had met at the New York conference. Monti's reviews are written with wit and simplicity, emphasising the pleasurable and entertaining aspects of cinema going, trying to look at the film from a teenager's perspective. Melandri and Monti's work for this popular magazine was in line with the elaborations of the Milanese groups, and specifically of the Gruppo dell'Inconscio, which concentrated on the specificity of women's writing, and its ability to express what Melandri calls the *fuori tema* (off-topic), the desires and tensions that derive from the ordinary experience of everyday life.[23] Specifically, in her reviews, Monti tried to combine the interests of her readership with her (feminist) ideas about cinema, art and girlhood. In this respect, her experience is a good example of *femminismo diffuso*, to the extent that two feminists, out of economic necessity and by their individual writings, circulated their feminist ideas among an audience that didn't engage with politics, and who possibly didn't know about feminism at all.

Conclusions

Adriana Monti's archive has guided us through a variety of political and creative experiences that reflect the evolution of the feminist movement, and the complicated positioning of an activist and filmmaker within the Italian feminist space, as well as in the precarious context of the film industry. The development of her personal cinematic vision went hand in hand with her activism, leading to experiments in film education and attempts to introduce feminist topics within non-activist structures, like the Albedo and the magazine *Ragazza In*. This archive also teaches us the importance of looking through and beyond the film to retrace the complex entanglement of creative expression and activism in feminist filmmaking. As explored in the previous chapter, political, economic and productive (infra)structures heavily influenced women's opportunities to make films. Monti's archive illuminates the extreme fragmentation and precariousness of the feminist networks of the 1980s, making an exploration of the characters and legacies of *diffused feminism* urgent. This latter project is certainly a compelling one, if we want to understand the trends that followed the 1970s. This means challenging a narrative located in the 1980s – simply, the ending of the second-wave movement, or a moment of *riflusso* and backlash: as we have seen through Monti's experience, feminist ideas and agendas continued to circulate and be carried out, although the practices and spaces of politics had inevitably changed.

Notes

1. Specifically, Marazzi digitalised the films *Ciclo continuo* (Continuous cycle, n.d.), *Bagagli* (Luggage, 1981) and *Il piacere del testo* (The pleasure of the text, 1977). Marazzi's film reconstructs the history of the Italian second-wave movement, drawing on three personal diaries and assembling old footage and animation.
2. Indeed, Monti's work is mostly known thanks to Giuliana Bruno and Maria Nadotti's book *Off Screen* (1988), which prevalently focuses on one of her films, *Scuola senza fine* (School without end).
3. The school was founded in 1952. In 1960 it was acquired by the municipality of Milan, and until 1980 it offered only evening and weekend classes. This is important, because at the time of her enrolment Monti had a daytime job.
4. Adriana Monti, Interview with the author, 4 June 2019.
5. The visual montage was eventually dismantled after the campaign, but the text accompanying the images was published by an independent feminist publisher linked to the Wages for Housework campaigners based in Mestre and Padua, and reached a broader circulation. The text accompanying the visual show was published in Chiara Gamba, Franca Geri, Adriana Monti, Grazia Zerman, 1975, *Siamo tante siamo donne siamo stufe!* (Padua: Collettivo editoriale femminista).
6. Traces of these creative practices are present in Lotta Femminista's archive, donated by Mariarosa Dalla Costa to the public library of Padua. For an introduction to the archive see Mariarosa Dalla Costa, 2015, 'Introduction to the Archive of Feminist Struggle for wages for housework'. Donation by Mariarosa Dalla Costa, *Viewpoint Magazine*. Available at https://viewpointmag.com/2015/10/31/introduction-to-the-archive-of-the-feminist-struggle-for-wages-for-housework-donated-by-mariarosa-dalla-costa/, accessed 21 December 2020. See also the

pictures in Mariarosa Dalla Costa and Camille Barbagallo (eds), 2019, *Women and the Subversion of the Community: A Mariarosa Dalla Costa Reader*, PM Press.
7. This publication collected texts stemming from a consciousness-raising group on the theme 'Sexuality and the Symbolic'. Gruppo Sulla Scrittura e la Sessualità 1978 (*A Zig Zag*).
8. The 150-hours was a scheme introduced in 1973 that gave workers 150 hours' paid leave to attend classes and obtain a middle school diploma. The scheme was a big achievement of the workers' movement, and also became an important laboratory for democratic pedagogy, which also attracted a considerable number of female students. Lesley Caldwell, 1983, 'Courses for Women: The Example of the 150 Hours in Italy', *Feminist Review*, no. 14 (Summer): 71–83. This article also includes reproductions of original promotional materials of the Affori classes, which elaborated on the popular format of the photoromance.
9. The programme, held in a middle school of the popular neighbourhood of Affori, was so successful that it was repeated until the mid 1980s, with many students asking to continue beyond the statutory 150 hours. In order to obtain funding for the continuation of the programme, students and teachers subsequently founded the Gervasia Broxson cooperative.
10. For instance, Monti filmed the body awareness class with the Super 8. Part of this footage is in Monti's archive, and has been digitalised by Marazzi.
11. The students and teachers who took part in the project were Amalia Molinari, Rina Aprile, Antonia Daddato, Lea Melandri, Ada Flaminio, Teresa Paset, Micci Toniolo, Paola Mattioli and Maria Martinotti. Persistent economic and technical issues eventually hampered the completion of the project, which almost reached a dead end after a group of women working at Rai in Rome visited the school and saw some of the footage, judging its style and intentions outdated. Adriana Monti, Interview with the author, 4 June 2019.
12. The year 1979 was also a turning point for Monti's creative development, as she had the opportunity to go to the Edinburgh Film Festival. This experience also impacted the visual style of *Scuola senza fine* as well: '[At] the Edinburgh Film Festival I got my fill of North American and North European feminist cinema, and this actually changed my image of feminist cinema a bit. In Italy we had RAI as an example, with a group of women who did a good job, but not interesting enough in my opinion. Instead, this Neapolitan group, the Nemesiache, did interesting things in their lunacy. 1979 gave me a more international dimension of women's cinema and from there came ideas for [the second part of the film]'. Adriana Monti, Interview with the author, 4 June 2019.
13. Adriana Monti, Interview with the author, 4 June 2019.
14. Monti made only a full-length feature film in 1998, *Gentili signore* (White lady).
15. Adriana Monti, Interview with the author, 4 June 2019.
16. Preserved in Monti's archive are all the papers referring to the school's programme and selection criteria.
17. Adriana Monti, email exchange with the author, 21 November 2020.

18. Letter from Giuliana Bruno and Maria Nadotti to Adriana Monti, 25 October 1984, Adriana Monti Archive, Folder 3.
19. Specifically, the film consisted of seven parts, put together by Monti into a single film: *La memoria e la vita* by Anna Piemonte; *Il pieno della sguardo* by Paola Melchiori; *Desiderio senza fine* by Giulia (Bundi) Alberti; *Andante can mala* by Maria Rosario Uribe; *Interno/esterno* by Gabriella Buora; *Tracce sulla pelle incantata* by Adriana Monti; *A volte un'emozione* by Nella Papa.
20. The class consisted of collective screenings followed by the analysis of the film, and a practical assignment in which each participant had to put together the images from the films that had the biggest impact on them. Born as research and working materials, *Frammenti per sé* (Fragments for the self, 1984) is the result of a collective work of analysis about the specificity of women's spectatorship, which Monti subsequently put together in a single videotape.
21. A selection of the letters has been published in Lea Melandri, 1992, *La mappa del cuore. Lettere di adolescenti a un giornale femminile* (Rubettino: Soveria-Mannelli). A new edition of this book will be published in 2021, following the success of the theatrical play inspired by Melandri's column ideated by the art collective Ateliersi of Bologna.
22. The style and format of this magazine can be compared to the UK teen weekly *Jackie* and the US *Seventeen*. Like these publications, *Ragazza In* included several articles about music and film stars, advice on relationships and sexuality, 'how-to' articles, and popular photoromances.
23. Melandri's exploration of the off topic is in Lea Melandri, 2017, *Alfabeto d'origine* (Vicenza: Neri Pozza).

Conclusion – Feminist Film Culture(s): Collectivities, Archives and Futures

In this book, women occupy multiple positions: they are spectators, fictional characters, actresses and directors, as well as activists and practitioners. Personal beliefs, class, sexual orientation and race concur to shape these positions, participating in a very precarious collectivity that reflects a scattered, contradictory and imperfect feminist film culture. Similarly, the archives explored and assembled throughout the book organise, disperse and omit information in a complex and contradictory fashion.

To make sense of these heterogeneous and magmatic histories, I have followed Iris Marion Young invitation to adopt 'pragmatic theorisation', an approach that understands women as a non-essentialist, multifaceted collectivity, rejecting neo-liberal individualism as a political solution and epistemic stance (Young 1994). The empirical nature of archival research, indeed, is a powerful tool for 'pragmatic theorising' as it acknowledges plurality and potentially asks for collaborative and accountable scholarship. The case studies analysed in this book aim at the exploration and assemblage of new archives, methodologies and paths of inquiry in clear opposition to essentialist and individualistic notions of women and research. For this reason, in conclusion to this project, I am going to suggest some pathways for future investigation and make some reflections on the many meanings of 'pragmatic theorising' within the framework of an archive-based project.

ARCHIVES AND HISTORIES AS 'AFFECTIVE CODES'

In the first two chapters of the book, I explored the role of women in the cinema audiences of the 1950s and 1960s and investigated how media and cultural consumption participated in the gendering of the public and the private sphere. To do so, I analysed both popular magazines and quantitative sources, which provided complementary and sometimes contradictory information, and pictured women as an imagined collectivity reflecting specific ideological and cultural projects. However, such images and practices didn't always find correspondence in the materiality of women's lives and their experiences with cinema. This is particularly evident in women's magazines, whose ideologically and emotionally bounded discourses on femininity and film spectatorship were often at odds with the perspectives and aspirations of the readers. These sources, then, are marked by an 'affective code' that recalls Richard Dyer's considerations on entertainment and utopia (Dyer 1992): the porous affective dimension of the women's magazines, then, offers a key to understanding the ways in which women negotiated their collective and individual position in popular culture, asking us to come to terms with the opacity of archival materials.

HISTORICISING THROUGH SENSORY ENCOUNTERS

There are some continuities between the 'affective code' of the women's magazines and cinema audiences, and the collectivities pictured in the activist sources surveyed in Chapters 3, 4 and 5. In the feminist archives of the 1970s, popular culture and cinema continued to offer invaluable sites for community building and imagination, but they were also sources of concern and conflict. Indeed, most of the activist histories emerging in these chapters are marked by sentiments of anger and despair, feelings that arise from the experience of patriarchal oppression, in which I can find myself too. At the same time, paraphrasing Audre Lorde, it was evident that when these women expressed and translated their anger into action, anger became an invaluable source of information and political energy (Lorde 1981). To better understand this shift in women's relationship with popular culture, in its emotional and political implications, I adopted a 'sensory approach' to my research materials. By borrowing and adapting the methodological tools suggested by Sarah Pink's work on 'sensory ethnography' (Pink 2015) I reflected on these activist materials 'as evocative of the research encounter through which they were produced and of the embodied knowledge they involved' (Pink 2015, 144). This also meant understanding anger and disappointment as inevitable aspects of feminist research, as a source of information and political traction that has a legitimate space in the analysis of the archival materials and at the moment of writing.

MAKING SENSE OF OUR EPISTEMOLIGICAL LIMITATIONS

Indeed, we should take seriously and engage with the emotional implications, for the feminist researcher, of dealing with archival materials originated in or reacting to experiences of gender violence, misogyny, racism and homophobia. Working on this project, and subsequently writing this book, made me aware that my emotional engagement with these archives has increased, rather than compromised, my understanding of the archival materials. This is especially true of the section about representation (Part II), which posed me several methodological and theoretical challenges. Analysing the comedies of the 1960s, reconstructing the experience of Ines Pellegrini, and studying Federico Fellini's *City of Women* were, for different reasons, emotionally charged research encounters. In many instances, the gendered meanings I was reconstructing exceeded the boundaries of the film text, whose evidence left little room for a feminist reading, while the historical reconstructions made evident the epistemological limitations of historical feminist debates. These limitations pushed me to find a different interpretative framework within and beyond the archives, forcing me to interrogate the opportunities of anachronism, while balancing out my primary objective of providing an accurate historical reconstruction.

Beyond Absence: Propositions for a New Research Culture

Emotion and imagination can help us in reading through the opacities and omissions in the archives, encouraging a productive engagement with the limitations of our theoretical frameworks. However, as the section about women in the film industry demonstrates, there are absences and limitations that could be fixed only by retracing and assembling new archives. To this extent, it is important to confront issues of access and visibility. I have conducted this research individually, yet it has also been, in a way, a collective endeavour. I have talked and discussed with dozens of researchers, archivists, librarians and activists about my findings, and only thanks to their generous testimonies and support have I been able to complete this book. At the same time, the lack of funding, infrastructure and support from many others has made this project something closer to a struggle than a 'simple' study. In a way, I am grateful to these obstacles and objections, as they gave me the opportunity to understand the meanings and importance of conflict in my research, but they also reminded me of the marginality and precarious space for feminist scholarship in Italian film studies.

A research culture based on values such as collegiality and collaboration, one that is willing to commit to a long-term project of valorisation, digitalisation and networking of existent archives would help to fix these issues at least in part, attracting to archival research a wider community of scholars, including more feminists and other marginalised folks. Open-access projects in digital humanities like the media history digital library Lantern,[1] and the Women Film Pioneers Project go precisely in this direction. Such tools can't replace the pleasures and strengths of 'analogue' archival research, but could certainly overcome some of its limitations, like the fetishisation of the 'discovery' of rare documents and the high costs for travelling and digital reproduction that are untenenable for students and precarious researchers. Drawing on these experiences, then, I am calling for a research culture that rejects the individualistic and romanticised ideal of the solitary researcher to prioritise access, relationships and accountability. Indeed, as long as archival sources remain difficult to access and study, especially for some of us, it will be also difficult to improve our scholarship and narratives. This is certainly a particularly compelling issue for feminist researchers, but a more sustainable and accessible scholarship must be a priority for the whole community of film researchers out there.

Note

1. See Lantern's Media History Digital Library, an open-access international collection of digitalised film magazines, available at https://lantern.mediahist.org/, accessed 5 May 2021.

Works Cited

A.M. 1959. 'Due soluzioni', *Cosí* 5, no. 15 (12 April): 3.
AA.VV. 1977. *Io sono mia*. Florence: Guaraldi.
Adelina. 1960. 'Alla mia età è vietato vedere spettacoli per adulti?' *Famiglia Cristiana* 30, no. 14 (3 April): 6.
Ahmed, Sara. 2010. *The Promise of Happiness*. Durham, NC and London: Duke University Press.
Ahmed, Sara. 2017. *Living a Feminist Life*. Durham, NC: Duke University Press.
Alberti, Bundi Giulia. 1980. 'La donna nel sistema di significazione', in Rony Daopoulo and Annabella Miscuglio (eds), *Kinomata. La donna nel cinema*, 37–53. Bari: Dedalo.
Almanacco. 1978. *L'Almanacco. Luoghi, nomi, incontri, fatti, lavori in corso del Movimento femminista italiano dal 1972*. Rome: Edizioni delle donne.
Altea, Giuliana. 2019. 'Con Papà. Creatività, domesticità e dinamiche familiari nella vicenda di Luce ed Elica Balla', in Monica Farnetti and Giuliana Ortu (eds), *L'eredità di Antigone. Sorelle e sorellanza nelle letterature, nel teatro, nelle arti e nella politica*, 359–76, Florence: Franco Cesati Editore.
Andreazza, Fabio. 2019. 'Il culto della patria, del littorio e della decima musa. Nazionalismo e cosmopolitismo negli allievi del CSC (1935–1938)', in Stefania Parigi, Christian Uva and Vito Zagarrio (eds), *Cinema e identità italiana*, 67–74. Rome: Roma Tre Press.
Anon. 1979. 'E . . . a proposito della produzione', *Quotidiano Donna 2*, no. 27 (4 July): 7.
Aprà, Adriano and Adriano Carabba. 1976. *Neorealismo d'appendice. Per un dibattito sul cinema popolare: il caso Matarazzo*. Rimini: Guaraldi.
Arvidsson, Adam. 2003. *Marketing Modernity: Italian Advertising from Fascism to Postmodernity*. London: Routledge.
Aspesi, Natalia. 2017. 'Weinstein, Natalia Aspesi: Se mi chiedi un massaggio in ufficio e io te lo concedo, poi non mi posso stupire su come va a finire', *Vanity Fair*, https://www.vanityfair.it/news/approfondimenti/2017/10/11/weinstein-commento-natalia-aspesi, accessed 16 December 2020.
Avalli, Ippolita (1979), 'Il bene da una parte il male dall'altra: come siete categoriche!', *Quotidiano Donna*, 11 July.
Baldi, Alfredo. 2010. '"Tutti in tuta bleu", Cronache del CSC (1934–1945)', *Bianco e Nero* 566.
Banks, Miranda. 2018. 'Production Studies', *Feminist Media Histories* 4, no. 2 (April): 157–61.
Barina, Antonella, Elena Castagni, Moira Miele and Maria Pia Toscano. 1977. 'Autodocenza: università in disfunzione della donna', *Effe* 5, no. 9 (September): 25–8.
Baschiera, Stefano and Francesco Di Chiara. 2011. 'Once Upon a Time in Italy: Transnational Features of Genre Production, 1960s–1970s', *Film International* 8, no. 6: 30–9.
Bayman, Louis. 2014. *The Operatic and the Everyday in Post-war Italian Melodrama*. Edinburgh: Edinburgh University Press.

Bellassai, Sandro. 2011. *L'invenzione della virilità. Politica e immaginario maschile nell'Italia contemporanea*. Bologna: Il Mulino.

Bellumori, Cinzia. 1972. *Le donne del cinema contro questo cinema*. Rome: Edizioni Bianco e Nero.

Belmonti M. G., A. Carini, R. Daopoulo, P. De Martiis and Annabella Miscuglio. 1981. *Veronique. La vera storia di A.A.A. Offresi*. Milan: Sperling & Kupfer.

Ben-Ghiat, Ruth. 2001. *Fascist Modernities: Italy 1922–1945*. Berkeley: University of California Press.

Berlant, Lauren. 2008. *The Female Complaint: The Unfinished Business of Sentimentality in American Culture*. Durham, NC, London: Duke University Press.

Bettini, Betty, ed. 1978. *Lessico Politico delle donne. Teorie del femminismo*, Vol. 3. Milan: Gulliver.

Biagini, Elena. 2018. *L'emersione imprevista: il movimento delle lesbiche in Italia negli anni '70 e '80*. Pisa Edizioni: ETS.

Bisoni, Claudio. 2009. *Gli anni affollati. La cultura cinematografica (1970–1979)*. Roma: Carocci.

Bondanella, Peter. 1992. *The Cinema of Federico Fellini*. Princeton, NJ: Princeton University Press.

Bonifazio, Paola. 2020. *The Photoromance: A Feminist Reading of Popular Culture*. Cambridge, MA, London: MIT University Press.

Bono, Paola and Sandra Kemp. 1991. *Italian Feminist Thought: A Reader*. Oxford: Blackwell.

Boyle, Karen. 2005. *Media and Violence: Gendering the Debate*. London: Sage.

Bracke, Maud Anne. 2014. *Women and the Reinvention of the Political: Feminism in Italy, 1968–1983*. New York, London: Routledge.

Brancati Daniela. 2011. *Occhi di maschio. Le donne e la televisione in Italia: una storia dal 1954 a oggi*. Rome: Donizelli.

Brasi, Anna and Fausta Gabrielli. 1979. 'Regia/Ruolo', in Adelaide Frabotta (ed.), *Lessico Politico delle donne*, Vol. 6: 42–51.

Brigate Saffo. 1978. 'TV secondo canale', in *Brigate Saffo*, insert of *Lambda* 3, nos. 18–19 (November–December): 1–3.

Bronstein, Carolyn. 2011. *Battling Pornography: The American Feminist Anti-Pornography Movement, 1976–1986*. New York: Cambridge University Press.

Brosio, Valentino. 1956. *Manuale del produttore di film*. Rome: Edizioni dell'ateneo.

Bruno, Giuliana and Maria Nadotti. 1988. *Off Screen: Women & Film in Italy*. London, New York: Routledge.

Buffoni, Laura, ed. 2018. *We Want Cinema. Sguardi di donne nel cinema italiano*. Venice: Marsilio.

Buhle, Mary Jo.1998. *Feminism and its Discontents: A Century of Struggle with Psychoanalysis*. Cambridge, MA: Harvard University Press.

Buonanno, Milly. 1978. *La donna nella stampa. Giornaliste, lettrici e modelli di femminilità*. Rome: Editori Riuniti.

Buonanno, Milly and Franca Faccioli. 2020. *Genere e media. Non solo immagini: soggetti, politiche, rappresentazioni*. Milano: Angeli.

Burke, Frank. 2002. 'Federico Fellini: Reality/Representation/Signification', in Frank Burke and Marguerite R. Waller (eds), *Federico Fellini: Contemporary Perspectives*, 26–46. Toronto: University of Toronto Press.

Bursi, Giulio. 2010. 'Inquadrare la materia. Tracce di un metodo pedagogico', *Bianco & Nero*, no. 566 (January–April): 52–7.

Calabró, Anna Rita and Laura Grasso. 2004. *Dal movimento femminista al femminismo diffuso: storie e percorsi a Milano dagli anni '60 agli anni '80*. Milan: Franco Angeli.

Caldwell, John Thornton. 2008. *Production Culture: Industrial Reflexivity and Critical Practice in Film and Television*. Durham, NC: Duke University Press.

Cambria, Adele. 1973. 'Un antifemminista al mese: Federico Fellini', *Effe 1* (December).

Cambria, Adele. 1979a. 'Luci rosse per il manifesto', *Quotidiano Donna* 2, no. 44, 12 December.
Cambria, Adele.1979b. 'L'ultimo Fellini vuole svendere il femminismo', *Quotidiano Donna* 2, no. 26 (27 June): 24–5.
Cambria, Adele. 2010. *Nove dimissioni e mezzo: le guerre quotidiane di una giornalista ribelle*. Rome: Donizelli.
Cami-Vela, María. 2009. 'Entre la esperanza y el desencanto. El cine militante de Helena Lumbreras', in María Ruído (eds), *Plan Rosebud: sobre imágenes, lugares y políticas de memoria*, 543–54, Galicia: Xunta de Galicia/Centro Gallego de Arte Contemporáneo.
Cantini, Maristella. ed. 2013. *Italian Women Filmmakers and the Gendered Screen*. Basingstoke: Palgrave Macmillan.
Cantore, Francesca and Giulia Muggeo. 2021. 'Federico Fellini and the debate in Italian feminist magazines (1973-80)', *Journal of Italian Cinema & Media Studies* 9, no. 1 (January): 45–62.
Cardone, Lucia. 2004. *Con lo schermo nel cuore. Grand Hôtel e il cinema (1946–1956)*. Pisa: ETS.
Cardone, Lucia. 2009. *Noi donne e il cinema: dalle illusioni a Zavattini (1944–1954)*. Pisa: ETS.
Cardone, Lucia and Sara Filippelli, eds. 2015. *Filmare il femminismo. Studi sulle donne nel cinema e nei media*. Pisa: ETS.
Care Collective. 2020. *The Care Manifesto*. London: Verso.
Carrano, Patrizia. 1977. *Malafemmina. La donna nel cinema italiano*. Florence: Guaraldi.
Cassamagnaghi, Silvia. 2007. *Immagini dall'America. Mass media e modelli femminili nell'Italia del secondo dopoguerra, 1945–1960*. Milan: Franco Angeli.
Cavallaro, Daniela. 2007. 'The making of a feminist film: Sofia Scandurra's Io sono mia', *Studies in European Cinema* 4, no. 3: 199–209.
Cavarocchi, Francesca. 2010. 'Orgoglio e pregiudizio. Note sul movimento gay e lesbico italiano', *Zapruder. Storie in movimento*, no. 21: 75–86.
Centro di Documentazione Donna di Padova. 1976a. *Effe* 4, nos 7–8 (July): 46.
Centro di Documentazione Donna di Padova. 1976b. 'Autoadesivi per noi', *Effe* 4, no. 12 (December): 45.
Cerankowski, Karli June and Megan Milks. 2010. 'New Orientations: Asexuality and Its Implications for Theory and Practice', *Feminist Studies* 36, no. 3: 650–64.
Chandler, Charlotte. 1995. *Io, Federico Fellini*. Milan: Mondadori.
Chironi, Daniela. 2019. 'Generations in the Feminist and LGBT Movements in Italy: The Case of *Non Una Di Meno*', *American Behavioral Scientist* 63, no. 10 (March): 1469–96.
CIF (Centro Italiano Femminile). 1977. *La donna e il cinema 1974–1975: indagine di analisi di contenuto*. Rome: Arti Grafiche Iasillo.
Cine Foro. 1965. 'Noticias', *Cine Foro. Revista Oficial Cine Club de Viña del Mar* 1, no. 5: 27.
Cinema. 1940. 'Marisa Romano', *Cinema. Quindicinale di divulgazione cinematografica* 5, no. 93 (10 May): 312.
Cinema Illustrazione. 1937. 'Dorothy Azner non é', *Cinema Illustrazione* 12, no. 47: 10.
CLI (Collegamento tra Lesbiche Italiane).1992. *Femminismo e Lesbismo. Incontro con Teresa de Lauretis*. Rome: Self published.
CoDis. 1962. *Il cinema e il suo pubblico. Indagine statistica e ricerca motivazionale sulla validità pubblicitaria del mezzo cinematografico*. S.l.: S.n.
Comand, Maria Pia. 2010. *La commedia all'italiana*. Turin: Il Castoro.
Connell, R. W. 1997. 'Sexual Revolution', in Lynne Segal (ed.), *New Sexual Agendas*. London: Palgrave Macmillan.
Conor, Bridget, Rosalind Gill and Stephanie Taylor. 2015. 'Gender and Creative Labour: Introduction', *Sociological Review* 63, no. 1: 1–22.
Conte, Maria Stella. 1982. 'Zanzibar: qui da noi cosa vogliono?' *Effe* 10, no. 4 (April): 15–17.

Cooperativa Arcobaleno. 1977. 'Cinque storie de L'arcobaleno', *Effe* 5, no. 4 (April): 29–30.
Cortés, María Lourdes. 2002. *El espejo imposible. Un siglo de cine en Costa Rica*. San José, Costa Rica: Farben Grupo Editorial Norma.
Cottino-Jones, Marga. 2010. *Women, Desire, and Power in Italian Cinema*. New York: Palgrave Macmillan.
Crainz, Guido. 2005. *Storia del miracolo italiano. Culture, identità, trasformazioni fra anni Cinquanta e Sessanta*. Rome: Donzelli.
Cryle, Peter and Alison Moore. 2011. *Frigidity: An Intellectual History*. Basingstoke: Palgrave Macmillan.
Cullen, Niamh. 2013. 'Morals, modern identities and the Catholic woman: fashion *Famiglia Cristiana*, 1954–1968', *Journal of Modern Italian Studies* 18, no. 1: 33–52.
Cvetkovich, Ann. 2003. *An Archive of Feelings: Trauma, Sexuality, and Lesbian Public Cultures*. Durham, NC: Duke University Press.
Dalla Costa, Mariarosa. 1972. *Women and the Subversion of the Community*. Bristol: Falling Wall Press.
Dall'Asta, Monica ed. 2008. *Non Solo Dive: Pioniere del cinema italiano*. Bologna: Cineteca di Bologna.
Dall'Asta, Monica, Barbara Grespi, Sandra Lischi and Veronica Pravadelli. 2016. 'A Politics of Intimacy: A Conversation with Alina Marazzi and Ilaria Fraioli', *Feminist Media Histories* 2, no. 3 (1 July): 119–41.
Damiens, Antoine. 2020. 'Film Festivals of the 1970s and the Subject of Feminist Film Studies: Collaborations and Regimes of Knowledge Production', *Journal of Film and Video* 72, nos 1–2 (Spring/Summer): 21–32.
Daopoulo, Rony and Annabella Miscuglio (eds), *Kinomata. La donna nel cinema*. Bari: Dedalo.
de Aloysio, Gemma. 1932. 'Sensibilità e personalità nell'ambiente moderno', *Futurismo* 1, no. 9: 6.
De Grazia, Victoria. 1992. *How Fascism Ruled Women: Italy 1922–1945*. Berkeley: University of California Press.
De Grazia, Victoria. 2005. *Irresistible Empire: America's Advance Through Twentieth-Century Europe*. Cambridge, MA: Harvard University Press.
De Lauretis, Teresa. 1987. *Technologies of Gender. Essays on Theory, Film and Fiction*. Bloomington and Indianapolis, IN: Indiana University Press.
De Lauretis, Teresa. 1993. 'Feminist Genealogies: A Personal Itinerary', *Women's Studies International Forum* 16, no. 4 (July–August): 393–403.
De Villiers, Nicholas. 2012. *Opacity and the Closet: Queer Tactics in Foucault, Barthes, and Warhol*. Minneapolis; London: University of Minnesota Press.
DEA – Donne e Audiovisivo. 2019. *Gap & Ciak: Men and Women in the Audiovisual Industry*. IRPSS. Available at https://www.irpps.cnr.it/wp-content/uploads/2017/09/DEA-rapporto-ENG-web-01-04-19-1.pdf, accessed 16 December 2020.
Derrida, Jacques. 1995. 'Archive Fever: A Freudian Impression', *Diacritics* 25, no. 2: 9–63.
Dever, Maryanne, Sally Newman and Ann Vickery. 2009. *The Intimate Archive: Journeys Through Private Papers*. Canberra: National Library of Australia.
Dominijanni, Ida. 2005. 'Rethinking the Change: Italian Feminism Between Crisis and Critique of Politics', *Cultural Studies Review* 11, no. 2 (September): 25–35.
Doxa. 1966. *Il cinema e il suo pubblico*. Milan: Doxa.
Doxa. 1977. *Il pubblico del cinema. Indagine sulle caratteristiche, abitudini, motivazioni ed aspettative del pubblico (anno 1977)*. Milan: Doxa.
Dyer, Richard. 1992. *Only Entertainment*. London: Routledge.
Dyer, Richard. 2018. *La Dolce Vita*. London: BFI, Bloomsbury.

E.M. 1981. 'Riprendiamoci la vita: A.A.A. Offresi', *Effe* 9, no. 3 (March): 6.

Effe. 1979. 'Solidarietà vuol dire . . .' *Effe* 7, nos 10–12 (October): 2.

Ehrenreich, Barbara, and Deirdre English. 2005. *For Her Own Good: Two Centuries of the Experts' Advice to Women*. New York: Anchor Books.

Eichhorn, Kate. 2010. 'DIY Collectors, Archiving Scholars, and Activist Librarians: Legitimizing Feminist Knowledge and Cultural Production Since 1990', *Women's Studies* 39, no. 6: 622–46.

Eichhorn, Kate. 2015. 'Feminism's There: On Post-ness and Nostalgia', *Feminist Theory* 16, no. 3: 251–64.

Ellsworth, Elizabeth. 1990. 'Illicit Pleasures. Feminist Spectators and Personal Best', in Patricia Erens (ed.), *Issues in Feminist Film Criticism*, 183–96. Bloomington: Indiana University Press.

Elsaesser, Thomas. 2005. *European Cinema: Face to Face with Hollywood*. Amesterdam: Amsterdam University Press.

Enciclopedia della donna. 1964. *Enciclopedia della donna. Grande enciclopedia di nozioni pratiche e di cultura generale per la donna*. Milan: Fabbri.

Europa. 1976. 'Cinema chiusi contro l'autoriduzione', *Europa*, 23 November: 3.

EWA (European Women's Audiovisual Network). 2016. *Where are the Women Directors? Report on Gender Equality for Directors in the European Film Industry 2006–2013*, https://www.ewa-women.com/wp-content/uploads/2018/09/Complete-report_compressed.pdf, accessed 20 December 2020.

EYE. 2020. Lili Rademakers. https://www.eyefilm.nl/en/collection/film-history/person/lili-rademakers, accessed 11 December 2020.

Faldini, Franka and Goffredo Fofi (eds). 1981. *L'avventurosa storia del cinema italiano raccontata dai suoi protagonisti 1961–1969* (Milan: Feltrinelli).

Faleschini-Lerner, Giovanna and Maria Elena D'Amelio, eds. 2017. *Italian Motherhood on Screen*. Basingstoke: Palgrave Macmillan.

Fanchi, Mariagrazia. 2010. '"Tra donne sole": Cinema, Cultural Consumption and the Female Condition in Post-war Italy', in Irmbert Schenk, Margrit Tröhler, and Yvonne Zimmermann (eds), *Film-Kino-Zuschauer: Filmrezeption. Film-Cinema-Spectator: Film Reception*, 305–18. Marburg: Schüren.

Federici, Silvia. 1975. *Wages Against Housework*. Bristol: Falling Wall Press.

Federici, Silvia. 2012. *Revolution at Point Zero. Housework, Reproduction and Feminist Struggle*. Oakland, CA: PM Press.

Federici, Silvia. 2018. 'On the Meaning of Gossip', in *Witches, Witch-hunting and Women*. New York: PM Press.

Fellini, Federico. 1980. *La città delle donne. Con una nota di Liliana Betti e una lettura di Andrea Zanzotto*. Milan: Garzanti.

Ferracuti, Franco, and Luigi Maria Solivetti. 1976. *La pornografia nei mezzi di comunicazione di massa con speciale riguardo alla televisione*. Turin: ERI.

Fisher, Mark. 2014. *Ghosts of My Life Writings on Depression, Hauntology and Lost Futures*. Winchester: Zero Books.

Forgacs, David. 1988. *The Gramsci Reader: Selected Writings (1916–1935)*. New York: Schocken Books.

Forgacs, David and Stephen Gundle. 2007. *Mass Culture and Italian Society from Fascism to the Cold War*. Bloomington: Indiana University Press.

Forte, Gioacchino. 1966. *I persuasori rosa. Sociologia curiosa del rotocalco femminile in Italia*. Naples: Edizioni Scientifiche Italiane.

Foucault, Michel. 1980. *The History of Sexuality*. New York: Vintage Books.

Frabotta, Adelaide, ed. 1979. *Lessico Politico delle donne. Cinema, letteratura, arti visive*, Vol. 6. Milan: Gulliver.
Fraire, Manuela. 1978–9. *Lessico politico delle donne*. Milan: Gulliver.
Franzinelli, Mimmo. 2000. *I tentacoli dell'Ovra. Agenti, collaboratori e vittime della polizia politica fascista*. Turin: Bollati Boringhieri.
Fraterrigo, Elizabeth. 2009. *Playboy and the Making of the Good Life in Modern America*. Oxford: Oxford University Press.
Freeman, Elisabeth. 2010. *Time Binds: Queer Temporalities, Queer Histories*. Durham, NC: Duke University Press.
Frontoni, Angelo. 1974a. 'Una stella dopo mille e una notte', *Playboy* 2, no. 9 (September): 41–50.
Frontoni, Angelo. 1974b. 'Macia e una notte', *Playmen* 7, no. 6 (June): 96–101.
Fullwood, Natalie. 2015. *Cinema, Gender, and Everyday Space: Comedy, Italian style*. New York: Palgrave Macmillan.
Gabrielli, Fausta. 1976. 'Essere donne nel cinema', *Donne e politica* 6, no. 34 (June): 27–9.
Gaines, Jane. 2008. '"Are They Us?": Women's Work in the Silent International Film Industries', in Monica Dall'Asta (ed.), Proceedings of the 'Non Solo Dive' Conference. Bologna: Cineteca di Bologna.
Garaguso, Patrizia and Eleonora Renzetti. 1978. *La mercificazione dell'immagine femminile nel cinema italiano 1960–71*. Trento: UNIcoop.
Garofalo, Damiano and Dalila Missero. 2018. '"Lontane da Voghera". Italian Housewives as Consumers and Spectators between Public and Private Spheres 1954–1964', *The Italianist* 38, no. 2: 174–88.
Gildea, Robert, James Mark and Anette Warring, eds. 2013. *Europe's 1968: Voices of Revolt*. Oxford: Oxford University Press.
Gill, Rosalind. 2007. 'Postfeminist Media Culture: Elements of a Sensibility', *European Journal of Cultural Studies* 10, no. 2: 147–66.
Ginsborg, Paul. 2003. *A History of Contemporary Italy: Society and Politics, 1943–1988*. New York: Palgrave Macmillan.
Giordiani, Enrico. 1980. 'Guida Gay: Roma', *Lambda* 5, no. 26 (Spring-Summer): 10–11.
Giuliani, Gaia. 2019. *Race, Nation and Gender in Modern Italy: Intersectional Representations in Visual Culture*. London: Palgrave Macmillan.
Giuliani Caponetto, Rosetta. 2012. 'Blaxploitation Italian Style: Exhuming and Consuming the Colonial Black Venus in 1970s Cinema in Italy', in Cristina Lombardi-Diop and Caterina Romeo (eds), *Postcolonial Italy: Challenging National Homogeneity*. New York: Palgrave Macmillan.
Gobbato, Emma. 2015. *Goliarda Sapienza scenggiatrice. Il caso 'I delfini' attraverso un carteggio inedito*. PhD Dissertation, University of Sassari.
Gorfinkel, Elena. 2017. *Lewd Looks: American Sexploitation Cinema in the 1960s*. Minneapolis: University of Minnesota Press.
Gramsci, Antonio. 1975. *Quaderni del carcere*. Vol. 1. Turin: Einaudi.
Grattarola, Franco and Andrea Napoli. 2014. *Luce rossa. La nascita e le prime fasi del cinema pornografico in Italia: cronaca, registi, attori, film*. Iacobelli.
Gruppo Sulla Scrittura e la Sessualità. 1978, *A zig zag: non scritti scritti*. Milan: Tipografia Celegraf.
Gundle, Stephen. 2000. *Between Hollywood and Moscow: The Italian Communists and the Challenge of Mass Culture, 1943–1991*. Durham, NC: Duke University Press.
Günsberg, Maggie. 2004. *Italian Cinema: Gender and Genre*. Basingstoke: Palgrave Macmillan.
Harding, Sandra. 1992. 'Rethinking Standpoint Epistemology: What is Strong Objectivity?' *Centennial Review* 36, no. 3: 437–70.

Harris, Jessica. 2017. '"In America è vietato essere brute": Advertising American beauty in the Italian women's magazine Annabella, 1945–1965', *Modern Italy* 22, no. 1, 35–53.

Hartsock, Nancy. 1983. 'The Feminist Standpoint: Developing the Ground for a Specifically Feminist Historical Materialism', in Sandra Harding, and M. B. Hintikka (eds), *Discovering Reality*. Dordrecht: Springer.

Heath, Theresa. 2018. 'Saving space: Strategies of Reclamation at Early Women's Film Festivals and Queer Film Festivals Today', *Studies in European Cinema* 15, no. 1, 41–5.

Hemmings, Claire. 2011. *Why Stories Matter: The Political Grammar of Feminist Theory*. Durham, NC, London: Duke University Press.

Herzog, Dagmar. 2005. *Sex After Fascism: Memory and Morality in Twentieth-Century Germany*. Princeton, NJ: Princeton University Press.

Higson, Andrew. 1989. 'The Concept of National Cinema', *Screen* 30, no. 4, October: 36–46.

Hill, Erin. 2016. *Never Done: A History of Women's Work in Media Production*. New Brunswick, New Jersey; London: Rutgers University Press.

Hipkins Danielle. 2016. *Italy's Other Women: Gender and Prostitution in Italian Cinema, 1940–1965*. Oxford, Bern, Berlin, Bruxelles, Frankfurt am Main, New York, Wien: Peter Lang.

Holdaway, Dom and Dalila Missero. 2020. 'The Neglected Spaces of Feminism and Queer in Contemporary Italian Political Cinema', in Daniel Fairfax, André Keiji Kunigami and Luca Peretti (eds), *Zapruder World: An International Journal for the History of Social Conflict* 6.

Holub, Renate. 1992. *Antonio Gramsci: Beyond Marxism and Postmodernism*. London, New York: Routledge.

Huyssen, Andreas. 1986. 'Mass Culture as Woman', in *After the Great Divide: Modernism, Mass Culture, Postmodernism*, 44–62. Bloomington: Indiana University Press.

IAD (Istituto accertamento diffusione). 1962–73. *Bollettino IAD*. Milan: s.n.

Illouz, Eva. 2007. *Cold Intimacies: The Making of Emotional Capitalism*. Cambridge: Polity.

Informaset. 1979. *Informaset: guida professionale per lo spettacolo*. Rome: Gulliver.

Kamleitner, Katherine. 2018. 'Closing the Gaps: Researching the Women's Event at the Edinburgh International Film Festival 1972', *Women's Film and Television History Network-UK/Ireland*, 27 March, available at https://womensfilmandtelevisionhistory.wordpress.com/2018/03/27/closing-the-gaps-researching-the-womens-event-at-the-edinburgh-international-film-festival-1972/, accessed 5 May 2021.

Kezich, Tullio. 1979. *Il filmsessanta: il cinema degli anni 1962–1966*. Milan: Il Formichiere.

Kipnis, Laura. 1992. '(Male) Desire and (Female) Disgust: Reading Hustler', in Lawrence Grossberg, Cary Nelson and Paula A. Treichler (eds), *Cultural Studies*. New York: Routledge.

Krutnik, Frank and Steve Neale. 1990. *Popular Film and Television Comedy*. London, New York: Routledge.

Kuhn, Annette and Jackie Stacey. 1998. 'Screen Histories: An Introduction', in *Screen Histories: A Screen Reader*. Oxford: Clarendon Press.

La Repubblica. 2018. 'Le donne del cinema italiano contro le molestie: "Contestiamo l'intero sistema"', *La Repubblica*, 1 February, https://bit.ly/3yqftil, accessed 20 May 2021.

La Stampa. 1976. 'Con un'inchiesta di Dacia Maraini tra Le ragazze di Capoverde', *La Stampa Sera*, 28 July: 6.

La Stampa. 1977. 'Le donne africane di Dacia Maraini', *La Stampa*, 30 November: 7.

L.T. 1975. 'Le donne cattoliche chideranno solidarietà di sesso alle attrici', *Corriere della Sera* (17 October): 7.

Labanyi, Jo. 2010. 'Doing Things. Emotion Affect and Materiality', *Journal of Spanish Cultural Studies* 11, nos 3–4: 223–33.

Lanaro, Silvio. 1992. *Storia dell'Italia repubblicana*. Padua: Marsilio.

Laura, Ernesto G. 1976. 'Il centro sperimentale di cinematografia. Dal fascismo allo statuto democratico', in Ernesto G. Laura (ed.), *Il CSC tra tradizione e riforma* edited by, *Bianco & Nero* 5/6 (May–June): 4–29.

Ledesma, Eduardo. 2014. 'Helena Lumbreras' *Field for Men* (1973): Midway between Latin American Third Cinema and the Barcelona School', *Studies in Spanish and Latin American Cinemas* 11, no. 3: 271–88.

Lilli, Laura. 1976. 'La stampa femminile', in *La stampa italiana del neocapitalismo*, edited by Valerio Castronovo and Nicola Tranfaglia 253–311, Rome: Laterza.

Livi, Grazia. 1965. 'L'Italia pornografica', *Epoca*, no. 754 (7 March).

Lombardi-Diop, Cristina. 2012. 'Postracial/Postcolonial Italy', in Cristina Lombardi-Diop and Caterina Romeo (eds), *Postcolonial Italy: Challenging National Homogeneity*, 175–90, New York: Palgrave Macmillan.

Longino, Helen. 1990. *Science as Social Knowledge: Values and Objectivity in Scientific Inquiry*. Princeton, NJ: Princeton University Press.

Lorde, Audre. 1981. 'The Uses of Anger', *Women's Studies Quarterly* 25, nos 1–2: 278–85.

Luciano, Bernardette and Susanna Scarparo. 2013. *Reframing Italy: New Trends in Italian Women's Filmmaking*. West Lafayette, IN: Purdue.

Lussana, Fiamma. 2012. *Il movimento femminista in Italia: esperienze, storie, memorie (1965–1980)*. Rome: Carocci.

Luzzatto-Fegiz, Pierpaolo. 1966. *Il volto sconosciuto dell'Italia. Seconda serie, 1956–1965*. Milan: Giuffrè.

Maccari, Dino. 1959a. 'Come sono le ragazze di oggi. I primi risultati della grande inchiesta', *Cosí* 5, no. 48 (29 November): 12–13.

Maccari, Dino. 1959b. 'Come si divertono', *Cosí* 5, no. 51 (20 December): 6–9.

Madeo, Liliana. 1976. 'La presa di Roma delle Femministe', *La Stampa*, 29 November: 7.

Maina, Giovanna. 2018. *Corpi che si sfogliano. Cinema, generi e sessualità su Cinesex (1969–74)*. Pisa: ETS.

Maina, Giovanna. 2019. *Play, man! Un panorama della stampa italiana per adulti (1966–1975)*. Milan: Mimesis.

Maina, Giovanna and Federico Zecca. 2012. 'Le grandi manovre. Gli anni Settanta preparano il porno', *Bianco e nero* 73, no. 1: 59–69.

Maltby, Richard. 2011. 'New Cinema Histories' in Daniel Biltereyst, Richard Maltby and Philippe Meers (eds), *Explorations in New Cinema History*, 1–40. Oxford: Blackwell.

Mangiacapre, Lina. 1979. 'Da quando Prometeo ci ha rubato il fuoco continua il saccheggio: è la volta di Fellini', *Quotidiano Donna 2*, no. 27 (4 July): 7.

Maria Clara. 1980. 'Basta con gli stupidi fiori in testa', *Quotidiano Donna* 3, no. 1, 16 January: 3.

Martin-Márquez, Susan. 2012. 'Editing in Women Auteur', in Jo Labanyi and Tatjana Pavlović (eds), *A Companion to Spanish Cinema*, 176–89. Chichester, West Sussex: Wiley-Blackwell.

Matilde. 1979. 'Caro padre, caro etero', in *Brigate Saffo*, insert of *Lambda* 4, no. 20 (January–February): 1–3.

Maule, Rosanna. 2009. *Beyond Auteurism: New Directions in Authorial Film Practices in France, Italy and Spain since the 1980s*. Bristol: Intellect.

Mayne, Judith. 1981. 'The Woman at the Keyhole: Women's Cinema and Feminist Criticism', *New German Critique*, no. 23: 27–43.

McClintock, Anne. 1995. *Imperial Leather: Race, Gender and Sexuality in the Colonial Contest*. London: Routledge.

Melandri, Lea. 2000. *La pratica dell'inconscio nel movimento delle donne degli anni Settanta*. Milan: Franco Angeli.

Meyerowitz, Joanne. 1993. 'Beyond the Feminine Mystique: A Reassessment of Postwar Mass Culture, 1946-1958', *Journal of American History* 79, no. 4: 1455–82.
Miele, Moira. 1978. 'Quale mare ci ha chiamate?' *Effe* 6, nos 10–11 (October): 34.
Miller, Tony. 2003. 'James Bond's Penis', in Christopher Lindner (ed.), *The James Bond Phenomenon*, 232–47. Manchester: Manchester Universtity Press.
Milliken, Christie. 1990. 'Fair to Feminism? Carnivalising the Carnal in Fellini's City of Women', *The Spectator* 10, no. 2 (Spring): 28–45,100.
Minuz, Andrea. 2012. *Viaggio al termine dell'Italia: Fellini politico*. Soveria Mannelli: Rubettino.
Mirizio, Annalisa. 2017. 'El anacronismo visual en el cine militante de Helena Lumbreras. Notas a propósito de la influencia de Pasolini y Zavattini', *Journal of Spanish Cultural Studies* 18, no. 4: 425–41.
Miscuglio, Annabella. 1979. 'Un occhio mobile che possiamo usare tutte', *Quotidiano Donna* 2, no. 22 (2 July): 7.
Missero, Dalila. 2016. 'Cecilia Mangini: A Counterhegemonic Experience of Cinema', *Feminist Media Histories* 2, no. 3 (1 July): 54–72.
Missero, Dalila. 2017. 'Non solo bambole: lo stardom femminile della commedia a episodi e il dibattito sul cinema immorale (1964–1966)', *Schermi. Storie e culture dei cinema e dei media in Italia* 1, no. 1: 119–33.
Missero, Dalila. 2018. 'Titillating Cuts: Genealogies of Women Editors in Italian Cinema', *Feminist Media Histories* 4, no. 4 (1 October): 57–82.
Missero, Dalila. 2019. 'Playboys and the Cosmo Girls: Models of Femininity in Italian Men's and Women's Magazines and the Popularization of Feminist Knowledge', *About Gender* 8, no. 16: 80–99.
Moe, Nelson J. 1990. 'Production and its Others: Gramsci's "Sexual Question"', *Rethinking Marxism* 3, nos 3–4: 218–37.
Morris, Penelope. 2006. 'The Harem Exposed: Gabriella Parca's Le italiane si confessano', in Penelope Morris (ed.), *Women in Italy, 1945–1960: An Interdisciplinary Study*, 109–30. Basingstoke: Palgrave Macmillan.
Morris, Penelope. 2007. 'A Window on the Private Sphere: Advice Columns, Marriage, and the Evolving Family in the 1950s Italy', *The Italianist* 27, no. 2: 304–32.
Morris, Penelope. 2013. '"Let's not talk about Italian sex". The Reception of the Kinsey Reports in Italy', *Journal of Modern Italian Studies* 18, no. 1: 17–32.
Mulvey, Laura. 2004. 'Looking at the Past from the Present: Rethinking Feminist Film Theory of the 1970s', *Signs: Journal of Women in Culture and Society* 30, no. 1: 1286–91.
Muñoz, José Esteban. 1996. 'Ephemera as Evidence: Introductory Notes to Queer Acts', *Women & Performance: A Journal of Feminist Theory* 8, no. 2: 5–16.
Nair, Parvati and Julián Daniel Gutiérrez-Albilla, eds. 2019. *Hispanic and Lusophone Women Filmmakers: Theory, Practice and Difference*. Manchester: Manchester University Press.
Nixon, Sean. 2003. *Advertising Cultures: Gender, Commerce, Creativity*. London: Sage.
Noi Donne. 1962. Che tipo di spettatrice sei?, *Noi Donne* 17, no. 21 (27 May): 38–41.
Noi Donne. 1977. 'Il cinema e la donna, qualcosa è cambiato. Ma l'attrice è sempre negra', *Noi Donne* 32, no. 34 (28 August): cover.
O'Healy, Áine. 1992. 'Unspeakable Bodies: Fellini's Female Grotesques', *RLA: Romance Languages Annual* 4: 325–9.
O'Healy, Áine. 2000. 'Toward a Poor Feminist Cinema: The Experimental Films of Dacia Maraini', in Rodica Diaconescu-Blumenfeld and Ada Testaferri (eds), *The Pleasure of Writing: Critical Essays on Dacia Maraini*. West Lafayette, IN: Purdue University Press: 246–63.

Ossi, Lina. 1979. 'Spettatrice', in Adelaide Frabotta (ed.), *Lessico Politico delle donne. Cinema, letteratura, arti visive*, Vol. 6, 22–8. Milan: Gulliver.

Paasonen, Susanna. 2007. 'Strange Bedfellows: Pornography, Affect and Feminist Reading', *Feminist Theory* 8, no. 1: 43–57.

Pallotta, Clelia. 1981. 'Il gioco dello specchio', *Effe* 9, no. 1 (January): 14–15.

Parca, Gabriella. 1959. *Le italiane si confessano*. Florence: Parenti Editore.

Pasolini, Pier Paolo. 1962. 'Introduzione', in Gabriella Parca, *Le italiane si confessano*, 2nd edition. Florence: Parenti Editore.

Pasolini, Pier Paolo. 1964. 'Per una visione del mondo epica-religiosa', *Bianco & Nero* 25, no. 6 (June): 12–41.

Pasqua, Mariella and Maricla Tagliaferri. 1978. 'I mille volti di Eva', *Effe* 10–11, no. vi: 27–9, http://efferivistafemminista.it/2014/12/i-mille-volti-di-eva/, accessed 5 May 2021.

Patriarca, Silvana. 2010. *Italianità. La costruzione del carattere nazionale*. Rome, Bari: Laterza.

Perilli, Vincenza. 2007. 'L'analogia imperfetta. Sessismo, razzismo e femminismi tra Italia, Francia e Stati Uniti', *Zapruder. Rivista di storia della conflittualità sociale*, no. 13 (May–August): 9–25.

Perona, Piero. 1976. 'Scrittrice con cinepresa', *La Stampa Sera*, 17 August: IV.

Petro, Patrice. 1990. 'Feminism and Film History', *Camera Obscura* 8, no. 22 (1 January): 8–27.

Petrovich Njegosh, Tatiana. 2015. 'La finzione della razza. La linea del colore e il meticciato', in *Il colore della nazione* edited by Gaia Giuliani 215–27. Milan: Le Monnier.

Picchietti, Virginia. 2002. *Relational Spaces: Daughterhood, Motherhood and Sisterhood in Dacia Maraini's Writing and Films*. Madison, NJ: Dickinson University Press.

Pini, Andrea. 2011. *Quando eravamo froci. Gli omosessuali nell'Italia di una volta*. Milan: Il Saggiatore.

Pink, Sarah. 2015. *Doing Sensory Ethnography*. 2nd edition. London: Sage.

Playboy. 1973. 'Playboy intervista: Federico Fellini. Candida conversazione sul sesso, il cinema, il matrimonio, le donne grasse', *Playboy* 2 (December): 37–48.

Playboy. 1980. 'Fellini scopre la sua D.D.', *Playboy* 9, no. 6 (June): 45–51.

Polina. 1978. 'A proposito di locali gay!' *Brigate Saffo*, insert of Lambda nos 14–15 (Summer): 9–10.

Pollock, Griselda. 1999. *Differencing the Canon: Feminist Desire and the Writing of Art's Histories*. London, New York: Routledge.

Ponzanesi, Sandra. 2005. 'Beyond the Black Venus: Colonial Sexual Politics and Contemporary Visual Practices', in Jaqueline Andall and Derek Duncan (eds), *Italian Colonialism: Legacies and memories* edited by. Oxford: Peter Lang.

Portaccio, Stefania. 1982. 'Buona e bella. I periodici femminili cattolici negli anni Cinquanta', *Memoria. Rivista di storia delle donne*, no. 4: 140-145.

Portelli, Alessandro. 2003. 'The Problem of the Color Blind: Notes on the Discourse on Race in Italy', in Paola Boi and Sabine Broeck (eds), *Cross Routes – The Meaning of 'Race' in the 21st Century*, 29–39. Münster, Hamburg, London: LIT Verlag.

Pravadelli, Veronica. 2014. *Le donne del cinema. Dive, registe, spettatrici*. Rome, Bari: Laterza.

Przybylo, Ela. 2011. 'Crisis and Safety: The Asexual in Sexusociety', *Sexualities* 14, no. 4 (August): 444–61.

Quotidiano Donna. 1980. 'Troppo poco lo spray sui vetri', *Quotidiano Donna* 3, no. 1, 16 January: p. 3.

Quotidiano Donna. 1981a. 'La mia sessualità, per fortuna, é altrove', *Quotidiano Donna* 4, no. 5 (13 March): 10–11.

Quotidiano Donna. 1981b. 'Dietro la telecamera un occhio limpido' *Quotidiano Donna* 4, no. 5 (13 March): 10.

RAI Servizio Opinioni. 1965. *Il pubblico della TV nel 1964. Quaderni del servizio opinioni RAI no. 10.* Turin: Servizio Opinioni RAI.

Rashkin, Elissa J. 2001. *Women Filmmakers in Mexico: The Country of Which We Dream.* Austin, TX: University of Texas Press.

Rassegna Kinomata. 1976. *La donna con la macchina da presa.* Exhibition Catalogue, Milan.

Rassegne del cinema di Sorrento. 1978. *Catologo della 4° edizione delle Rassegne del cinema di Sorrento.* Naples.

Reich, Jacqueline. 2004. *Beyond the Latin Lover: Marcello Mastroianni, Masculinity and Italian Cinema.* Bloomington, Indianapolis: Indiana University Press.

Rich, Adrienne. 1980. 'Compulsory Heterosexuality and Lesbian Existence', *Signs* 5, no. 4: 631–60.

Rich, B. Ruby. 1998. 'Prologue: Angst and Joy on the Women's Film Festival Circuit', in *Chick Flicks: Theories and Memories of the Feminist Film Movement*, 29–39. Durham, NC: Duke University Press.

Rigoletto, Sergio. 2017. 'Against the Teleological Presumption: Notes on Queer Visibility in Contemporary Italian Film', *The Italianist* 37, no. 2: 212–27.

Ronza, Elvio. 1975. 'Dicono no alla solidarietà di sesso', *La Stampa Sera.* 20 October: 1.

Rotunno, Daniela. 1979. 'Arriva un bastimento carico di film delle donne', *Quotidiano Donna* 2, no. 32 (19 September): 15.

Russell, Catherine. 2002. 'Parallax Historiography: The Flâneuse as Cyberfeminist', in Jennifer M. Bean and Diane Negra (eds), *A Feminist Reader in Early Cinema*, 552–70. Durham, NC: Duke University Press.

Saarenmaa, Laura. 2017. 'Adventures of an export salesman: travel, race, and sex abroad in a 1970s Finnish pornographic magazine', Porn Studies 4, no. 1: 35–49.

Saraceno, Chiara. 1993. 'The Italian Family: Paradoxes of Privacy', in Philippe Ariès and Georges Duby, *A History of Private Life*, Vol. 5, 451–502, Cambridge, MA: Harvard University Press.

Scalfari, Eugenio. 1979. 'Con il Maestro parlando di donne', *La Repubblica* (17 July).

Scego, Igiaba. 2015. *Adua.* Milan: Giunti.

Scerbanenco, Giorgio. 1960a. 'Un problema delicato per la donna moderna. Vivere con gli altri', *Annabella*, 19 July: 20–1.

Scerbanenco, Giorgio. 1960b. 'Uomini che molestano le donne. Il gallismo', *Annabella*, 31 July: 20–1.

Schaefer, Eric. 2015. *Sex Scene: Media and the Sexual Revolution.* Durham, NC: Duke University Press.

Sedgwick, Eve Kosowsky. 1985. *Between Men. English Literature and Male Homosocial Desire.* New York: Columbia University Press.

SIAE. Annuario dello Spettacolo SIAE [1958–1968], www.siae.it/statistica.asplink_page= Statistica_BibliotecaDelloSpettacoloDal1936Al1999.htm&open_menu=yes [link expired?]

Skeggs, Beverley. 1997. *Formations of Class and Gender: Becoming Respectable.* London: Sage.

Soussloff, Catherine M. and Bill Nichols. 1996. 'Leni Riefenstahl: The Power of the Image', *Discourse* 18, no. 3: 20–44.

Staayer, Chris. 1984. 'Personal Best, Feminist/Lesbian Audience', *Jump Cut. A Review of Contemporary Media*, no. 29 (February): 40–44.

Stacey, Jackie. 1994. *Star Gazing: Hollywood Cinema and Female Spectatorship.* London: Routdledge.

Stanfield, Peter. 2008. 'Notes Toward a History of the Edinburgh International Film Festival, 1969–77', *Film International* 6, no. 4: 62–71.

Tagliaferri, Maricla. 1977. 'Amore di cinema', *Effe* 5, no. 4 (April): 26–8.

Tagliaferri, Maricla. 1978. 'Una rassegna itinerante', *Effe* 6, nos 10–11 (October–November): 35.
Tamburrini, Filomena. 1979. 'No care compagne, io non vi scuso', *Quotidiano Donna 2*, no. 27 (4 July): 7.
Teobaldelli, Ivan, Sergio Sella, Roberto Polce and Fulvio Ferrari. 1980. 'Milano: sulle orme di re Desiderio. Guida gay', Lambda 5, no. 25 (January–February).
Tola, Miriam. 2002. 'Mara Blasetti', *Cinecittà News*, 29 August, https://news.cinecitta.com/IT/it-it/news/54/61366/mara-blasetti.aspx, accessed 16 December 2020.
Tonelli, Anna. 2003. *Politica e amore. Storia dell'educazione ai sentimenti nell'Italia contemporanea*. Bologna: Il Mulino.
Tornabuoni, Lietta. 1980. 'Fellini: vi spiego perché gli uomini hanno paura', *La Stampa* (29 March): 3.
Treveri Gennari, Daniela, Catherine O'Rawe, Danielle Hipkins, Silvia Dibeltulo and Sarah Culhane. 2020. *Italian Cinema Audiences: Histories and Memories of Cinema-going in Post-War Italy*. New York: Bloomsbury Academic.
Turina, Isacco. 2013. *Chiesa e biopolitica. Il discorso cattolico su famiglia, sessualità e vita umana da Pio XI a Benedetto XVI*. Milan, Udine: Mimesis.
Una lettrice [A reader]. 1960. 'Non sono anch'io una ragazza? Ebbene sto degli anni senza andare al cinema. *Famiglia Cristiana* 30, no. 7 (14 February): 7.
Una mamma preoccupata [A worried mum]. 1959. 'Andare al cinema', *Noi Donne* 14, no. 15 (12 April): 3.
Una tredicenne lombarda [A 13-year-old Lombard]. 1959. 'Non mi lasciano andare al cinema', *Famiglia Cristiana* 32, nos 32–3 (9 August): 7.
Viola, Sandro. 1964. 'È stufo di farci ridere', *L'Espresso* 6, no. 25 (21 June).
Wanrooij, Bruno. 2008. 'Carnal Knowledge: The Social Politics and Experience of Sex Education in Italy, 1940–1980', in Lutz D. H. Sauerteig and Roger Davidson (eds), *Shaping Sexual Knowledge: A Cultural History of Sex Education in Twentieth Century*. New York: Routledge.
Warner, Michael. 2002. 'Publics and counterpublics (abbreviated version)', *Quarterly Journal of Speech* 88, no. 4: 413–25.
Weeks, Jeffrey. 1985. *Sexuality and its Discontents: Meanings, Myths and Modern Sexualities*. London: Routledge & Kegan Paul.
White, Patricia. 2006. 'The Last Days of Women's Cinema', *Camera Obscura* 21, no. 3: 145–51, available at https://doi.org/10.1215/02705346-2006-015, accessed 5 May 2021.
Williams, Linda. 1989. *Hard Core: Power, Pleasure and the 'Frenzy of the Visible'*. Berkeley: University of California Press.
Williams, Melanie. 2013. 'The Continuity Girl: Ice in the Middle of Fire', *Journal of British Cinema and Television* 10, 3: 603–17.
Williams, Raymond. 1978. 'Structures of Feeling', in *Marxism and Literature*. Oxford, New York: Oxford University Press, 128–35.
Williams, Raymond. 1989. 'Culture Is Ordinary', in *Resources of Hope: Culture, Democracy, Socialism*, 3–14. London: Verso.
Young, Iris Marion. 1994. 'Gender as Seriality: Thinking about Women as a Social Collective', *Signs* 19, no. 3: 713–38.
Zapponi, Bernardino. 1979. 'Fellini '80', *Playboy* 8, no. 12 (December): 73–118.
Zecchi, Barbara. 2019. 'Intervening in the Present: Catalan Cinema's Radical Years (1968–1978)', *Film Quarterly* 72, no. 3 (1 March): 69–77.

Index

#*metoo*, 111, 119n10
#*quellavoltache*, 111, 120n12
#*wetogether*, 111

8 Marzo, giornata di festa e di lotta (*8 March, Day of Celebration and Struggle*, Arcobaleno Cooperative, 1977), 144–5, 147
8½ (Federico Fellini, 1963), 33, 98

A Zig Zag, 157, 162n7
AAA Offresi (FCC, 1981), 143, 148–9
Abbrescia, Silvana, 144, 152n10
Aborto, parlano le donne (*Abortion, Women Talk*, Iskra Cooperative, 1975), 146, 153n18
Acquaviva, Ada, 133
affective memory and codes, 40, 43, 63, 70, 109, 164–5
Ahmed, Sarah, 8, 35
Ajello, Nello, 85n6
Alba, 16, 22, 26n11, 28, 33, 38n4
Albano, Lucilla, 159
Albedo Cooperative, 156–7, 159, 161
Alberti, Giulia (Bundi), 43–4, 158–9, 163n19
Alessandri, Luisa, 125–6, 133
Almanacco, 43, 45, 47, 50n8, 140, 142, 144–5, 150, 152n12, 152n17, 156
Alta infedeltà (*High Infidelity*, Mario Monicelli, Elio Petri, Franco Rossi, Luciano Salce, 1964), 77
   episode *Peccato nel pomeriggio* (*Sin in the Afternoon*), 80–1
Altea, Giuliana, 124
Alternative Cinema Conference, 41
Altoviti, Antonio, 113, 116

Altri tempi (*Infidelity*, Alessandro Blasetti, 1952), 112
Amarcord (Federico Fellini, 1973), 100
Amore e Rivoluzione (*Love and Revolution*, 1976), 13n1
Angelilli, Paola, 131
Annabella, 16, 22, 28, 30–1, 37, 84n5
Anni ribelli (*Laura: The Rebel Years*, Rosalia Polizzi, 1997), 133
Aprà, Adriano, 25n3, 26n13
Araya, Zeudi, 96n5
Arbasino, Alberto, 19, 90
Archibugi, Francesca, 150
archival research
   archival turn, 3–4
   Archivia, 21, 40, 50n1, 151n6
   Archivio Fondazione Elvira Badaracco, 40, 50n4, 50n7–8
   colonial archive, 86–7. 90, 96n1, 96n7
   feminist archives, 7, 21, 50n1 84, 118, 165
   Fondazione Badaracco, 40, 50n7–8
   Fondazione Micheletti, 108, 155
   Fondo Movimento Femminista, 50n4
   Fondo Pompeo Magno, 151n6
   queer archive, 55
   pragmatic theorisation, 164
ARCI, 42, 50n2
Argento, Asia, 111, 119n10
Art Kino, 146, 153n23
Arvidsson, Adam, 27
Aspesi, Natalia, 111, 119n11
Associazione Organizzatori e Direttori di Cineteleproduzioni, AODC, 116, 120n20

autocoscienza (consciousness raising), 21, 45, 56, 141–3, 147, 150, 157
Autonomia Operaia (Workers Autonomy), 50n1
Avalli, Ippolita, 100
Aviv, Nurith, 142, 146
Azcona, Rafael, 65
Azner, Dorothy, 127

Baldi, Alfredo, 122, 134n3
Balsamo, Saro, 96n3
Barina, Antonella, 47
Bartalini, Isa, 113, 120n15
Bella, 23
Bellumori, Cinzia, 93, 110, 113, 116, 120n19
Belmonti, Maria Grazia, 149, 151n7, 154n29
Ben-Ghiat, Ruth, 127, 136n16
Berlanga, Luis, 10, 62, 65
Berlant, Lauren, 28
Bettini, Betty, 96n2, 141
Biagi, Enzo, 94
Biagini, Elena, 53, 56, 67, 150
Bianchi, Olga, 123, 130–1, 133, 137n23
Bianco e Nero, 110, 129, 134n3
Birri, Ferdinando, 130
Black Venus, 86–8
Blasetti, Alessandro, 109, 113, 117, 136n11
Blasetti, Mara, 11, 107, 109, 112–13, 115–18, 120n14, 120n15, 120n16, 120n17, 120n18, 120n20, 120n21, 155
Blood For Dracula (Paul Morrissey, 1974), 113
Bloom, Claire, 79–80
Boden, Vivien, 114
Bolero Film, 22
Bologna, 40, 54, 67
Bona, Matilde, 56–7
Bosé, Lucia, 53
Boyle, Karen, 65–6
Brancati, Daniela, 143–4
Brasi, Anna, 144–5, 152n12
Brass, Tinto, 80, 106n10
Bravissimo (*Very good*, Luigi Filippo D'Amico, 1955), 113
Breakfast at Tiffany's (Blake Edwards, 1961), 36
Bresler, Jerry, 113, 116
Brigate Rosse (Red Brigades), 56, 68, 135n8

Brigate Saffo (Sappho Brigades), 10, 52, 55–60
British Film Institute, BFI, 44
Brosio, Valentino, 114
Bruno, Giuliana, 2, 40, 135n6, 144, 148, 157, 159, 161n2, 163n18
Buffoni, Laura, 3, 153n26
Buonanno, Milly, 3, 20–1, 93, 119n7

Caligula (Tinto Brass, 1979), 106n10
Calvino, Italo, 90
Cambria, Adele, 5, 13n2, 68, 100–1, 105n7
Campese, Silvana/Medea, 40, 44–6, 49
Capomazza, Tilde, 133, 153n27
Carabba, Claudio, 25n3
Cardinale, Claudia, 29
Carrano, Patrizia, 67, 100, 110–11, 114–15, 120n20, 125–6
Casa Internazionale delle Donne (Rome), 50n1, 146
Casanova (Federico Fellini, 1976), 104n4
Catholic Action (Azione Cattolica), 38n4
Cavani, Liliana, 9, 43, 54, 123, 132–3
Cavarocchi, Francesca, 54
Centro Cattolico Cinematografico, CCC, 31, 38n5
Centro di Documentazione Donna di Padova, 68, 71n10
Centro Italiano Femminile, CIF, 38n9, 93
Centro Sperimentale di Cinematografia, CSC, 11, 66, 108, 114, 121–31, 133, 134n2, 135n9, 136n11, 136n12, 136n13, 136n16, 140, 152n12
Chiarini, Luigi, 122, 125
Cine Foro, 130
Cinecittà, 53, 100
Cinema, 127
Cinema Illustrazione, 127
Cineteca di Bologna, 108–9, 120n21–2
Ciotta, Mariuccia, 133
Circeo Massacre, 62, 64–6, 68, 70n1
CoDis, 24
Colasanti, Donatella, 64–5, 70n1
Collegamento tra Lesbiche in Italia, CLI, 54
Collettivo Femminista di Cinema, FCC, 42–3, 47, 140–3
Colli, Ombretta, 58

comedy, Italian style 73, 75–7, 79
Comencini, Cristina, 150
Comencini, Francesca, 150
Comencini, Luigi, 77, 80, 160
Comin, Jacopo, 127, 136n16
Compagne Organizzate per il Contropotere Femminista, COFC, 63, 68
Confidenze, 23
Connell, R. W., 88
Conor, Bridget, 110
Conte, Maria Stella, 150
Controsesso (*Countersex*, Marco Ferreri, Renato Castellani, Franco Rossi, 1964), 77
Cooperativa Arcobaleno (Arcobaleno Cooperative), 108, 144–5, 152n12, 152n16
Cooperativa spettatori produttori cinematografici, 144
Cosí, 16, 22, 26n11, 28, 33–5, 38n4
Cosmopolitan, 23, 85n7
cruising (gay spectatorship), 24, 57, 59–60
Cuore (Luigi Comencini, 1984), 160

Dalla Costa, Mariarosa, 83
Damiani, Damiano, 45
Damiani, Donatella, 98, 101–2, 104
D'Amico, Luigi Filippo, 113
Daopoulo, Rony, 4, 42–3, 50n5, 53–6, 140–3, 149, 151n5, 151n7
Darling (John Schlesinger, 1965), 113
databases, 135n10, 137n25
de Aloysio, Gemma, 123–5, 136n12–13
De Céspedes, Alba 18, 25n1
De Laurentiis, Dino, 116
de Lauretis, Teresa, 5, 13n2, 54, 74, 84, 97, 153n25
De Sica, Vittorio, 125
Deadly Weapons (Doris Wishman, 1974), 67
Del Pozzo, Giovanna, 37
Derrida, Jacques, 117
Deserto rosso (*Red desert*, Michelangelo Antonioni, 1964), 81
Desperately Seeking Susan (Susan Seidelman, 1985), 160
di Nola, Laura, 5, 123, 135n8
Dietrich, Marlene, 36
diffused feminism (femminismo diffuso), 156, 158, 160–1

Diotima, 13n4
discursive self-production, 39
Divorzio All'Italiana (*Divorce Italian Style*, Pietro Germi, 1961), 36
Doane, Mary Ann, 159
Dominijanni, Ida, 13n4, 141
Donne e Audiovisivo, DEA, 111
Dopoguerra (*Postwar*, Marisa Romano, 1937), 127
Doxa, 22–4, 26n8, 40–1

economic boom, 12, 15, 22–3, 27–8, 35, 37, 73, 75, 80
Edinburgh International Film Festival, 40, 44, 162n12
Edizioni San Paolo, 33
Effe, 21, 23, 40, 42, 47–8, 50n1, 66, 69, 138n28, 145, 147–9, 152n17, 156
Eichhorn, Kate, 5–7
Ekberg, Anita, 101
El cuarto poder (Helena Lumbreras, 1970), 129
Emmanuelle Nera (Bitto Albertini, 1975), 91
Enciclopedia della donna, 29
Ente per la Gestione Cinema (Cinema Management Board), 116
Epoca, 77
Europa di notte (*European Nights*, Alessandro Blasetti, 1959), 113
European Women's Audiovisual Network, EWA, 150
Extraconiugale (*Extramarital*, Massimo Franciosa, Mino Guerrini, Giuliano Montaldo, 1964), 77
EYE institute of Amsterdam, 131, 137n24

Famiglia Cristiana, FC, 16, 28, 30–5, 37 38n4–5
Federazione Italiana Cineclub, Fedic, 41–2
Federici, Silvia, 3–4, 75, 83
Felix, Maria, 53, 59
Fellini, Federico, 11, 33, 73–4, 81, 97–103, 104n1–2, 104n4–5, 105n7–8, 105n10, 131, 160, 166
feminist film culture, 3–5, 47, 164
Feminist Media Histories, 13n1
Fenech, Edwige, 94
Ferracuti, Franco, 71n5
Ferraù, Alessandro, 120n20

Index

Ferreri, Marco, 65, 77, 78, 80–2
Film-makers' Cooperative, 144
Filmstudio, 42–3, 50n5, 140, 151n4
Fisher, Mark, 7
Flesh For Frankenstein (Paul Morrissey, Antonio Margheriti, 1973), 113
Fo, Dario, 156
Fofi, Goffredo, 81, 109, 118n3
For Your Eyes Only (John Glen, 1981), 113
Frabotta, Maria Adelaide, 4, 93, 146–7, 152n12, 153n19
Fraioli, Ilaria, 155
Fraire, Manuela, 50n3
Frammenti per sé (*Fragments for the self*, Adriana Monti, 1984), 159, 163n20
Franco, Francisco, 92, 129, 136n18
Friedan, Betty, 20
Froncillo, Rosetta, 144, 152n13
Frontoni, Angelo, 90, 96n6
FUORI, 56, 58, 135n8
futurismo, 124

Gabrielli, Fausta, 144–5, 152n12, 152n16
Galileo (Liliana Cavani, 1968), 54, 133
García Márquez, Gabriel, 130
Gassman, Vittorio, 77, 80
Gatti Rossi in un Labirinto di vetro (*Eyeball*, 1975), 92
Gaze Theory, 43
Gemser, Laura, 91
Geri, Franca, 157, 161n5
Ghira, Andrea, 70n1
Giancaro, Maria Pia, 94
Gidget Goes to Rome (Paul Wendkos, 1963), 113
Ginger e Fred (*Ginger and Fred*, Federico Fellini, 1986), 160
Gioia, 22, 26n11, 38n4
Giorgi, Eleonora, 94
Girosi, Mimmola, 143
Giulietta degli spiriti (*Juliet of the spirits*, Federico Fellini, 1964), 81, 97
Good, Roger, 116, 120n22
Gramsci, Antonio, 5, 13n2, 19–20, 24, 25n2, 82
Grand Hotel, 23
Grandi, Barbara, 89
Grazia, 22, 84n5

Greer, Germaine, 99, 104n4–5
Gruppo dell'Inconscio (Group of the Unconscious), 155–7, 160
Guida, Gloria, 94
Guidetti, Lorenzina, Suor, 33–4, 38n8
Guifo, Gianni, 70n1
Gurley Brown, Harley, 85n7
Guy-Blanche, Alice, 4

Hefner, Hugh, 89–90, 96n4
Hepburn, Audrey, 36
Holub, Renate, 13n1, 82
How to Murder Your Wife (Richard Quine 1965), 78
Hustler, 95

I mille volti di Eva (*The Thousand Faces of Eve*, Ada Acquaviva, Tilde Capomazza, Mariuccia Ciotta, Rosalia Polizzi), 133, 138n28
Il brigadiere Pasquale Zagaria ama la mamma e la polizia (Luca Davan, 1973), 92
Il Decameron (*The Decameron*, Pier Paolo Pasolini Pasolini, 1971), 64
Il Fiore delle mille e una notte (*Arabian Nights*, Pier Paolo Pasolini, 1974), 86, 89–90, 96n6
Il Giardino dei Finzi-Contini (*The Garden of the Finzi-Contini*, Vittorio De Sica, 1970), 125
Il lavoro (*Boccaccio '70*, Luchino Visconti, 1962), 81
Il mito (*The Myth*, Giorgio Pellaro, Rosalia Polizzi, 1966), 132
Il Mondo, 19
Il passo (*The Step*, Marisa Romano, 1937), 127
Il piacere del testo (*The Pleasure of the Text*, Adriana Monti, 1978), 157, 161n1
Il rischio di vivere (Anna Carini, Annabella Miscuglio, 1977), 148
Il passatore (Piero Nelli, 1978), 54
Il seme (*The seed*, Marisa Romano, 1937), 127
International Film Festival de Viña del Mar, 130
International Film Meetings, 44
Invernizio, Carolina, 18–19, 25n1
Io sono mia (*I Belong to Me*, Sofia Scandurra, 1978), 21, 54, 108, 140, 142–3

Irigaray, Luce, 13n4
Iskra Cooperative, 145–6, 152n18, 153n23
ispettore di produzione, 114
Istituto Accertamento Diffusioni, IAD, 22
It Started with a Kiss (George Marshall 1959), 78
Italian and American Directions: Women's film Theory and Practice, 156, 159
Italian Cinema Audience project, ICA, 17, 24, 30, 34
Italian Communist Party, PCI, 35, 132, 136n19
Italian Ministry of Tourism and Show, 116
Izzo, Angelo, 70n1

James Tont, Operazione U.N.O. (Bruno Corbucci, 1965), 132
Johnston, Claire, 42
Judgement in Nuremberg (Stanley Kramer, 1961), 36

Kinomata Festival, 42–44, 50n6, 53, 146, 150, 151n4
Kinsey Report, 78

L'amore coniugale (*Conjugal Love*, Dacia Maraini, 1970), 146
La bella governante di colore (A Beautiful Black Housekeeper, Luigi Rosso, 1976), 92
La ciociara (*Two Women*, Vittorio De Sica, 1952), 125
La città delle donne (*The City of Women*, Federico Fellini, 1980), 11, 73–4, 97–104, 104n1–2, 106n10, 166
  Notes on City of Women (Ferruccio Catronuovo, 1980), 103, 104n2
La dolce vita (Federico Fellini, 1960), 103, 106n12, 131
La Donna nella Resistenza (*Women of the Resistance*, Liliana Cavani, 1965), 54
La giovane Arabia (*The Young Arabia*, Giorgio Pellari, Rosalia Polizzi, 1966), 132
La lotta non é finita (*The Struggle is not Ended*, FCC, 1972–3), 141
La Madama (*Sexycop*, Duccio Tessari, 1976), 92
La Maddalena collective, 5, 48, 71n3, 135n8
La moglie più bella (*The Most Beautiful Wife*, Damiano Damiani, 1970), 45

La Parmigiana (Antonio Pietrangeli, 1963) 33
La ragazza dalla pelle di luna (Luigi Scattini, 1972), 96n5
La Ricotta (in *Ro.Go.Pa.G.*, Pier Paolo Pasolini, 1963), 33
Ladri di Biciclette (*Bicycle Thieves*, Vittorio De Sica, 1948), 125
Lambda, 52, 56–60, 61n8
Lamera, Atanasio 31
Lantern Media History Digital Library, 166, 167n1
Lao, Méri, 101, 105n8–9
Lattuada, Bianca, 115
Le bambole (*The Dolls*, Mauro Bolognini, Luigi Comencini, Dino Risi, Franco Rossi, 1965), 77, 80
  episode *La telefonata* (*The Phone Call*), 80
Le casalinghe di via Plinio (*The Housewives of via Plinio*, Adriana Monti, 1976), 157
Le donne del Risorgimento (*The Women of the Risorgimento*, Franca Maranto, 1960), 131, 137n25
Le italiane e l'amore (Gabriella Parca, 1961), 20
Le italiane si confessano, 19–20, 25n4
Le Nemesiache, 40, 44–6, 50n7–8, 100
Le nostre mogli (Nanni Loy, 1966), 132
Le ragazze di Capo Verde (*The Girls from Cape Verde*, Dacia Maraini, 1976), 146
Le Rassegne del Cinema Femminista, 42, 44
Leone, Lù, 5, 142
L'Espresso, 78, 85n6, 120n12
Lessico politico delle donne, 42, 141, 156
Liala (Amalia Liana Negretti Odescalchi), 18, 25n1
Liberazione Omosessuale, 56
Life Size (*Tamaño natural (Grandeur nature)* Luis Berlanga, 1975), 10, 62, 64–5, 70n2, 71n3
Lilli, Laura, 20–1
Lion of the Desert (Moustapha Akka, 1980), 113
Lisi, Virna, 80, 84n4
Lo Sceicco Bianco (*The White Sheik*, Federico Fellini, 1952), 18
L'Occhio Negato, 42, 46
Lollobrigida, Gina, 43, 77, 84n4
London Film-Maker Co-op, 144

Index

Lonzi, Carla, 83, 153n26
Lopez, Rosaria, 65, 70n1
Lorde, Audre, 165
Loren, Sophia, 43, 53
Lotta Femminista, LF, 42, 155–6, 161n6
L'Uccellino (in *La mia signora, My Wife*, Mauro Bolognini, Tinto Brass, Luigi Comencini, 1964), 80
Lumbreras, Helena Giménez, 123, 128–30, 132–3, 136n18–19, 137n20–1
Luna Park, 19

Maccari, Dino, 33–5
Macrelli, Rina, 54–5
Madeo, Liliana, 68
Maestranze Tecnici e Cinema (MTC), 143, 148, 151n7
Maina, Giovanna, 3, 63–4, 91, 96n3
Manfredi, Nino, 53
Mangano, Silvana, 43, 80
Mangiacapre, Lina/Nemesi, 44–5, 100–1
Manni, Ettore, 98
Maraini, Dacia, 65, 71n3, 108, 142, 145–7, 153n18–21, 153n24
Maranto, Franca, 123, 126, 131, 137n25
Marazzi, Alina, 155, 161n1, 162n10
Marcasciano, Porpora, 61n7
Marcuse, Herbert, 66, 83
Marghera come Marienbad (*Marghera like Marienbad*, Anna Brusi, Fausta Gabrielli, 1974), 144–5
Marx, Karl, 145
  Marxism, 82–3, 141
Mastroianni, Marcello, 77, 79–80, 98, 102
Maternale (Giovanna Gagliardo, 1978), 159
Melandri, Lea, 21, 26n7, 141, 159–60, 162n11, 163n21, 163n23
Melchiori, Paola, 159, 163n19
melodrama, 18, 25n3, 136n16
Menuet (Lili Rademekers, 1982), 131
Mezzano, Daniela, 67
Miceli, Alda, 94
Miele, Moira, 40, 48, 147
Milan, 13, 29, 40, 43, 47, 59, 67, 84n5, 90, 155–156, 160, 161n3
Milks, Megan, 76
Miracolo a Milano (*Miracle in Milan*, Vittorio De Sica, 1951), 125

Miscuglio, Annabella, 4, 42–3, 50n5, 140, 143–4, 148–50, 151n5, 151n7, 159
Missero, Dalila, 6, 19, 24, 70n2, 77, 96n9, 126, 152n14
Mister Moses (Ronald Neame, 1965), 116, 120n22
Modesty Blaise: The Beautiful One Kills (Joseph Losey, 1966), 113
Monicelli, Mario, 77
Monti, Adriana, 11, 47–8, 51n11, 108, 155–61, 161n2, 161n3–5, 161n10–17, 163n18–20
Moravia, Alberto, 71n3, 85n6, 90
Moreno, María de los Ángeles 'Kitico', 130
Moretti, Nanni, 20
Morris, Penelope, 19, 25n1, 28, 78, 113
Mouvement de libération de la femme, 53
Movimento Femminista Romano, 42, 64, 135n8
Muller, Frederick, 116
Mulvey, Laura, 42–4, 49, 159
Muñoz, José Esteban, 7, 55
Mura (Maria Assunta Giulia Volpi Nannipieri), 18
Musidora-Femme/Media, 44
Muzzi, Paola, 144
Myles, Lynda, 44

Nadotti, Maria, 2, 40, 144, 148, 157, 159, 161n2, 163n18
Naples, 40, 44–6, 50n9, 122, 132
National Conference of Lesbian Women, 54
neorealismo rosa/neorealismo d'appendice, 19, 25n3
New Chilean Cinema, 130
New Cinema History, 3–4
New Latin American Cinema, 131, 137n20, 137n22
Noi Donne, 16, 26n5, 28, 35–7, 38n9, 40, 47, 50n1, 93, 95
Non Una di Meno, NUDM, 6, 13n3
  Ni Una Menos, 13n3
Not a Love Story: A Film About Pornography (Bonnie Sherr Klein, 1981), 66
Notari, Elvira, 4, 43, 122, 135n6
Novella, 23

objectified woman, 93–5
O'Healy, Áine, 97, 153n24

opacity of the closet/archive, 7, 54–5, 165
Orazi e Curiazi 3–2 (Giorgio Mariuzzo, 1977), 92
Ossi, Lina, 42

Paasonen, Susanna, 63
Pala, Giovanna, 10, 53–6, 59, 61n3
Pallotta, Clelia, 46
Paoli, Vanna, 66, 142, 152n11
pappagalli, 29
Parca, Gabriella, 19–21, 24–5, 25n4, 26n6
Pasolini, Pier Paolo, 20, 25n4, 26n6, 33, 64, 81, 86–7, 89–90, 96n6–7, 129
Pellegrini, Ines, 11, 73, 86–92, 94–5, 96n5, 166
Per un cinema clitorideo vaginale (For a Clito-Vaginal Cinema, FCC, 1971), 43, 140
Personal Best (Robert Towne, 1982), 39, 61n4
Petri, Elio, 80–2
Piccola, 26n5
Piccola posta (The letters page, Steno, 1955), 18
Piccoli, Eva, 144
Piccoli, Michel, 65
Pietro Micca (Aldo Vergnano, 1938), 127
Pillow Talk (Michael Gordon 1959), 78
Pinochet, Augusto, 130
Pinori, Pino, 115
Pittatore, Rossana, 56
Placido, Michele, 142
Playboy, 63, 87, 89, 91, 95, 96n3–4, 96n6, 99, 101–2
Playmen, 63, 89, 96n3, 96n6
Polizzi, Rosalia, 123, 132–3, 137n27, 138n27
Pompeo Magno (Collective), 53, 56, 62, 71n3, 141
Proibito (TV Show), 94
Processo per stupro (Trial for rape, Maria Grazia Belmonti, Anna Carini, Rony Daopulo, Paola De Martis, Annabella Miscuglio, Loredana Rotondo, 1978), 68, 143

quantitative sources, 10, 17–18, 22, 26n9, 34, 164
queer counterpublics, 6–7, 10, 24, 52, 54–5, 59–60, 102, 105n5, 112
queer asynchronies, 103, 106n12
Questa Volta Parliamo di Uomini (Let's Talk About Men, Lina Wertmüller, 1965), 77

Quotidiano Donna, 40, 50n1, 63, 68–9, 100–1, 104n2, 147, 149, 154n28, 156

Racconti d'Estate (Gianni Franciolini, 1958), 53
Rademekers, Fons, 131
Ragazza In, 21, 156, 158, 160–1, 163n22
ragazzate, 30
RAI Servizio Opinioni, 22, 26n8
Raider, Yvonne, 159
Rambo: First Blood (Ted Kotcheff, 1982), 160
Rame, Franca, 156
Rassegne del Cinema di Sorrento, 147–8
Reich, Wilhelm, 66, 71n7, 83, 104n3
Remiddi, Laura, 62, 64–6, 69, 70n2, 71n4
revisionist histories, 7
Rich, Adrienne, 52
Rich, B. Ruby, 41, 128, 137n22
Riconciliati (Reconciled, Rosalia Polizzi, 2001), 133
Riefensthal, Leni, 128
riflusso nel privato, 12, 13n5, 73, 161
Risi, Dino, 77, 80
Riso Amaro (Bitter rice, Giuseppe De Santis, 1949), 18
Ritratti di donne africane (Portraits of African Women, Dacia Maraini, 1976–7), 146–7
Rizzoli, 28, 89
Rocca, Daniela, 36
Romano, Marisa (Maria Luisa Scala), 123, 127–9, 133, 136n16–17
Rome, 21, 42, 48, 56, 59, 63, 67–8, 70n1–2, 71n3, 86, 90, 96n3, 121–2, 129, 131, 146, 156
Ronza, Elvio, 94
Rosaleva, Gabriella, 159
Ross, Frank, 116, 120n22
Rossetto, Gabriella, 123, 126
Rotondo, Loredana, 143, 151n7
Rotunno, Daniela, 147
Royal Academy of Santa Cecilia, 125
Russell, Catherine, 39–40

Salce, Luciano, 77
Salò o le 120 giornate di Sodoma (Salò, and the 120 Days of Sodoma, Pier Paolo Pasolini, 1975), 86
Sandrelli, Stefania, 142

Index

Sans Toit ni Loi (*Vagabond*, Agnes Varda, 1985), 160
Scego, Igiaba, 86–7
Scerbancenco, Giorgio, 29, 38n1
Schicchi, Riccardo, 94
Schneider, Maria, 58, 59, 61n6, 142
Schub, Esfir, 43
Schucht sisters (Eugenia, Giulia, Tatiana), 5
Scuola senza fine (School without end, Adriana Monti, 1979–83), 108, 157–9, 161n2, 162n12
Se permettete parliamo di donne (*Let's talk about women*, Ettore Scola, 1964), 80
second-wave feminism, 2, 6, 10–12, 16, 21, 52, 62, 74, 83, 88, 93–4, 100–1, 104, 148, 156, 161, 161n1
Sedgwick, Eve Kosowski, 24
Segnalazioni Cinematografiche, 38n4
segretaria di produzione/edizione, 114, 125–6, 132
sex wars, 62, 66
sexual revolution, 73, 86–9
sexualisation, 1, 10, 64, 88, 145
Sherazade (Association), 46
SIAE, 23
Simoncelli, Carla, 156
Sinfonia in Bianco (*Simphony in White*, Marisa Romano, 1937) 127
Sogni d'oro (*Sweet Dreams*, Nanni Moretti, 1981), 19
Sogno, 19
Sordi, Alberto, 53, 75
Sotto la corce del sud (*Under the Southern Cross*, Guido Brignone, 1938), 127
Soussloff, Catherine, 128
Spaak, Catherine, 77–9
Spagna '68 – El hoy es malo, pero el mañana es mio (Helena Lumbreras, 1968), 129
Spinazzola, Vittorio, 26n13
Spolato, Mariasilvia, 56, 61n5
Staller, Ilona, 94
standpoint theory, 8–9
Stanfield, Peter, 44
Stegers, Bernice, 98
Stern, Darine, 89
Super 8, 2, 47, 50n8, 137n 23, 140, 147–8, 151n3, 152n17, 153n24, 155, 157, 162n10

Tagliaferri, Maricla, 40, 42, 48, 138n28
Take Back the Night (movement), 63, 67–9, 71n8
Tamburi, Jenny, 94
Tamburrini, Filomena, 101
Tartara, Marina, 143
Tattilo, Adelina, 96n3
Tattoli, Elda, 43
television, 19, 22–5, 64, 123, 131–3, 143–47
Teorema (Pier Paolo Pasolini, 1968), 81
The Adventurers (Lewis Gilbert, 1970), 116
The European Women's Audiovisual Network (EWA), 119n8, 150
The Feminine Mystique (Betty Friedan, 1963), 20
The Goonies (Richard Donner, 1985), 1960
The Group Therapy (in *Marcia Nuziale, The wedding march*, Marco Ferreri, 1965), 78, 81
The Tender Trap (Charles Walters 1955), 78
Tognazzi, Ugo, 77–79, 80
Tola, Miriam, 115
Tornabuoni, Lietta, 99
Townsend, Joan, 59
transformative publics, 39, 49
Tre notti d'amore (*Three nights of love*, Renato Castellani, Luigi Comencini e Franco Rossi, 1964), 77–8
Trevisan, Miriana, 111
Tronti, Mario, 145
Troppo Forte (*Great!*, Carlo Verdone, 1986), 160
Turin, 29, 67, 132, 146, 153n22
Tuzi, Jone, 115, 126

Ultimo tango a Parigi (*Last tango in Paris*, Bernardo Bertolucci 1972), 62, 64
Umberto D. (Vittorio De Sica, 1952), 125
Una razione mensile di atrocità (*A monthly ration of atrocity*, Gianluigi Bruni, Serenella Isidori, Vanna Paoli, Nieves Zenteno, 1977), 66, n152
Unione Donne d'Italia, UDI, 35–6, 38n9, 138n27

Valeri, Franca, 18
Vasio, Ornella, 123, 126
Venman-Rademekers, Lily, 123, 131, 133

Vie Nuove, 37
Villa, Claudio, 53
Viola, Franca, 45, 50n10
Violenza Segreta (*Secret violence*, Giorgio Moser, 1963), 33
Vittori, Benilde, 123, 126
Vogliamo anche le rose (*We want roses too*, Adriana Monti, 2007), 155
Voglio vivere con Letizia (Cammillo Mastrocinque, 1938), 125
Von Trotta, Margharete, 46

Wages for Housework campaign, 47, 51n11, 83, 156, 161n5–6
Warner, Michael, 52, 60
Weinstein, Harvey, 111
Wertmüller, Lina, 9, 77
What? (Roman Polanski, 1972), 113
What's New Pussycat? (Clive Donner 1965), 78
Williams, Raymond, 2, 6
Women Film Pioneers Project, 134n4, 135n6, 166
Women's International League for Peace and Freedom, 130

years of lead (anni di piombo), 12, 46
Young, Iris Marion, 164

Zabriskie Point (Michelangelo Antonioni, 1970), 54
Zapponi, Bernardino, 99
Zavattini, Cesare, 20, 25n4, 130
Zenteno, Nieves, 66, 142, 144, 152n11
Zeppieri, Giorgio, 68
Zerman, Grazia, 48, 157, 161n5
Zimmerman, Mary K., 26n9

EU representative:
Easy Access System Europe
Mustamäe tee 50, 10621 Tallinn, Estonia
Gpsr.requests@easproject.com

www.ingramcontent.com/pod-product-compliance
Lightning Source LLC
Chambersburg PA
CBHW07082525O426
43671CB00036B/2071